INSPIRING TEACHING

INSPIRING TEACHING

Preparing Teachers to Succeed
in Mission-Driven Schools

SHARON FEIMAN-NEMSER
ERAN TAMIR
KAREN HAMMERNESS

Editors

Harvard Education Press
Cambridge, Massachusetts

Library of Congress Control Number 2014936826

Paperback ISBN 978-1-61250-724-8
Library Edition 978-1-61250-725-5

Published by Harvard Education Press,
an imprint of the Harvard Education Publishing Group

Harvard Education Press
8 Story Street
Cambridge, MA 02138

Cover Design: Joel Gendron
Cover Photo: LWA–Dann Tardif/Blend Images/Getty Images

The typefaces used in this book are Chapparal Pro for text and Franklin Gothic for display.

Contents

Teacher Preparation in Context

SHARON FEIMAN-NEMSER

The growing consensus that teachers matter is not matched by a similar recognition that teacher education matters. Policy makers and teacher educators want to know how to prepare high-quality teachers and how to measure their effectiveness and the effectiveness of their preparation for teaching. The public has a right to expect that teacher preparation influences how teachers teach and what students learn. Yet, we lack a strong research base for understanding how to prepare and support teachers to meet the challenges of teaching, especially in hard-to-staff schools serving low-income, minority students.[1]

Some argue that reducing the requirements for becoming a teacher is necessary in order to attract high-quality candidates. Others counter that classroom teaching requires serious professional preparation and on-the-job support. While the debate is often cast in terms of traditional versus alternate route programs, recent studies show that there is more variation within pathways to teaching than between them.[2] Instead of setting up artificial dichotomies, we need studies that identify features of teacher education programs, whether university based or alternative routes, which contribute to the success of teachers and their students.

> Future research will be more useful for improving teacher education and teaching if it . . . looks for individual features of those programs that have an impact on results. These important features—including high quality supervision of student teachers, coursework tied to the practice of teaching, and selection of applicants with given propensities or skills—can cut across pathways and programs. By understanding and incorporating these features, we will accelerate the improvement of all routes into teaching.[3]

In the current accountability climate, policy makers favor achievement test scores as the ultimate measure of a program's quality and a teacher's effectiveness. While student achievement gains are important, they are hardly an ideal indicator of teacher effectiveness or student learning. Some regard the value-added "revolution," which is spreading across the country with support from the U.S. Department of Education, as the magic bullet we have been waiting for. Because value-added studies seek to measure an individual teacher's contributions to increases in student achievement, the assumption is that such research can assess the quality of graduates from particular teacher education programs. But connecting the dots between teacher preparation and student achievement is fraught with difficulty.[4] Not only are the statistical tools unstable, but such measures do not provide an accurate picture of the quality of teacher education programs.[5]

Researchers studying more proximal outcomes of teacher education argue that if we want to know whether a particular teacher is prepared to carry out her classroom responsibilities, we need assessments that measure teachers' actual skills in the classroom, such as their ability to explain content, lead a discussion about a particular text, and diagnose students' learning difficulties and progress.[6]

In the last decade, the policy emphasis has shifted from inputs (e.g., candidate characteristics, faculty qualifications) to outcomes (e.g., teaching performance, student learning, teacher retention, career decisions). But teacher educators and policy makers also need to understand the role of selection and preparation and how they affect a variety of outcomes, including who chooses to teach in what kind of school; how well teacher education prepares them for the practice of teaching; why teachers from different programs stay, move, or leave; what their teaching is like; and what kind of careers they seek. These outcomes are not affected by selection or preparation alone, but by the interaction of teachers' backgrounds and personal qualities, their professional preparation and the schools where they work. So we need research that probes the interaction of person, program, and setting and examines how different combinations of this central dynamic affect teachers' learning, practice, and retention.[7]

Finally, we must distinguish the issues and questions that lend themselves to empirical study from those that are based in values and cannot be resolved by science alone. Research can tell us who goes into teaching, what they learn in teacher education, what their practice is like, even what their students learn. Research can also link teaching practice and student learning, although this value-added methodology is far from neutral and leaves out other important learning outcomes. But research alone cannot determine who is qualified to teach, because decisions about teacher quality and qualifications depend, in part, on beliefs about good teaching and what we value most in teachers. With different views about what makes a good teacher, there will be different expectations about what teachers should know, care about, and be able to do.

This book contributes to contemporary discussions and debates about teacher education policy and practice, including the question of whether and how different approaches to teacher preparation make a difference. It does so by examining how three teacher education programs help teachers develop the context-specific understandings, commitments, stances, and practices they need to respond to the learning needs of their students by tracking their professional growth and by documenting the challenges they encounter in their respective school sectors. We argue that context is more than just the setting for teaching and learning to teach. With their histories, resources, people, cultural patterns and values, contexts have content. They also have the power to shape our perceptions and actions, which gives them agency.[8] We offer in this volume a conceptual framework to illuminate different layers of context—from the classroom to the cultural, geographic, and political surroundings that interact with classroom teaching and shape teachers' work—and show how each program defines and teaches the *content* of their particular context.

The programs we study do not fit neatly into the categories of traditional or alternate routes. Like some alternate paths to teaching (e.g., Teach For America), they attract academically able students from highly selective colleges. They also offer extended opportunities for guided practice, as do some urban residency programs. Unlike most alternate route programs, however, these three programs provide a coherent professional curriculum organized around a vision of teaching in a particular context. We call them "hybrids" because they have some features of reform-minded, university-based teacher education and some features of innovative alternate routes.[9]

In keeping with recent calls for research across different pathways to teaching, these programs are especially interesting cases to study.

By focusing on programs that prepare teachers for particular kinds of schools, this book advances the concept of *context-specific* teacher education, which has a long history extending back to the 1920s and 1930s, when progressive teacher education programs prepared teachers with a progressive ideology and pedagogy.[10] In 1963 the Washington, DC, school district took teacher education into its own hands because universities were not adequately preparing teachers for the District's public schools.[11] In the 1970s and 1980s, federal programs like the National Teacher Corps prepared teachers for urban or rural settings.[12] More recently, rural programs like Teachers for Alaska and the Ka Lama Education Academy in Hawaii and urban programs like those operated by UCLA, Boston College, Mills College, and Clark University explicitly embrace the mission of preparing teachers for particular kinds of schools in particular contexts. [13]

While programs to prepare teachers for particular settings have existed in different forms for decades, studies of these programs have not always shed light on those aspects of the context that may present specific or unique challenges or *how* and *in what ways* such programs define and prepare teachers for those targeted settings. Yet, understanding and examining these context-specific aspects of teaching and teacher education are central to understanding their effects on students and teachers. This book explores and illustrates the ways in which three context-specific programs prepare teachers for particular school contexts, the extent to which schools support teachers in developing their practice, and how teachers negotiate the challenges in their work.

The Choosing to Teach Study

The Choosing to Teach Study, which forms the basis for this book, had its origins in a conversation between Father Tim Scully, vice president of the University of Notre Dame and founder of the Alliance for Catholic Education (ACE), and Sharon Feiman-Nemser, a professor of Jewish Education at Brandeis University and intellectual leader of Brandeis' Day School Leadership Through Teaching Program (DeLeT). The conversation took place at a meeting on building the field of Catholic education hosted by the Carnegie Foundation for the Advancement of Teaching. Both ACE and DeLeT, relatively new programs at the time, were created to address a shortage of teachers in their respective school sectors. Scully and Feiman-Nemser hatched the idea of bringing together a group of graduates from each program to explore the experience of teaching in faith-based schools.[14]

In 2005 they held a two-day retreat in Boston with ten beginning teachers from each program and five faculty members from each program. The retreat surfaced many fascinating similarities and differences in the teachers' motivations and experiences. This piqued our interest in learning more about why these young adults chose to teach in Jewish and Catholic schools and how their identities and practices as teachers and as Jews and Catholics were shaping and being shaped by the programs where they were being prepared to teach and the schools where they taught. Thus, the Choosing to Teach Study was born.

To increase the social relevance of the study, and because comparative work can be invaluable in making visible aspects of a complex phenomenon that are easily overlooked or taken for granted, we expanded the sample to include a cohort of urban public school teachers prepared in a teacher education program with a strong commitment to social justice. Thus, what began as an effort to understand the character, quality, and impact of mission-driven teacher education became, with the addition of this urban teacher education program, a comparative, longitudinal study of context-specific teacher education and its effects on the teaching practices, career aspirations, and retention patterns of a sample of beginning teachers in urban public, urban Catholic, and suburban Jewish schools.

The Choosing to Teach Study addressed one overarching question: How do teacher education programs and school contexts interact with teachers' backgrounds to shape their identities, practices, and career commitments? The question assumes that what teachers learn and where and how they teach result from the interaction of personal qualifications, professional education, and school settings. The study investigates three programs with clear missions and strong commitments to their respective school sector: the Urban Teacher Education Program (UTEP) at the University of Chicago, the Alliance for Catholic Education at the University of Notre Dame, and the Day School Leadership Through Teaching at Brandeis University. We call these programs "context specific" because each is designed to prepare teachers for a particular kind of school that serves particular populations of students.[15] Each has a coherent curriculum based on a shared vision of good teaching, and each communicates clear role expectations for teachers and offers tools, understandings, and practices to help teachers succeed in these settings (see table I.1).

The Urban Teacher Education Program, University of Chicago. Founded in 2003, UTEP began by recruiting undergraduates mainly from the University of Chicago who were interested in promoting social justice through teaching. The program also seeks candidates outside the University of Chicago who share the UTEP's commitment, captured in its tag line: "Be the change you wish to see in the world." The two-year master of arts in teaching (MAT) program began as a program preparing elementary school teachers for jobs in the Chicago Public Schools. All students do some practicum work in the University of Chicago Charter School operated by the Urban Education Institute, which also launched and currently operates UTEP, and complete part of their residency in "neighborhood" Chicago schools. UTEP offers classroom-embedded induction support to its graduates during their first three years of teaching.

Alliance for Catholic Education, University of Notre Dame. Established in 1994 by the Institute for Educational Initiatives, ACE is among the premier suppliers of Catholic teachers in the United States, preparing 180 elementary and secondary teachers annually in a two-year alternate certification master's program. The program begins with seven weeks of summer preparation, after which candidates, primarily from the University of Notre Dame, serve as full-time teachers in underresourced Catholic schools across the southern and southwestern United States. The program aims to integrate Catholic values of serving the poor and making the world a better place with solid teaching practice. During their first two years of teaching, ACE teachers live in small communities and receive frequent visits from program faculty and staff who offer pedagogical and spiritual support and work with schools to maintain on-site mentoring systems.

TABLE I.1 Program overviews

	UTEP	ACE	DeLeT
Founding	2003	1992	2002
Size; level*	Cohorts of 25; elementary & secondary	One cohort of 180; elementary & secondary	One cohort of 10–12; elementary & secondary
Institutional home	University of Chicago	University of Notre Dame	Brandeis University
Length of prep	2 years	2 years	14 months
Degree/License	MAT, state certification	MEd, state certification	MAT, state certification
Education level	Post-BA	Post-BA	Post-BA
School sector	Chicago public schools	Urban & rural Catholic schools	Non-Orthodox Jewish day schools
Structure	2 academic years, including a residency year and 2 summers	2 summers and 2 academic years of teaching	2 summers and 1 academic year of internship

* At the time of the study, UTEP and DeLeT prepared only elementary teachers. Now both programs also prepare secondary teachers. ACE continues to prepare both elementary and secondary teachers.

Day School Leadership Through Teaching, Brandeis University. Founded in 2002 by the Mandel Center for Studies in Jewish Education, DeLeT is a postbaccalaureate program that prepares elementary teachers of general and/or Jewish subjects for non-Orthodox Jewish day schools. The program meets requirements for a MAT degree and a state teaching license. The centerpiece of the program is a yearlong mentored internship in one of Boston's Jewish day schools. Overall, the thirteen-month program is designed to help teachers learn to plan, teach, and reflect on their teaching and their students' learning and to build classroom learning communities infused with Jewish values and experiences. After graduation, DeLeT supports new teachers and offers resources and professional development opportunities to experienced alumni through the DeLeT Alumni Network (DAN).

UTEP, ACE, and DeLeT represent an interesting subgroup within the category of nontraditional teacher education programs. Each was created by and is part of a research center at an elite university dedicated to developing and studying effective ways to prepare teachers who have a positive effect on their schools, students, and communities. All grant master's degrees and meet certification requirements, two (ACE and DeLeT) as alternate routes. While these programs reflect a sense of innovation that policy makers hoped to stimulate by easing regulations on teacher certification, they hardly fit the image of scanty preparation that most educators and policy makers have in mind when they think of alternate route programs. Thus, they represent an important phenomenon in the vast market of nontraditional teacher education programs that aim to prepare teachers who can make a positive difference in their schools and in the lives of their students.

Data for the Choosing to Teach Study come from

- Two semi-structured interviews, each approximately ninety minutes in length, with thirty randomly selected teachers (ten from each program) that took place in years two and four after graduation
- Classroom observations and interviews with a subsample of these teachers chosen by program leaders because their instructional practice reflects the vision and pedagogy fostered by their programs
- Semi-structured interviews with faculty, mentor teachers, and program leaders
- Focus group discussions with program faculty
- Program documents (e.g., syllabi, handbooks, Web sites)
- Semi-structured interviews with more than twenty school principals who hired and supervised the teachers in Boston, Los Angeles, and Chicago.[16]

This rich set of qualitative data, combined with the comparative and longitudinal nature of the Choosing to Teach Study, allows us to examine how factors and findings from large-scale, correlational research actually play out in particular teacher education programs and in the lives and work of individual teachers and to generate hypotheses for future studies.

The six members of the research team—a mix of "insiders" and "outsiders" to the three programs—come from five different universities and have expertise in the substantive foci of the research. Each program is represented by a researcher who played a central role in its founding and/or who serves on the program's faculty or staff. Having researchers with intimate knowledge of each program helped ensure that descriptions and claims were trustworthy. The presence of outside researchers, who are not affiliated with any of these programs, and the comparative nature of the study helped sharpen our perceptions, refine our interpretations, and protect the study against bias. The research team also brought to bear its expertise in teacher education, teacher policy, identity formation, new teacher induction, Jewish education, Catholic education, and urban education. This book is the final product of our long-standing, generative collaboration.

Overarching Themes

Inspiring Teaching offers conceptual frameworks and empirical insights related to four cross-cutting themes, none of which has received sustained attention in research on teacher education and learning to teach. These themes shaped our inquiry and unify the book.

Context-Specific Teacher Education

Although teacher educators have experimented for decades with programs aimed at preparing teachers for particular school contexts, a generic approach to teacher education still dominates the field.[17] Yet, an approach to teacher education that treats context as a source of knowledge and a constituent of learning fits with contemporary theories of situated learning and builds on the work of educators who consider sociocultural and historical influences on learning, including learning to teach.[18]

We advance a multifaceted idea of context-specific teacher education by exploring what "context" means for the three programs in our study and by analyzing how each program understands and responds to what it perceives as pressing needs and unique affordances and constraints in its respective school sector. Building on a rich literature that studies and theorizes learning as embedded in particular social, cultural, and physical environments and histories, we show how UTEP, DeLeT, and ACE approach the history, ecology, and culture of their respective communities and what kinds of learning opportunities they offer to prepare teachers for the challenges awaiting them at these schools.[19] In each of the three cases, we explore the ways in which the programs help new teachers understand the multiple and overlapping layers of contexts in which they will teach and show how that knowledge enables new teachers to develop agency and efficacy in such settings.

All three program chapters treat context as a set of nested layers, starting with the most proximate (the classroom and school) and then moving out to the community (or parish), to the district (or diocese), and expanding still further to the policy context, the broader society, and even the global community. While the three programs give differential attention to these layers of context, all of them understand context as more than the setting in which schools are located. Rather, the specific contexts of urban public schools, urban Catholic schools, and Jewish day schools place substantive demands on teacher educators, influencing both what and how they teach future teachers.

Visions of Good Teaching

We are interested in the visions of teaching advanced by the three programs, how those visions shape teacher education curriculum and program design, and how they are reflected in teachers' classroom stance and practice. This work builds on current thinking and research about the role of vision in teachers' practices and careers and the widespread belief that strong teacher education programs rest on a clearly articulated vision of good teaching.[20] We examine teachers' evolving visions of good teaching as they are influenced by their teacher education programs and their teaching practice and show how these visions affect learning opportunities for students. In so doing, we consider other valued learning outcomes, besides student achievement, that programs advocate and teachers work toward.

This theme highlights the mission-driven nature of the three programs and the normative basis of teaching and teacher education. People hold different views of what good teaching entails and what good teachers should be like. As we analyze the kind of teaching each program embraces and the associated expectations about what teachers should know, care about, and do, we uncover the program's guiding values. Then we can ask how the visions teachers bring to teacher education and teaching align with the visions they encounter in their teacher education program and schools and how this influences their instructional practice, identity, and professional commitments.

Identity and Agency in Learning to Teach

Learning to teach involves more than the acquisition of knowledge, skills, and commitments. It involves the formation of a professional identity that integrates ways of knowing, doing, and being in the world. As Parker Palmer puts it, "Good teaching cannot be reduced to technique. Good teaching comes from the identity of the teacher [which] is a moving intersection of the inner and outer forces that make me who I am."[21]

Recent comparative research on the preparation of clergy, nurses, lawyers, engineers, and doctors highlights identity formation as a key element of professional education. This element or dimension derives from the aim of professional education: to develop dispositions, knowledge and skills that cohere in a professional identity and practice.[22] Through what researchers call a "normative apprenticeship" or an "apprenticeship of professional identity," novice professionals learn to "be the kind of person entitled to serve others.[23]

We are interested in the development of teachers' professional identity in relation to their religious, cultural, and ideological commitments. How are teachers' identities as teachers and as Catholics, Jews, and social activists formed through their upbringing, schooling, teacher education, and teaching? What is the relationship between this process of formation and the exercise of agency? To explore these questions, we draw on studies of professional identity formation, early socialization, the concept of habitus, and research on social or collective identities.[24]

Past experience, familiarity, and immersion shape but do not determine a person's religious or ideological commitments or their professional choices. People also get new input from experiences that cause them to review their earlier ideas. We are interested in the complex interplay of the already cultivated habitus and identity that teachers bring from their upbringing and the new possibilities they encounter.

Career Commitments

Finally, we are interested in the ideas about career advanced by teacher education programs, understood and pursued by beginning teachers, and supported by schools. Our inquiry builds on seminal studies of the sociology of teaching and the life cycle of teachers, as well as on more recent studies of teacher retention, leadership, and career commitments.[25] We explore how beginning teachers from UTEP, DeLeT, and ACE develop a concept of (good) teaching before, during, and after their teacher preparation and how they negotiate, imagine, and enact a career as teachers and leaders based on that concept. We explain the high levels of commitment to teaching and leadership demonstrated by these teachers compared with the kinds of career commitments reported by teachers in other surveys.[26]

Our research shows that teacher education programs with a focused mission and a clear vision of good teaching, along with opportunities to learn to enact that vision in practice, can foster exceptional career commitments. At the same time, beginning teachers adjust and reinterpret their initial career aspirations based on the kinds of students they teach and the school's working conditions, professional culture, and administrative support. This theme is particularly timely in light of changing career expectations on the part of new teachers, compared with those of the retiring generation of teachers.[27]

Overview of the Book

Inspiring Teaching tells a coherent story about what it means and what it takes to recruit, prepare, and retain teachers for particular kinds of schools. Some chapters foreground the programs, the teachers, or the schools while other chapters explore the interaction of two or more of these factors as they shape teachers' visions of good teaching, instructional practices, retention, and career decisions. To illustrate these complex dynamics and to bring to life the motivations, perspectives, learning, and teaching of the beginning teachers in our study, we also present detailed cases of teachers from the larger sample. The cases demonstrate the value of qualitative data to animate concepts and provide a nuanced understanding of the forces and factors that lead emerging adults to choose teaching and then to renew or reject that choice.

The first three chapters explore context-specific teacher education through case studies of the three programs. These program chapters address the following questions: What do faculty believe beginning teachers need to know, care about, and do in order to teach in their particular school sector?

What dimensions of this context are most salient in the program's curriculum? And what opportunities do teacher candidates have to learn about these aspects of context?

Chapter 1 unpacks the "urban" in urban teacher education, detailing the signature pedagogies and learning opportunities by which UTEP prepares teachers for the Chicago Public Schools, the third largest district in the United States. Kavita Kapadia Matsko and Karen Hammerness show how the program fosters a stance toward social justice while teaching the practices and local knowledge needed to operationalize that commitment.

Chapter 2, written by Christian Dallavis and Anthony Holter, describes how ACE prepares teachers for urban and rural Catholic schools that serve poor, minority students. Like UTEP, ACE teachers mainly come from white, middle-class backgrounds, so the program must help them learn to work with children whose backgrounds differ from their own. As an alternative preparation program with a condensed schedule, ACE deals with this challenge and other aspects of the Catholic school context through formal and informal curricula that integrate academic preparation, communal support, and spiritual/vocational growth.

Chapter 3 describes how DeLeT prepares elementary teachers for liberal Jewish day schools, a recent addition to the U.S. private school landscape. Sharon Feiman-Nemser shows how DeLeT frames the role and practice of a day school teacher around three layers of context: classroom culture, school community, and a vision of what it means to be a Jewish American in the twenty-first century. The DeLeT curriculum addresses tensions between universal and particular, religious and secular.

Chapter 4 focuses on the thirty beginning teachers, ten from each program, the study followed from the time they entered their teacher education programs through their fourth or fifth years of teaching. Bethamie Horowitz analyzes how these participants decided to embark on teacher education, how they came to think of themselves as teachers, and how they developed a sense of competence and agency. To explore the interplay of identity and agency, Horowitz presents cases of six teachers, two per program, who came to teaching and teacher preparation with somewhat tentative commitments.

The influence of teacher preparation takes center stage in the next two chapters, which examine how the commitments beginning teachers bring to their program and the learning opportunities they encounter shape their visions of good teaching and their practice. Prominent teacher educators argue that strong teacher education programs rest on a well-articulated vision of teaching that undergirds coursework and clinical experiences and provides a shared language for faculty, teachers, and teacher candidates.[28] Researchers have also documented the role of vision in teaching and teacher development.[29] In chapter 5, Karen Hammerness shows how each program is motivated by a distinct vision (or combination of visions) and how these influence the purposes, sense of agency, and visions that beginning teachers carry into teaching.

Recent research draws renewed attention to the importance of centering teacher education on the practice of teaching.[30] Teaching is, after all, a professional practice. So learning to teach means learning to enact a principled practice in a particular context. Chapter 6 offers portraits of six teachers who enact the commitments and pedagogical practices advocated by each program. These cases of individual teachers-in-action illustrate the impact that context-specific teacher preparation can have on teachers' commitments and practice and on their understandings of the settings where they work.

Chapters 7 and 8 bring the impact of schools and the perspectives of school leaders to the fore. Considerable research underscores the effects of administrative leadership and professional culture on teacher retention and attrition, especially in the early years of teaching.[31] In chapter 7, drawing on interviews with the principals who hired and supervised these teachers, Eran Tamir examines what school leaders do to orient, support, and develop new teachers and how this varies within and across school sectors. Then, in chapter 8, Tamir describes and analyzes how those factors shaped the decisions of teachers who participated in the Choosing to Teach study to stay in their first school, move to a different school, or leave teaching altogether.

In the final chapter, Sharon Feiman-Nemser revisits the overarching themes of the book, gathers together the major findings, and considers what the study has to say to teacher educators, policy makers, and researchers. The three programs presume that some contextual understandings and practices are critical to successful teaching in a given school sector, but they differ in how they define "the content of context" and what they do to help teachers learn to teach in those settings. These differences affect teachers' practice, sense of agency, and career decisions.

While school conditions often trump teacher preparation, programs that link a broad social mission and a vision of teaching with contextualized teaching practices can play a critical role in preparing and retaining strong teachers for hard-to-staff schools.

CHAPTER 1

Preparing Teachers for the Chicago Public Schools

The Urban Teacher Education Program, University of Chicago

KAVITA KAPADIA MATSKO AND KAREN HAMMERNESS

Urban school districts face a variety of complicated, interrelated issues that are important for aspiring teachers to understand, including racial and ethnic heterogeneity, concentrations of poverty, dense bureaucracies, and large scale.[1] In light of these complexities, an increasing number of teacher education programs identify themselves as preparing teachers specifically for urban schools. Some colleges and universities are also offering specialty programs that focus on urban teacher preparation, alongside more traditional programs. Similarly, the emerging model of urban teacher residencies, which takes an approach to teacher preparation based on the medical model, works in partnership with a specific school district and aims to provide a more comprehensive and "clinically rich," or practice-based, experience for prospective teachers. Yet, in all these cases, "urban" is rarely explicitly defined.

In this chapter we move beyond the notion of urban teacher preparation to examine how the University of Chicago's Urban Teacher Education Program prepares teachers for the challenging work of teaching in the Chicago Public Schools (CPS). We describe *what* new teachers learn about the specific context of Chicago and *how* they learn that context-specific knowledge. We explain what UTEP faculty think teachers need to know about CPS and the varied ways that UTEP defines the urban context. We illustrate the opportunities UTEP candidates have to learn about these features of the context and point to key themes that run through the program: inquiry into self, inquiry into children, inquiry into practice, and inquiry into socially just activist teaching in order to develop a responsive stance and teaching practice that is tailored, in particular, to the CPS setting.

Unpacking the "Urban" Context of the Chicago Public Schools

The Chicago Context

In the late 1980s, Chicago received notoriety when U.S. Secretary of Education William Bennett proclaimed its public schools to be the worst in the nation. Operating as the third-largest district in the country, CPS is responsible for educating 18 percent of the students in the state of Illinois. The district is comprised of 681 schools and serves more than 404,000 students, the majority of whom are from low-income families (87 percent). Approximately 85 percent of the student body is made up of African American (42 percent) and Latino (44 percent) students, while about 9 percent of the students are white.[2]

CPS has been at the forefront of school reform since it was one of the first districts taken over by the office of mayor in 1995, a move that was catalyzed by chronic student underperformance. Since that time, many of the country's educational policies and debates have been spurred to life in Chicago, including increased attention to standardized assessments; the organization of local school councils that draw from the community to oversee the work of school leaders; the opening of one hundred new schools in the name of offering school choice to families; controversial school closings and "turnarounds" as mechanisms for school improvement; and a new system for teacher evaluation. These moves, coupled with the financial hardships faced by the state in recent years, have resulted in a vast array of processes and initiatives that all teachers in the system must navigate. Novices preparing to enter the workforce must manage the implications of all of these policies while also learning how to teach in settings that have been influenced by these policies.

UTEP

The Urban Teacher Education Program resides within the Urban Education Institute (UEI) at the University of Chicago. Reviving the tradition of teacher education at the university that flourished in the 1960s and 1970s,

UTEP and UEI embrace the mission of preparing teachers who will work toward reliably excellent schooling in Chicago and across the nation.

UTEP began in the fall of 2003 with two goals: to prepare high-quality teachers to enter the CPS system and to develop an innovative model for teacher preparation. The program awards a MAT degree and Illinois certification in one of three pathways: elementary school teaching (grades K–9), secondary school (grades 6–12) teaching, or endorsement in either mathematics or the biological sciences. The program design is intentionally crafted as a hybrid between a theoretically focused university-based model and a residency model, where clinical experiences are central.

Students. Students seeking to learn how to teach with UTEP express a strong commitment to social justice and equity and a deep desire to work in the Chicago system and have typically had some kind of life or work experience in urban communities. Through interview processes, students who are accepted into the program demonstrate strong content knowledge, reflective abilities, and effective interpersonal skills. The student body is comprised of University of Chicago undergraduates, graduates of other colleges and universities nationwide, and a few candidates seeking a change in career. The program is organized around a cohort model and therefore remains intentionally small; a maximum of twenty-five candidates are accepted into each certification pathway each year.

Curriculum. UTEP explicitly promotes teaching as "intellectual work" that requires nuanced understanding of the context, subject-matter expertise, extensive clinical and pedagogical training, and knowledge of self. Toward that end, several themes of inquiry are embedded in an interdisciplinary manner into the UTEP curriculum (see table 1.1). These inquiries result in exploration of self, children, practice, and of social justice–oriented teaching.

The first academic year of the program, called the Foundations year, integrates four strands of work: academic and methods coursework, guided tutoring, fieldwork experiences, and an introspective "soul" strand. This structure provides candidates multiple opportunities to learn about the history of public schooling in Chicago; participate in facilitated discussions about race, class, culture, and educational equity; and work with children and adolescents in structured, supervised school settings. By virtue of these various entry points into the work of being a teacher in CPS, candidates are simultaneously engaged in interrogating and exploring the aforementioned themes in the curriculum. For example, through the work of soul strand, candidates are pushed to understand their own motivations, perspectives, and identities as a way to consider how they might get to know students. Tutoring requirements and related assignments in the program provide extensive opportunities to know and *see* children and begin to engage in child-centered instructional practices. Collectively, this combination of work is intended to further candidates' commitments and understandings about social justice teaching.

During the next phase of the program, candidates spend a summer in methods coursework and become immersed in a clinical residency that spans the academic school year. Candidates are placed in two classroom settings over the course of the year that provide complementary schooling and teaching experiences. UTEP's preservice residents are hosted and mentored by carefully selected classroom teachers who serve as the program's clinical instructors. Methods and equity coursework are wrapped tightly around the extensive clinical immersion during residency; coursework intentionally builds on and draws from the experiences in the field. During the second year of the program, the themes of inquiry deepen as the extensive work and relationships with children become the mechanisms through which to better understand pedagogy and self. Becoming participants in a school community helps residents begin to understand how systemic inequities such as institutionalized racism and classism and linguistically/culturally subtractive and assimilationist policies might play out at the school level. Residents are also equipped with conceptual frameworks, vocabulary, and instructional practices to help them begin to work across dimensions of difference—thus adding to their understandings of what it means to be a teacher of social justice.

During the last summer of the program, candidates complete a final course co-taught by residency instructors and postgraduate induction coaches in which the activities and assignments are designed to smoothly transition candidates into their own classrooms. As teachers of record, program graduates continue learning across the themes of inquiry set forth at the start of the program about the self, children, practice, and social justice teaching. It is during this challenging novice teacher phase that graduates must continue to apply strategies to enact socially just choices in the classroom as well as in the larger society. A major focus of the program's postgraduation support is developing alumni to be classroom-based teacher-leaders and future clinical instructors for the program, so that they can assist and support the learning of their UTEP peers.[3]

Learning the Contexts of the Chicago Public Schools

Although the features of the CPS context that the program deems important are nested, overlapping, and often interrelated in the program's day-to-day work, they hold unique content for teachers who are preparing to enter the Chicago teaching workforce. UTEP's context-specific focus attends to the historical, political, racial, economic, and cultural particularities of Chicago as well as localized knowledge about the district's routines, procedures, and curriculum. In comparison to the other two programs, which define context more in terms of communities and groups, UTEP pays more attention to the geographical and regional context.

Federal/State Policy Context

UTEP recruits and attracts candidates who are invested in social justice and have the potential to become culturally competent teacher-leaders in the Chicago Public Schools. Through coursework, candidates explore the notion of teaching as political and moral action, so that even students who initially do not consider themselves especially political develop an awareness of the potential connections among the work of teaching, adherence to moral principles, and participation in social action. One candidate remarked, "We've learned about the extent to which kids are subjected to things that just shouldn't be happening to [them] . . . It just seems like our [country's] motives are completely amiss."

The study of landmark court cases such as *Brown v. Board of Education,* significant federal initiatives such as No Child Left Behind, and debates around standardized testing, school finances, and the movement toward national standards and assessments all inform candidates' political-

TABLE 1.1 UTEP elementary program overview

Quarter	Year 1: Internship	Year 2: Residency	Years 3–5: Induction
Autumn	Schools and Communities; Number Theory; additional courses as needed to fulfill the state's general education and/or endorsement requirements	Introduction to Math Concepts and Pedagogy; Elements of Literacy Instruction III: Reading and Writing across the Content Areas	Postgraduate supports: ongoing job-embedded coaching bimonthly in conjunction with first-year teacher meetings and/or interest-based inquiry groups
Winter	Teaching and Learning in Urban Schools; Geometry	Elements of Social Studies Instruction	
Spring	Human Development and Learning; Elements of Literacy Instruction I: Reading	Unit Design and Assessment; Elements of Science Instruction	
Summer	Elements of Literacy Instruction II: Writing		
Autumn	Fieldwork (guided observations of schools, classrooms, teachers, students, and curriculum); tutoring (mathematics and literacy); assistant teaching	Seminar & Practicum: Professional Teaching I	
Winter	Fieldwork (guided observations of schools, classrooms, teachers, students, and curriculum); tutoring (mathematics and literacy); assistant teaching	Seminar & Practicum: Professional Teaching II	
Spring	Fieldwork (guided observations of schools, classrooms, teachers, students, and curriculum); assistant teaching	Seminar & Practicum: Professional Teaching II	
Summer	Practicum: Small-group work	Transition to Teaching Seminar	
Autumn	Soul strand: Interns analyze how forms of privilege and oppression impact their identities and views and affect teaching and learning in the educational system. This strand prepares interns for developing multiple lenses to evaluate social institutions and policies and ways to enact conscious, just, and inclusive choices in their classrooms and schools.	Critical Analysis of Key Issues in Urban Education	
Winter		Justice-Centered Teaching in Urban Schools	
Spring			
Summer	Working with Students with Special Needs	Language and Linguistic Diversity	

educational perspectives and the ways in which they may heighten challenges inherent in teaching for equity. Conversations about federal and state policy inevitably flow into and inform discussions about the Chicago context. For example, candidates learn about powerful local organizations such as Teachers for Social Justice and local education reporting such as Catalyst. In this way, aspiring teachers become informed about issues pertinent to educators in Chicago and learn the value of remaining so. Candidates' exploration into education policy and politics begins during the Foundations year and continues into the second, when, for instance, they see the intended and unintended consequences of shifting accountability structures that are emblematic of the current education environment.

The Public School Context

During the first year, candidates begin defining and exploring large public schools by studying their general characteristics and associated macro-level constraints. These constraints include the density and size of an urban school district, working with limited resources, limited teacher influence in schoolwide and classroom decision making, high teacher turnover, and depersonalized working environments that are manifest, for example, in large class sizes or prescribed curricula.[4]

Candidates read portraits of urban schools, in particular those captured in seminal works by Jonathan Kozol and Charles Payne, and research and develop school portraits of the sites in which they intern, obtaining a more nuanced perspective of the public school context in Chicago.[5] Engaging in these school studies, according to faculty, is the first step in highlighting the differences within and across schools and in establishing a counter-narrative to generalizations about urban schools. At the completion of the nine-month Foundations year, candidates enter the residency better armed to experience the Chicago urban school landscape. As one UTEP faculty member put it, "The reality of urban education is that we have to produce teachers who are capable of functioning in this environment of urgency; but also to come away with a larger vision of what schooling can look like in Chicago."

Neighborhood/Community Context

Chicago is recognized as one of the most segregated cities in the nation, with recent gentrification in the midsouth neighborhoods exacerbating the city's pattern of class isolation.[6] As a consequence, segregation in housing, schools, and virtually every other aspect of Chicago life is the backdrop against which UTEP graduates will teach. The program places most of its residents in schools on the city's South Side and West Side—regions that are predominantly African American and Latino, respectively.

Chicago's history as a destination of the Great Migration of the early twentieth century has indelibly shaped its African American communities.[7] Although 2010 census data suggest that the city's African American population is declining, the city's Latino population continues to grow. These demographic shifts have had profound influences on residential and economic patterns (and political agendas), which in turn affect CPS, including decisions around school closings. UTEP candidates study the effects of depopulation on jobs and social networks in working-class communities such as Woodlawn, a largely African American lakefront community adjacent to the University of Chicago, and Bronzeville, the historic African American neighborhood made famous by Gwendolyn Brooks and other black artists, businesspeople, and intellectuals.[8] After studying the geographical aspects of the entire city during their first year in the program, second-year residents complete their preservice teaching in two different neighborhoods. As part of this experience, they examine similarities and variations in each setting and analyze the impact of locality on the school environment. In this way, beyond the history of the communities and neighborhoods in Chicago, residents have opportunities to study specific African American and Latino neighborhoods—the very communities in which they may someday be employed.

Such exposure to the richness, traditions, and diversity of these communities aims to counter commonly held, monolithic views of African Americans and Latino families and prepares candidates to establish respectful and effective relationships with families and students. The social-political context candidates study as part of their learning about the communities includes teasing out nuanced relationships between culture and learning— a vital skill to acquire as they prepare to teach in Chicago.

Candidates also reflect on preconceived notions they bring to the program. For instance, the term "urban" often functions as a coded marker for "the conditions of cultural conflict grounded in racism and economic oppression."[9] Without explicit attention to existing generational, class, and familial differences within the African American and Latino communities, stereotypes can be unintentionally perpetuated or reinforced. UTEP therefore actively helps candidates debunk misconceptions associated with low-income communities of color. The University of Chicago, for example, is located in a mixed-income, multiethnic community surrounded by high-need African American neighborhoods. One student recalled, "Being at the University of Chicago makes you aware of the situation around you . . . Ideas were (unintentionally) perpetuated that these were dangerous communities . . . communities you should not enter." Forced to reconcile conflicting narratives about the local surroundings, the student concluded that she "just had to reject" prior messages after participating in UTEP.

To address stereotypical thinking directly, the Foundations curriculum (both academic courses and the soul strand) examines the history, structures, key institutions, and resources of the communities surrounding the university. In the second year residents participate in a yearlong seminar that provides a forum to share what they are observing in their preservice classrooms and learning about sociocultural context. One student recalled how the program "presented an image of parents that has a definite basis in reality . . . Most of the parents that I've come across want their children to succeed . . . but they work two jobs [making scheduling a conference with them challenging] . . . so it's sort of preparing me for those realities."

District Context

Like many of its counterparts across the country, CPS is a high-need school district that primarily serves students of color. Despite many similarities, large urban districts across the country can differ profoundly in terms of curricula, standards, expectations, and ways of operating. For example, CPS has a strong central office, yet first-time employment is the function of principals who hire teachers for their schools. A novice entering the district must also understand the role of Local School Councils as a feature of many CPS schools' governance as well as the city's long-term school reform effort to open many new charter schools, to reconstitute "failing" neighborhood schools for turnaround, and to close others. Candidates attend Local School Council meetings and community meetings when possible during their first year in the program to gain insight into these structures and their varying effectiveness. District policy in Chicago also promotes a wide variety of school types with different philosophies and approaches to instruction. By visiting a variety of schools across the city through the program's guided fieldwork strand, candidates become familiar with the array of public school options in Chicago that include, in addition to turnarounds and charters, contract, magnet, selective admissions, regional gifted centers, and neighborhood schools.[10]

Prospective teachers who have grappled with details of localized context will better understand the tensions inherent in how significant decisions are made. As one faculty member noted, "Residents receive 'CPS 101' throughout the program as a way of understanding the ins and outs of navigating the system to find useful resources." If the program's mission is to prepare students to enter Chicago's public school system, awareness about structural details such as these will promote candidates' success. Furthermore, understanding the variety of schools—and the philosophies emanating from them—may also be helpful in enabling new teachers to select school settings for their early careers that are particularly supportive or aligned with their own preparation.

Classroom/School Context

The CPS classroom is where UTEP candidates learn about instructional practice. Required clinical training at select University of Chicago and CPS partner schools creates a common "text" for candidates, allowing them to become familiar with the balanced literacy and *Everyday Mathematics* curricula that strongly align with instructional frameworks candidates learn about in their coursework. Candidates are also exposed to other commonly used instructional material in the district to learn local curricular expectations and practices, thus putting them on a much firmer footing when they enter their classrooms as teachers of record. Early exposure to local curricula also provides candidates with opportunities to consider how to use the material in a manner that meaningfully draws on their knowledge of their students.

Because schoolchildren themselves are key to context, UTEP staff and faculty want candidates to understand relationships among students and teacher, their respective cultures, and the subject matter—all of which converge in the classroom. During the Foundations year, preparation for classroom context is infused in signature assignments such as a school study, a student study, and a study of a CPS teacher. Candidates are taught to *see* individual pupils by developing astute observation skills and awareness of the various lenses through which their behavior is interpreted. Additive frameworks such as "funds of knowledge" help candidates acknowledge and tap into the multiple strengths in students' families and communities.[11] In the same way, candidates create cases about a teacher. Through both the student and teacher study assignments, generalizations about urban schoolchildren and teachers are dismantled; what is instead emphasized is the relationship between the individual and the forces in the environment and the ways that they act on and react to one another.

More broadly, opportunities to understand classroom context are embedded in candidates' learning about culturally relevant pedagogy. Making curriculum relevant and engaging to students by building on their own knowledge, interests, and experiences receive great emphasis in the program. According to one faculty member, "We want teachers to find out what kids are interested in and tailor the curriculum to meet those interests." At the same time, UTEP candidates understand that cultural relevance is only one deciding factor in instructional material. One graduate elaborated, "[Just because my students say] . . . we want to read about 50 Cent . . . doesn't mean that I'm going to structure my unit around 50 Cent or some other rapper. I'm only willing to use [material that is] useful in their learning . . . and tied to goals." This observation highlights how content about the context—in this case the children—along with meaningful learning goals inform UTEP candidates' instructional decision making.[12]

From "Universal" to "Context-Specific" Teacher Preparation: A Stance and Practice in Action

UTEP faculty emphasize that in addition to agreement around what new teachers need to know about the features of the Chicago context, they share certain beliefs about what effective teachers need to know and be able to do in urban school settings. This requires nurturing students' stances toward social justice as well as practices to operationalize that commitment. It is worth noting that the practices that the program values are not urban or even Chicago specific, per se; instead, the program argues that cultivating particular perspectives and skills in light of knowledge gleaned from the context makes their *enactment* context specific.

Nurturing a Social Justice Stance Through Schooling

UTEP was founded on the assumption that a high-quality education is a critical lever to achieve social justice. The program selects individuals who are interested in making this kind of social commitment and capitalizes on these preexisting interests in intentional ways. This particular commitment, or stance, is deepened by providing students with the knowledge to recognize and name various forms of inequities and tools to act on them, particularly as they relate to a school setting.

Although this work occurs throughout the program, it is particularly emphasized through the soul strand, an introspective set of course experiences. The soul strand component of the Foundations year is designed to engage candidates in developing their teaching identities through conversations, readings, critical analysis, and reflections about how multiple forms of privilege and oppression have influenced their individual perspectives as well as the larger educational system. For example, through the development and sharing of an autoethnography assignment, candidates identify and interrogate the socializing forces that have shaped their personal identity development in order to broaden their perspectives on the experience of others, particularly those who are traditionally underrepresented in the mainstream culture and media.

Participation in a community walk activity establishes the foundation for a practice that will be critical to candidates' success as urban classroom teachers: their ability to move beyond the schoolhouse and to integrate with the communities in which they teach in order to understand the social, cultural, and systemic forces that surround their students and influence their development. This strand of work rests on a theory of action which posits that individuals must both know and understand themselves as cultural beings before they can know their students and that recognizing structural inequities will motivate and strengthen their commitments to social justice activism, thus highlighting key program themes of inquiry into self and into social justice activism. This commitment is required not only for UTEP's aspiring teachers but also encouraged for their pupils as well. One UTEP graduate explained that this means "asking kids about what's going on and getting their opinions and letting them know that they're a part of social justice . . . they're citizens and it's their job to have opinions about this."

The Interactive Read-Aloud

Preparing candidates to teach schoolchildren how to read, write, and communicate is inarguably a universal focus of teacher education. However, in Chicago this core concentration takes on a special urgency given the number of students who enter school with multiple language experiences or with primary languages different from the language and related demands required in school. UTEP therefore emphasizes the teaching of high-quality, culturally informed instructional practices based on a balanced literacy framework. One goal of the elementary program is to prepare candidates to teach literacy across the curriculum and to provide highly differentiated instruction to the students they will have—a necessity, since a wide range of reading levels and disparities is the norm in most CPS classrooms. For these reasons, the program particularly emphasizes the interactive read-aloud, an instructional practice that can be used in virtually all content areas.

The format of the interactive read-aloud appears on the surface to be relatively straightforward: teachers read from a conceptually accessible text that, ideally, is slightly above the class grade or reading level. The teacher periodically stops reading to model authentic responses and to ask questions that encourage the class to engage with and think about the text's meaning.

Before candidates learn the specific practice of a read-aloud, they read texts that provide them with insight about language forms and use that are relevant to their neighborhood and school contexts, such as standard English, African American English, and English as a second language. They are also asked to engage in a variety of asset-based activities that help them look at their students' strengths. One particular experience they have is conducting multiple home visits to inform them of the students' familial, neighborhood, and community contexts. Together, these experiences inform text and instructional strategy selection.

Candidates then begin to learn about the practice by viewing video depicting a high-quality enactment of an interactive read-aloud in CPS classrooms and begin to articulate its characteristics. UTEP staff also model the interactive read-aloud, including their decisions around book selection, highlighting relevance, development of teaching points, and follow-up activities. Because staff members have been teachers in CPS schools, they explore the choices and decisions about book selection, goals, and assessments with reference to the strengths, needs, and resources of the children they themselves taught in the CPS schools. During visits to classrooms, candidates observe and document teachers reading to children and collect examples of student-teacher dialogue, with particular emphasis on questioning techniques. In this way, attention to the universal practice of read-aloud is coupled with understanding specific classroom conditions.

Classroom observation is followed by formal instruction in the UTEP methods classes. During the Literacy Methods class, candidates learn about the history of reading curriculum shifts in CPS, as well as the mechanics of leading an effective interactive read-aloud. The choice of textually complex and/or thought-provoking literature beyond children's independent reading level advances many important skills and dispositions, from comprehending and synthesizing factual information to spurring the imagination and fostering discussion evoked by literature. Providing repeated opportunities for children to learn and practice these skills is particularly important in CPS, where children's main exposure to books often occurs in the classroom. Candidates working with second language learners, for example, are taught to emphasize opportunities to engage in discussion and discourse to support oral language development. Candidates then prepare to conduct an interactive read-aloud in the classroom where they are assigned to work during the year. They rehearse their lessons with their cohort and incorporate suggestions for improving it, again with their particular students in mind. As a final assessment, candidates plan and create two follow-up read-aloud lessons that incorporate children's learning as well as the feedback obtained during the first cycle. Candidates then revisit their read-aloud lesson series during their second year in the program, when, as residents in a new CPS classroom, they develop a three-week literacy unit tailored to account for the interests, experiences, strengths, and needs of the children in front of them and assume responsibility for instruction.

These steps highlight the embedded emphasis on themes related to children and practice that run through the program. Moreover, the meticulous process of teaching a central literacy instructional practice draws intentional lines among student, context, and practice in a way that informs candidates' pedagogy more broadly and serves as an important example of how UTEP blends the imperative to teach both content and context.

The program's attention to the *particulars* of its local surroundings begins to illuminate how a teacher education program might move beyond a focus on generic notions of urban teacher preparation and begin to engage its aspiring teachers in the content of the specific context. Thus, *context* extends well beyond a conception of a candidate's immediate physical surroundings as simply the setting in which one learns to teach to include the setting-specific content that may be important for teacher candidates to learn as part of their preparation process. Knowledge about the community, the setting, and the children inform teacher's day-to-day decision making and instructional moves. In this manner, a teacher's interaction with and knowledge of various aspects of context deeply affect her development and ability to be successful in the work of teaching.

Lessons from UTEP's Chicago-Specific Design

The demands associated with working in urban schools continue to be highlighted by research across disciplines. In response, a growing number of programs of all types—university based, alternative, and residency—claim to prepare teachers for urban school settings. The term "urban," however, is rarely explicitly defined, and so what aspiring teachers ought to learn to be effective in urban settings is also not clear. The issues, both political and practical, that may be pertinent to new teachers in Los Angeles, for instance, are different that those entering the profession in Miami.

In examining the University of Chicago's Urban Teacher Education Program, we describe the features that the program faculty have considered as central to the Chicago context. These features represent important knowledge about how the classroom, school, community, district, and state and federal policy world all influence teaching and learning at the classroom level. Such a focus—coupled with an integrated emphasis on the themes of self, children, practice, and social justice activism—creates UTEP's "Chicago-specific" design for localized and nuanced teacher preparation. Our examination of the program's scope and sequence, assignments, and syllabi reveals an array of opportunities for candidates to grapple with various aspects of the Chicago context. UTEP not only helps its candidates learn the particulars of a stance toward social justice that is informed by the Chicago context, but it also helps candidates know themselves and learn to enact pedagogies with the specifics of the students as well as the landscape in mind.

CHAPTER 2

Preparing Teachers for Urban and Rural Catholic Schools

The Alliance for Catholic Education Service Through Teaching Program, University of Notre Dame

CHRISTIAN DALLAVIS AND ANTHONY HOLTER

The capacity of Catholic schools to provide high-quality, low-cost education to urban communities has been greatly diminished in recent years. Beleaguered by financial strains and concerns about Catholic identity, many of these schools are closing. At the same time, urban Catholic schools serve increasingly diverse student populations. In the 2013–2014 academic year, nearly 300,000 Latino children were enrolled in Catholic schools, accounting for 15 percent of all Catholic school students. In all, 34.8 percent of all Catholic school students were from racial and ethnic minority groups.[1]

Catholic schools also comprise the largest sector of faith-based schools, accounting for one in every three in the nation, and their viability in urban areas is often seen as a bellwether for urban faith-based schools broadly.[2]

Attracting and retaining high-quality teachers is essential to the success of urban Catholic schools. The Alliance for Catholic Education at the University of Notre Dame has tried to address this need by preparing teachers to serve in increasingly diverse Catholic schools through the ACE Service Through Teaching program (ACE STT). The largest preparer of Catholic school teachers in the nation, ACE STT annually places 180 teachers in more than 100 Catholic schools in thirty-three communities, and in twenty years ACE has prepared and placed nearly 1,500 teachers in Catholic schools across the United States.

In this chapter we present the results of an examination of ACE's preparation of teachers for the multiple contexts of their placements, providing a descriptive analysis of the Catholic school context in which ACE teachers served and salient demographic features of ACE teachers and schools. We examine course syllabi and program handbooks from the ACE academic program, looking closely, for example, at the content of a course called Teaching in the Catholic School that sought to prepare teachers specifically for Catholic schools. We also integrate interview data regarding core programmatic elements that specifically address the classroom context, identifying program leaders' beliefs about what ACE teachers needed to know to be effective in the specific communities in which they taught, including the religious, racial, ethnic, geographic, and socioeconomic aspects of the ACE schools. The chapter concludes with our suggestions for teacher educators who prepare students for schools with multiple salient contextual dimensions, describing ways that teacher preparation programs might learn from ACE's experience preparing teachers for multiple "nested" layers of school context.

The Alliance for Catholic Education

ACE offers a two-year alternative teacher preparation program that includes practicum teaching, content and pedagogical training, online coursework, and a supervised teaching placement in a Catholic school community (see table 2.1). Teachers spend fifteen weeks over two summers at Notre Dame taking teacher preparation courses and two academic years taking online coursework.

ACE attracts a strong applicant pool of college graduates, drawing more than 400 applications for ninety spots in 2014, nearly all of whom studied in an undergraduate major other than education. As a result, ACE has attracted teachers who have a strong academic background in the content area in which they will teach. Applicants come from a diverse array of selective undergraduate institutions and are selected through an intensive process that considers their academic record, leadership experiences, and commitment to service. ACE prepares these selected recent college graduates and novice teachers for the specific context of a Catholic school and for teaching students who often differ from them racially, socioeconomically,

TABLE 2.1 Overview of ACE STT program elements

Session	Activity	Location	Duration
Summer session 1	Academic coursework Practicum teaching	University of Notre Dame	8 weeks
Academic year 1	Academic coursework Supervised teaching	ACE placement site	10 months
Summer session 2	Academic coursework	University of Notre Dame	7 weeks
Academic year 2	Academic coursework Supervised teaching	ACE placement site	10 months
Summer session 3	Graduation	University of Notre Dame	1 week

and/or culturally. Even though the original mission of ACE was not focused on recruiting career educators, more than 70 percent of ACE graduates have remained in education beyond the two-year program, and the majority continues to teach in Catholic schools.[3] More importantly, approximately 98 percent of all ACE STT teachers persisted through the two years of the program, completing their term of service and earning a graduate degree.

ACE teachers are assigned by program administrators to live in rural and urban areas to teach in underresourced Catholic schools, primarily in the southern and southwestern United States. Nearly every ACE teacher works with students who come from a racial, ethnic, or socioeconomic background that is different from their own. As a result, the ACE experience reveals how multiple contexts of schooling intersect in complex ways for beginning teachers. Because they do not choose their placement, ACE teachers have struggled to adapt to the particular cultural and geographic contexts of their schools while also adapting to the Catholic school context. We have come to recognize these varied—and, in certain ways, competing—contexts as "nested layers" of context that ACE teachers worked to navigate and reconcile during their two years in ACE. Program administrators also struggled with these layers of context, as the condensed schedule of an alternative preparation program makes it difficult to address multiple contexts effectively.

Nested Layers of Context

Every teacher faces multiple layers of context in the classroom, and within each layer of context there are a variety of salient features. There is the immediate classroom context, which is determined by the grade level and subject area taught. There is the school context, some salient features of which may include its organizational structure as a traditional public, charter, private secular, or private religious school. There is the community context, which may reflect cultural contexts related to ethnic, racial, and/or socioeconomic dynamics. Here, we use "culture" to refer to a dynamic set of factors that shape how people view the world and act in it. We follow Sonia Nieto and Patty Bode in viewing cultural contexts as shaped by shared "history, geographic location, language, social class, [and] religion."[4]

The features that are most salient may vary from teacher to teacher, depending on one's personal background and experiences. For ACE teachers, the salient contexts were often those where the teachers experienced the greatest disconnect from their own lives, while those that resonated closely with the teachers' experience were often overlooked. Just as white teachers teaching white students often do not recognize the importance of race in the classroom, ACE teachers often did not notice the contexts in which they were already familiar and comfortable.[5] These were related to race, ethnicity, socioeconomic status, geography, or even the religious context of the school. For example, ACE teachers who attended Catholic schools themselves did not typically have trouble adapting to the Catholic school context, while those who had only attended public schools found it difficult to acclimate to the religious school environment. To prepare all ACE teachers effectively, program administrators have made decisions about which contexts receive the most programmatic attention. When the amount of time spent with teachers is greatly limited by the design of the program, some layers of context are necessarily given more attention than others. In particular, those layers that are addressed by state accreditation and certification requirements, like grade-level pedagogy and content area curriculum, receive more attention than layers that are not so explicitly prescribed by external forces, like cultural context.

Cultural Competence

Scholars concerned about the achievement gap and educational inequality argue that teacher preparation programs must prepare teachers for the contexts with which they are unfamiliar and uncomfortable, and researchers have developed and supported a framework of culturally responsive pedagogy that prepares teachers to work with students whose backgrounds differ from their own.[6] Teachers who are prepared to employ culturally responsive teaching practices are able to "make classroom instruction more consistent with the cultural orientations of ethnically diverse students."[7] One of the central goals of culturally responsive pedagogy is to foster cultural competence among students and teachers, which requires "that the teacher must become, in essence, a student of students' cultures."[8] To successfully operate in unfamiliar community contexts, teachers must acquire "thorough knowledge about the culture, values, learning styles, historical legacies, contributions, and achievements of different ethnic groups."[9] The culturally competent teacher is thus armed with an explicit understanding that multiple salient dimensions of context are at play in each particular school, and these teachers are equipped with tools they will need to understand these dimensions and their influence on classroom dynamics.

Figure 2.1 illustrates the nested layers of context that ACE teachers often encountered. The discussion that follows will provide a description of the contexts teachers encountered in ACE schools and a description of the contexts that were familiar to most ACE teachers, calling attention to the tension points where ACE teachers' backgrounds might demand more explicit programmatic preparation for specific layers of context. We will then describe how the program prioritized preparation for each of those layers of context, calling attention to specific ways that the program attended to each layer of context as well as areas of tension that emerged when these contexts competed for programmatic attention.

The Contexts for Which ACE Prepares Teachers

The founding mission of the ACE STT program was to recruit and prepare talented teachers for service in Catholic schools with limited resources,

FIGURE 2.1 Nested layers of context in ACE STT

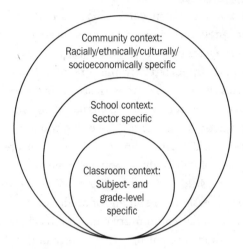

with the larger mission of strengthening and sustaining these Catholic schools over the long term. As such, over the two-year program, the course sequence for the master of arts in education degree is designed to address the specific classroom, school, and community contexts. The focus on specific contexts is weighted differently in each course and across the entire curriculum to meet the most pressing demands of teaching first and with the most depth (see table 2.2).

The Classroom Context

The classroom context (e.g., grade and content area) received the greatest attention in course syllabi and was the primary focus of the official academic programming. In fact, over 80 percent of all formal academic coursework focused specifically and primarily on the content area (e.g., mathematics), developmental level (e.g., high school), and general classroom teaching responsibilities (e.g., classroom management, instructional methods, assessment) that shaped the classroom context.

ACE STT teachers were new to the teaching profession, and because of the parameters for their certification and the conferral of a graduate degree in education, the academic curriculum has been highly constrained. ACE STT, however, provided a foundation in pedagogy, instruction, and assess-

TABLE 2.2 Course sequence and the Catholic school context in the curriculum

Session	Course	Primary context addressed
Summer session 1	Introduction to Teaching	Classroom
	Practicum	Classroom
	Introduction to Computers in Education	Classroom
	Teaching in Catholic Schools	Community/School

	Effective Elementary Classroom Teaching*
	  Introduction to Middle School Teaching
	  Introduction to High School Teaching
		Classroom

	Seminar in Content Area I*
	  Teaching of Reading
	  Math in Elementary Education
		Classroom

	Integrative Seminar	Community/School
Academic year 1	Supervised Teaching	Classroom
	Clinical Seminar	Classroom
	Topics in Educational Psychology	Classroom

Summer session 2	Exceptionality in Childhood*
	  Exceptionality in Early Adolescence
	  Exceptionality in Adolescence
		Classroom

	Child Development and Moral Education* Development and Moral Education in Adolescence	Classroom

	Seminar in Content Area II*
	  Language Arts
	  Content Methods
	  Elementary Language Arts Assessment
		Classroom

	Integrative Seminar	Community/School
Academic year 2	Supervised Teaching	Classroom
	Clinical Seminar	Classroom
	Assessment in Content Area II* Assessment in Elementary Education	Classroom

* Variation of course sequence due to content area or elementary, middle, or high school placement.

ment for novice teachers, especially compared to other alternative teacher certification programs. For example, teacher candidates in top-tier alternative teacher education programs complete an average of 432 hours of instruction. ACE STT Teachers completed 479 hours of instruction, 145 of which were completed before they entered the classroom as teachers of record. The high number of instructional hours completed by ACE STT teachers places ACE in the top quartile of all alternative teacher certification programs nationally.[10]

Interviews with key program personnel revealed that directors, faculty, and pastoral staff alike all indicated that a primary focus of the program is to help students develop "the knowledge and skills to be successful . . . in whatever school setting they are placed." Teachers were viewed as "professional educators who hold kids to really high standards." The programmatic emphasis on the classroom context—with a great deal of time dedicated to developing content and grade-level-specific pedagogical knowledge—has proven to effectively prepare teachers for the demands of this context.

The School Context

The specific school context, sometimes referred to as the school sector (e.g., public, private, etc.), refers to the salient school-level characteristics that shaped the learning experience and the ACE STT teachers' preparation for teaching. All ACE STT teachers were placed for service in Catholic schools across the United States. This sector has a rich history and documented positive effects that distinguish these schools from other public and private K–12 institutions, though the dynamics of this specific school context were explicitly addressed in only about 12 percent of the courses that comprised the official academic curriculum.[11]

The Catholic school context in which ACE STT teachers served often resonated deeply with their own educational experiences and personal religious identities and beliefs. Program evaluation data indicate that over 90 percent of ACE teachers were Catholic and that many had personal experience as students in Catholic schools (though it is important to note that a Catholic religious affiliation is not a prerequisite for participation in ACE STT). In fact, more than 50 percent attended Catholic primary school and secondary school, and a staggering 35 percent attended Catholic schools continuously from kindergarten through college or university. This common Catholic school experience and shared religious identity was more than a nominal connection between teacher and student, between teacher and school context. As the senior director of the ACE STT academic program, asserted, "There is, at root theologically, a relationship established before [ACE STT teachers] ever walk into a classroom."

The Community Context

Each Catholic school and classroom where ACE STT teachers served was situated within a local and geographic context that influenced teaching and learning, and those locales shaped the official ACE STT curriculum. Since ACE has partnered with a variety of Catholic schools across diverse geographic and local contexts, there were several salient dimensions of cultural context affecting ACE STT teachers and their competence and efficacy. Approximately 18 percent of the courses in the official academic curriculum were designed to address the geographic and cultural contexts where ACE STT teachers lived and worked.

The general economic status of the local community where ACE STT teachers served was perhaps one of the most important dimensions that characterize it. Because ACE's mission is targeted to service in underresourced schools, many ACE teachers encountered socioeconomic contexts that affected classroom dynamics, as they often educated large numbers of children from economically disadvantaged families and communities. The annual census of ACE placements sites—communities where ACE STT teachers live and work—revealed that over 90 percent of ACE STT schools were in communities where the child poverty rate exceeds the national average.

The common challenges expressed by children and communities facing economic hardship are exacerbated further by other cultural factors related to race and ethnicity, such as those evidenced in predominately Latino communities in Texas, Arizona, and southern California or in African American communities in Memphis and Atlanta, or to unique geographic context, as in rural communities in southern Louisiana or on a Native American reservation in southern Arizona. This rather large diversity in ACE placement sites—geographically, culturally, and economically—has the result of placing most ACE teachers into specific contexts that are unfamiliar, even to each other. As a result, ACE teachers are at a high risk of finding themselves in the situation described by Geneva Gay, who argues, "When the cultures of students and teachers are not synchronized, someone loses out. Invariably, it is the students."[12]

Since ACE teachers were typically placed in cities and states that were new to them and in school communities that served children from ethnic, racial, and socioeconomic groups that did not reflect their own background, what did they need to know to be successful educators in each of these contexts?

Programmatic Preparation for Context and the Three Pillars

ACE used the concept of three "pillars" to describe the ways that the program offered support to its participants. The three pillars of ACE are professional service, community life, and spiritual growth. New ACE teachers were introduced to this conceptual framework during the recruitment period, when the pillars were framed as the structure of programmatic support that beginning teachers should expect to receive from ACE. The pillars also represent the three formal dimensions of the program. ACE teachers were graduate students enrolled in an academic program that prepared them for the professional responsibilities of the classroom. ACE teachers were assigned to live together in an intentional Christian community in a particular locale and then participated in a series of retreats that offered opportunities for spiritual growth and reflection on the vocation of teaching.

The pillars are explicitly integrated into both the official and unofficial curriculum of the ACE STT program, and while it is somewhat artificial to separate them, it is helpful to consider how each of the three pillars provided support to beginning teachers, particularly with regard to how they prepared ACE teachers to deal with the nested layers of context that inflected their experience as teachers. In addition to the formal academic program and the retreat program, ACE STT also relied on an unofficial or informal curriculum to help prepare candidates for their specific school and community contexts. During both the summer sessions and academic year, ACE STT candidates lived, studied, prayed and worked in a community of peers.

First-year teachers learned about the school and city where they would be working and living from those who had just completed a year of service in those very places. Through these less formal interactions, they gained some insight into the school and cultural contexts (of course this insight is limited, because the second-year ACE teachers only held a one-year head start on the new teachers).

The Classroom Context

Professional service was the focus of the majority of the coursework in the ACE master of education program, and the emphasis in the academic program was on preparing teachers for the grade level and subject area of their particular classroom assignment. ACE teachers assigned to teach fifth grade were enrolled in a similar course of study as those teaching physics in high school, but the content of the courses varied to attend to the particular developmental level and content of the teaching assignment.

ACE teachers began preparing for the classroom context in earnest during the first week of the ACE summer program, when they took Introduction to Teaching, a five-day intensive course that combined all-group instruction in the history and philosophy of schooling in the United States with grade-level-specific workshops in classroom management. ACE teachers then took a variety of courses for the remainder of the summer (see table 2.2), including methods and assessment courses tailored to the particular grade level and content area of each teacher's assignment. During the first summer, teachers spent mornings in local summer school programs participating in a practicum experience that provided mentored opportunities to observe and practice teaching.

During the school year, ACE teachers were enrolled as full-time graduate students in online courses designed to strengthen their instruction and assessment practices. Professors from Notre Dame visited each ACE teacher every semester to provide professional support, and principals and mentor teachers in the schools conducted formal observations every semester. These formal observations, the feedback conversations that follow, and the online assignments were primarily focused on supporting teachers in their grade-level and content-specific classroom context. The focus on content knowledge and pedagogy was perhaps most clearly evident in the performance indicators used to assign grades to ACE teachers in the Supervised Teaching course.

During each semester of service, ACE teachers were observed and evaluated according to a set of indicators of performance in the classroom. There are twenty-eight performance indicators in all, and each semester supervisors focused on a different set of indicators.[13] During the first semester of teaching, teachers were evaluated as "proficient," "basic," or "unsatisfactory" in seven "necessary" indicators and seven additional "sufficient" indicators. The necessary indicators were related to classroom management, procedures, record keeping, professionalism, parent communication, establishing a respectful rapport with students, and organizing the physical space of the classroom. The sufficient indicators included content knowledge and pedagogy, instructional objectives, communication, questioning and discussion techniques, student engagement, assessment, and providing feedback to students (see table 2.3).

In the second semester, the seven sufficient indicators became necessary indicators and expectations for performance were raised. At the same time, four new sufficient indicators were considered: classroom culture, knowledge of resources, differentiating instruction, and contributions to the school community. In the third semester six additional sufficient indicators were considered, including demonstrating knowledge of students, designing coherent unit-based instruction, articulating instructional goals, designing assessments that provide evidence of learning, modifying instruction for exceptional learners, and promoting student engagement with community resources. Finally, during the fourth semester, the ungraded indicators were considered: contributing to the larger community, fostering character and ethnical development, fostering spiritual development, and serving as a spiritual and ethical role model.

Over the course of four semesters, teachers were evaluated on twenty-eight indicators, twenty-one of which are graded. Of the total indicators, twenty-one fell under the "professional teaching" pillar, three were classified as "community" related, and four were categorized under "spirituality." Three of the four spirituality performance indicators and one of the three community indicators were ungraded.

TABLE 2.3   ACE supervised teaching performance indicators

	Semester assessed			
	Fall 1	Spring 1	Fall 2	Spring 2

Pillar 1: Professional teaching

Domain 1: Planning and preparation

	Fall 1	Spring 1	Fall 2	Spring 2
Demonstrates knowledge of content and pedagogy	Sufficient	Necessary	Necessary	Necessary
Demonstrates knowledge of students			Sufficient	Necessary
Designs coherent unit-based instruction			Sufficient	Necessary
Selects instructional objectives	Sufficient	Necessary	Necessary	Necessary
Selects instructional outcomes/goals			Sufficient	Necessary
Design assessments to provide evidence of learning			Sufficient	Necessary
Demonstrates knowledge of resources		Sufficient	Necessary	Necessary

Domain 2: The classroom environment

	Fall 1	Spring 1	Fall 2	Spring 2
Establishes a culture for learning		Sufficient	Necessary	Necessary
Manages classroom procedures	Necessary	Necessary	Necessary	Necessary
Manages student behavior	Necessary	Necessary	Necessary	Necessary
Organizes physical space	Necessary	Necessary	Necessary	Necessary

Domain 3: Instruction

	Fall 1	Spring 1	Fall 2	Spring 2
Communicates clearly and accurately	Sufficient	Necessary	Necessary	Necessary
Uses questioning and discussion techniques	Sufficient	Necessary	Necessary	Necessary
Engages students in learning	Sufficient	Necessary	Necessary	Necessary
Provides feedback to students	Sufficient	Necessary	Necessary	Necessary
Modifies instruction according to developmental level, language proficiency, and learning styles of students		Sufficient	Necessary	Necessary
Modifies instruction for children with learning exceptionalities			Sufficient	Necessary
Assesses student learning	Sufficient	Necessary	Necessary	Necessary

Domain 4: Professional responsibilities

	Fall 1	Spring 1	Fall 2	Spring 2
Maintains accurate records	Necessary	Necessary	Necessary	Necessary
Communicates with parents and guardians	Necessary	Necessary	Necessary	Necessary
Demonstrates professionalism	Necessary	Necessary	Necessary	Necessary

Pillar 2: Community

	Fall 1	Spring 1	Fall 2	Spring 2
Contributes to the school community		Sufficient	Necessary	Necessary
Contributes to the larger community				Ungraded
Promotes student engagement with community resources			Sufficient	Necessary

Pillar 3: Spirituality

	Fall 1	Spring 1	Fall 2	Spring 2
Creates environment of respect and rapport	Necessary	Necessary	Necessary	Necessary
Fosters character and ethical development				Ungraded
Fosters spiritual development in children				Ungraded
Serves as spiritual and ethical role model				Ungraded

The School Context

Every ACE teacher worked in the Catholic school context, and the preparation for that context began during the orientation retreat held each April at Notre Dame—two full months before these future teachers began their formal academic training. The theme of this retreat—"Come and you will see"—echoed Christ's first invitation to his disciples, and the focus was on introducing ACE teachers to the model of Christ the teacher.[14]

The program also focused on the Catholic context of ACE teachers' schools through formal academic coursework. During the first week of the summer program, ACE teachers attended the Integrative Seminar each day. This one-credit course, as its name suggests, integrated the three pillars of professional service, community life, and spiritual growth. This seminar met each day of the first week and then weekly for the remainder of the summer, and all ACE teachers enrolled in the course during both their first and second summers. Most Integrative Seminar sessions were devoted to peer discussions explicitly, with the bulk of the course time dedicated to conversations within and among communities of ACE teachers, which provided a formal mechanism for ACE teachers to learn from peers about what it means to be a teacher in a Catholic school and about their community contexts. In particular, the seminar identified Jesus Christ as an exemplary model of teaching that all ACE teachers might emulate. Much of the course was dedicated to introducing ACE teachers to the philosophical foundations of Catholic education. Teachers studied the documents published by the U.S. Conference of Catholic Bishops, including its 1972 pastoral message *To Teach as Jesus Did* and the 2005 statement *Renewing Our Commitment to Catholic Schools*. *To Teach as Jesus Did* called on Catholic school educators to model their teaching after Christ in three particular ways: by teaching in a way that embraces "the message revealed by God which the Church proclaims; fellowship in the life of the Holy Spirit; service to the Christian community and the entire human community."[15] "To teach as Jesus did" is to transmit knowledge including the beliefs and tradition of the faith, to build community, and to engage in service to others.

According to the 2013 Integrative Seminar syllabus, the course also introduced beginning teachers to research literature that suggests the effectiveness of Catholic schools.[16] As the summer progressed, the seminar format encouraged conversations among community members on community life, community prayer, the social justice teachings of the Catholic Church, conflict resolution, communication issues, and service. Each session was grounded in a brief study of a relevant scriptural passage, and each week participants engaged in conversation with their housemates to prepare to live together and to serve in Catholic schools together.

Additionally, all ACE teachers enrolled in Teaching in a Catholic School, a one-credit course that met weekly throughout the first summer. This course, typically taught by a Holy Cross priest who was himself a former Catholic school teacher, introduced ACE teachers explicitly to the unique roles and responsibilities that teachers in Catholic schools experience. Instructors and teaching assistants, who often were also graduates of the ACE program, discussed scenarios, lessons, parent interactions, and school context issues that are uniquely inflected by the Catholic identity of the school. In this course, ACE teachers had the opportunity to explore social and political issues, moral dilemmas, and church teachings that could inform situations they may face in the classroom. Teachers who would be teaching religion also took the one-credit Religious Education course, which prepared them for the unique challenges of catechization, or teaching children about the Catholic faith. In this course, teachers learned the expectations that dioceses and parishes have for their teachers and spent time reading and discussing the catechism of the Catholic Church and engaging in focused assignments to explore how to approach sensitive issues and handle difficult conversations that may emerge in a religion class. In particular, they discussed how to facilitate conversations about politicized issues that their students see in the news and in their everyday lives, including abortion, sexuality, immigration, racism, poverty, birth control, health care, and the death penalty. This course sought to ensure that ACE teachers were prepared to facilitate those conversations in ways that are authentically informed by teachings of the Catholic Church.

The ACE STT retreat program also provided significant resources for preparing teachers for the Catholic context of their schools. All ACE teachers gathered in Texas during the first weekend of December for the annual

December Retreat, which was primarily dedicated to personal spiritual growth and community building but which also devoted significant time to reflecting on the experience of being a Catholic school teacher.

The Community Context

The community context received attention throughout the academic and retreat programs, and it was the focus of a series of additional sessions that accompanied the formal academic curriculum.

During the April Retreat, new ACE teachers met their future housemates as well as their superintendent, who provided a brief introduction to the local geographic, ethnic, and cultural context of their new community assignment. Over the course of that weekend, ACE teachers were encouraged to reflect on aspects of their own cultural identity when they responded to the question, "Who am I?" By sharing these conversations with their "future family and bosses"—their soon-to-be housemates and their superintendents—ACE teachers began to consider how elements of their own racial, ethnic, and class culture would differ from that of the students they were preparing to teach in the fall.[17] Identifying the areas of dissonance can be an important first step in ensuring that student learning does not suffer from a disconnect between teacher and student.[18]

During the summer program, ACE offered several opportunities for teachers to consider the role of cultural context. The Integrative Seminar devoted significant class time to preparing teachers to live together in community, and teachers were encouraged during this course to explore ways to integrate their lives into the local cultural community. During the first week of the first summer session, teachers spent a morning devoted to considering both their own cultural identities and the cultural contexts of the schools in which they would serve. Segments of the Introduction to Teaching course in the first week introduced the teachers to concepts like multicultural education, culturally responsive pedagogy, and sociocultural theories of learning.

Another session in the first week on multicultural education and diversity and two additional evening workshops on community, diversity, and cultural context augmented the formal curriculum and provided a broad overview of and introduction to the racial/ethnic and geographic diversity of the schools and communities in which ACE STT teachers would live and work. Participants attended six hours of sessions that paid particular attention to education in the African American and Latino communities and then another session pertaining to their own specific school context or their personal interest. In these workshops, ACE STT teachers had an opportunity to work together with other teachers who serve in similar cultural contexts. During one of the workshops, the program invited leaders of schools that serve a variety of communities to meet with ACE teachers. For example, a principal of an all–African American school spent time with the ACE teachers assigned to predominantly African American schools in Atlanta, Memphis, Jacksonville, and Los Angeles. In another workshop, ACE teachers serving in predominantly Hispanic communities in Texas gathered with principals of similar schools. Additionally, ACE graduates who served in those schools were also invited to join new ACE STT teachers to explore the unique opportunities and challenges that they experienced as teachers in these communities.

In these sessions, ACE teachers were encouraged to seek greater understanding of cultural differences, and they spent time discussing some salient elements of the culture they serve, though always with the caution that too great a focus can devolve into unhelpful stereotyping. For example, in one session on serving in Hispanic communities, a lively discussion emerged about the differences between Hispanic schools in the Rio Grande Valley and Hispanic schools in Los Angeles or Florida. One conversation focused on the deep respect that many teachers are afforded in Hispanic communities; the privileged place of *la maestra* was a new concept for many teachers who had never lived in Hispanic communities, and a discussion of this concept helped some teachers understand why their students' parents deferred to the teacher so completely. Conversations like these were designed to help ACE teachers begin the process of developing cultural competence, which has been described as becoming "a student of student cultures."[19]

Some syllabi revealed an introduction and integration of cultural competence and culturally responsive pedagogy throughout content-area pedagogy courses as well. For example, the middle school language arts content methods course devoted significant time and attention to the development of cultural competence, as did the middle and high school social studies methods course.

Informally, ACE's structure—as a two-year program with both first- and second-year teachers enrolled at the same time—created an additional layer of support for helping many ACE teachers engage the local community. Most first-year teachers shared a home with more experienced second-year teachers, who often served as live-in mentors to help new arrivals acclimate to the local culture and community. There were, however, a number of ACE communities that are "self-contained," where the entire community consisted of either first- or second-year teachers who did not receive the benefit of having housemates who have already lived in the community for a year.

Finally, most ACE teachers were highly engaged in service and other extracurricular activities in the school and local community, which exposed them to a wider array of community experiences and individuals than did classroom teaching alone. Through this intentional engagement outside the bounds of the classroom or even school context, most ACE teachers formed relationships with other adults in the community that fostered a greater integration into the local community and culture.

Enhancing an Integrated Approach

To more clearly address the primary and salient contexts in which ACE STT candidates taught, we have treated each context and pillar as discrete entities. We know, though, that the contexts our teachers navigated, and the support structures designed to help them do so successfully, were not so neatly delineated. In fact, we believe that a signature strength of the ACE STT program is precisely the intentional integration of support structures (professional service, community life, spiritual growth) across the nested layers of context (classroom, school, community) that ACE STT teachers navigated each day.

Although initially constructed in response to the constraints of an alternative teacher preparation program, and to meet the requirements for certification and degree conferral, this integrated approach has proven an effective scaffold for teacher preparation. Faculty and staff in the ACE STT program indicated that this integrated approach helps teachers develop a disposition of "constant improvement." The two-year course sequence and formal academic curriculum is framed as the base and launching pad from which these novice educators must seek ongoing formation to become highly effective and reflective educators. Faculty members noted that the central lesson conveyed to ACE teachers is that it is okay if "they don't have it figured out after one or two years, [because] good teachers are constantly improving."

ACE faculty and staff regularly sought opportunities to both evaluate and improve the formal and informal curriculum. A first consideration for enhancing this integrated approach to teacher preparation relates to the official curriculum. As we have already discussed, there is a potential danger in focusing too heavily on content knowledge and general pedagogy without commensurate coverage of the salient nested layers of context. As one faculty member stated, the teachers may "come in with facts and dates and a lot of knowledge, but they don't understand always how to make the cultural connections with the students." Because so many ACE teachers encountered cultural difference and dissonance in their ACE placements, this dynamic may create tension that could be ameliorated with a more balanced focus on context throughout the official curriculum.

Moreover, the tension created in the curriculum across the three contexts—the classroom, the school, and the local community—is in some ways artificial. Sound pedagogical or content knowledge absent an appreciation and incorporation of the religious identity of the school and the cultural identity of the community context is ineffective. Culture matters because how students learn is fundamentally social—because they learn from and with other people—and therefore learning is fundamentally cultural. In fact, careful alignment of culture and instruction can positively impact student achievement.[20]

The second consideration for enhancing the model relates to the timing and pacing of the curriculum. The ACE STT model of preparing teachers for the Catholic school context is constrained by time, and this time constraint can result in certain salient contexts being overlooked or underconsidered. One faculty member lamented the limited amount of time he had with his students, saying, "I just wish we had more time. That's the downside of a fifteen-week program, which is essentially what we have." The program could only afford, in terms of time, to offer one one-credit course dedicated to the Catholic school context and only a few short additive sessions to address the myriad concerns regarding cultural, racial, and ethnic contexts. After these formal encounters in the curriculum, the choice to incorporate these contexts into specific courses is left to each individual faculty member.

While our review of syllabi indicated that a context-specific focus is indeed present in many courses, there were still opportunities to enhance and integrate the cultural context more intentionally and consistently across the program. This alternative model of teacher formation—the short two-year cycle and compacted summer schedule—placed real limits on both the depth and breadth of the official curriculum. This model, though, highlights the potential for the program—including ethos, expectations, norms, and overall structure—to play an important role in the overall formation of highly effective teachers for the Catholic school context.

The Need for a Context Mind-Set

The contextual dynamics of a Catholic school have changed dramatically over the past several decades. Fifty years ago a Catholic primary school in Brooklyn would have resembled Catholic primary schools in Denver or Los Angeles or Minneapolis, largely serving a single European ethnic group and being staffed by religious men and women from the same ethnic community.[21] This is no longer the case, and it is often not true of Catholic schools even in the same town or neighborhood. The changing face of Catholic schools requires that school leaders and teachers—and the teacher educators who prepare them—be even more attentive to the nested layers of context that define these communities and shape the teaching and learning that happens in these schools.

The nested layers of context and the tensions they reveal call attention to the need for teacher preparation programs like ACE to specifically prepare teachers to understand the unique nature of the Catholic school context, to have strong content and pedagogical knowledge so they are prepared for the specific classroom context, and to be culturally competent so they are prepared to work with children from cultural groups different from their own. Programs like ACE need to be explicit when preparing teachers about the various salient contexts teachers will face on-site. Teacher educators in programs like ACE must instill in their beginning teachers a context-aware mind-set, preparing them to recognize the many ways different aspects of context might inflect the teaching and learning that happen in their classroom.

Given the ACE mission to sustain and strengthen Catholic schools "to ensure that all children, especially those from low-income families, have the opportunity to experience the gift of an excellent Catholic education," the preparation of teachers and leaders for these schools must maintain the important and precarious balance among religious understanding, content knowledge and pedagogical training, and cultural competence.[22] This focus on three distinct but intertwined elements of teacher preparation is irrevocably enmeshed in the Catholic tradition that animates these schools, which affirms Catholic schools as a privileged environment that provides "an exceptional educational experience for young people—one that is both truly Catholic and of the highest academic quality."[23]

CHAPTER 3

Preparing Teachers for Jewish Day Schools

The Day School Leadership Through Teaching Program, Brandeis University

SHARON FEIMAN-NEMSER

Since the 1980s, the number of Jewish all-day schools and the religious diversity of their students have increased.[1] Throughout the twentieth century, most day school students came from Orthodox Jewish families. Starting in the 1980s, however, increasing numbers of non-Orthodox families began choosing a day school education for their children. This was a most unexpected social development, given the long-standing commitment of the American Jewish community to public education.

The growth of non-Orthodox, or "liberal," Jewish day schools created a demand for skilled teachers who could address the academic and Jewish aspects of day school learning.[2] This spawned a handful of Jewish teacher training programs in the late twentieth and early twenty-first centuries, including DeLeT (Day School Leadership Through Teaching).[3] *Delet,* the Hebrew word for "door," was designed to open a door on a career in day school teaching. The program was the brainchild of a venture philanthropist who mobilized a group of generous funders to underwrite a pilot program at two academic sites, Brandeis University near Boston and the Hebrew Union College–Jewish Institute of Religion in Los Angeles. DeLeT mainly prepares generalist teachers for the elementary grades (1–6) in liberal Jewish day schools.[4]

Approved as an alternate route to certification in the state of Massachusetts, DeLeT combines professional studies with a yearlong internship in a local day school leading to a MAT degree and a state teaching license.

Graduates teach general and/or Jewish subjects depending on their background, the market, and the needs of their school. According to a program evaluation commissioned by the Jim Joseph Foundation, which has supported the program since 2007, DeLeT represents a "paradigm shift" in a field where teachers typically have a strong sense of vocation but lack professional training.[5]

In this chapter we describe and analyze how the DeLeT program at Brandeis University prepares beginning teachers for Jewish day schools and ask: What do program faculty think DeLeT graduates need to know, care about, and be able to do to succeed in this milieu? What aspects of the day school context receive explicit attention in the DeLeT curriculum? What opportunities do teacher candidates have to learn the content of this context and integrate it into their identity and practice as Jewish day school teachers? In answering these questions, we draw on interviews with program leaders and instructors, observations of key components of the formal and informal curriculum, and a focus group discussion with program leaders, instructors, and mentor teachers.[6] We also draw on program documents including course syllabi, handbooks, publicity, and the program's Web site. From these data we identified three layers of context that the program addresses in an explicit way, starting with the micro context of the *classroom* that interacts with the surrounding *school community* that in turn shapes and is shaped by the *wider Jewish and non-Jewish society*. Across these layers of context, three themes integral to teaching in Jewish day schools and to the program's stance play out: integration, inquiry, and community.

A Brief History of Jewish Day Schools

Between 1881 and 1914, unprecedented numbers of Jewish immigrants came to the United States from Eastern Europe and settled mainly in large cities. Facing enormous challenges in building a life and making a living, they embraced free public education as the key to becoming American and securing a better social and economic future. Initially they adopted the Protestant model of full-time public schooling and separate Sunday schools. Many immigrants, however, were more traditionally religious and less eager to assimilate. Frustrated with the limitations of truncated Jewish study, some gravitated to more intensive supplementary schooling, while others opened Orthodox all-day schools.[7]

Between 1940 and 1964, the number of Jewish day schools grew from thirty-five to 306.[8] Most were Orthodox, although the Conservative movement began establishing day schools in 1957. Reform Jews remained committed to public education and explicitly criticized day schools as inconsistent with a philosophy of integration into the larger society. In the 1970s, however, concerns about public schooling, disillusionment with civil rights, and a desire to provide Jewish educational alternatives led to the creation of a handful of Reform day schools in large cities.

A 2009 day school census commissioned by the AVI CHAI Foundation reported 800 day schools, up from 676 in 1998.[9] Of these, 200 (25 percent) were non-Orthodox, which included 98 community schools, 17 Reform schools, and 50 Conservative (Solomon Schechter) schools.[10] Most of the growth in the non-Orthodox sector has occurred in community day schools, which showed a 40 percent increase in the last decade, mainly at the high school level.[11] Community schools are pluralistic; they enroll students across the denominational spectrum of Judaism and welcome Jewish students with nonreligious, secular orientations as well.

Each Jewish day school functions more or less autonomously within its respective geographic community, and these local communities do not have a single authority structure. There are national associations of Jewish day schools connected with each major denomination of Judaism (Reform, Conservative, and Orthodox) as well as a national network of community day schools, but they do not exert control over school policy or practice. Outside the Orthodox community, day schools educate a relatively small segment of Jewish children compared to supplementary schools sponsored by local synagogues. Their student population is largely middle and upper middle class, and nearly all students are Jewish or have at least one Jewish parent.

The conventional history of Jewish day schools identifies two conflicting motivations for their establishment. Some day schools were founded to help young people integrate into the larger society; others were established to insulate them from the broader society, thereby ensuring their survival.

Today, however, all Jewish day schools coexist in and interact with a multi-layered milieu. As Alex Pomson explains, "Jewish day schools interact with a variety of communities and social forces located at varying proximity to their day-to-day operation."[12] The DeLeT program deals selectively with these external layers of context.

The DeLeT Program

The Day School Leadership Through Teaching teacher education program was started in 2001 because a visionary venture philanthropist, Laura Lauder, wanted to address the shortage of qualified teachers for liberal elementary day schools, particularly teachers who could teach general and Jewish subjects in an integrated way. Impressed with Teach For America (TFA), a service-oriented program that recruits talented graduates from elite colleges and universities for two years of teaching in hard-to-staff public schools, Lauder wanted to create a prestigious, selective, intensive fellowship to recruit and train day school teachers. She organized a group of funders who supported DeLeT during its first five years, when it functioned as a national fellowship program.[13]

Brandeis University, a nonsectarian, liberal arts college and research university with a history of service to the Jewish community, was selected as one of two academic sites for the program.[14] During the planning phase, a national design team articulated its beliefs about (good) teaching and learning and the mission of liberal Jewish day schools. It also agreed on a common structure—two summers of study and a yearlong internship during the intervening school year—and identified the subjects, both Jewish and general, that would be addressed. When DeLeT became part of the established educational offerings at both institutions, these ideas ensured a common framework and conceptual foundation for faculty, mentor teachers, and students.[15]

As a full-time, thirteen-month program, DeLeT combines Jewish and education studies with an intensive internship. Students spend two summers on campus taking courses and participating in cocurricular activities. During the intervening school year, they spend four days a week in a local day school learning to teach with the support and guidance of experienced teachers and clinical instructors. During their internship, students return to campus one day a week to continue their studies.

Students

DeLeT recruits teacher candidates who are Jewishly motivated, intellectually curious, passionate about learning and teaching, and keen to make a difference in the lives of Jewish children. A typical cohort of ten to twelve students consists of two-thirds recent college graduates and one-third career changers. Students bring varied Jewish backgrounds. The majority grew up in Conservative and Reform families, with some from Orthodox homes. In terms of their own Jewish education, about a third attended Jewish day schools, while the rest participated in other forms of Jewish education, including supplementary Hebrew school and Jewish summer camps. Most have spent time in Israel, touring, visiting, or studying.[16]

Many DeLeT alums attended top-ranked universities where they majored in a variety of subjects in the humanities and social sciences.[17] A little over half majored in religion or Jewish studies. DeLeT does not have a Hebrew language requirement, and students enter the program with varying skill, ranging from basic to fluent.[18]

Those with strong Jewish studies backgrounds often end up teaching Jewish studies, but even those who become elementary generalists are expected to integrate Jewish themes into their teaching, situate classroom experiences in a Jewish frame of reference, and serve as Jewish role models.[19] Like their students, DeLeT teachers are Jewish and mainly middle or upper middle class.

Vision and Curriculum

The program links a vision of liberal day school education with a vision of the kind of teacher the program aims to prepare. According to the first *DeLeT Handbook,* the central task of Jewish day schools is to enable students "to form integrated identities as they study and experience their dual heritage and responsibilities as Americans and as Jews."[20] To advance this vision, DeLeT aims to prepare elementary day school teachers who "(a) take students and their ideas seriously; (b) create democratic classrooms infused with Jewish values and experiences; (c) make meaningful connections between general and Jewish studies; (d) welcome parents as partners in children's education; (e) value Jewish text study as a core Jewish activity; (f) learn in and from their teaching."[21]

Several elements stand out in these outcomes. The list gives primacy to knowing pupils and fostering their capacity to think. It signals the teacher's responsibility to model and teach both Jewish and democratic values and to help students learn to be citizens of two communities. It implies that such learning may be enhanced by curricular integration. It highlights the value of learning from texts and from experience for both students and teachers.[22]

At Brandeis, five intersecting strands make up the DeLeT curriculum: fundamentals of teaching; clinical studies; subject matter pedagogy; learners and learning; Jewish literacy and identity (see table 3.1). A seminar on classroom teaching, tightly coordinated with the yearlong internship, runs through the program and provides a forum for learning about planning, instruction, assessment and classroom organization, management, and culture. Subject-specific methods courses address the learning and teaching of core subjects in the elementary curriculum, both general (mainly reading/language arts and math) and Jewish (Bible, prayer, holidays, Israel). A seminar on becoming a Jewish educator enables DeLeT students to articulate and explore their personal stance on basic theological and ideological issues and to consider the implications for their identity and practice as day school teachers.

The first summer emphasizes teachers as learners—of teaching, of classical Jewish texts, of reading and mathematics. The DeLeT students "need to know themselves as math learners before they can become math teachers," the program's mathematics educator observed in the focus group discussion, and her sentiment was echoed by the Bible instructor, who said, "That resonates with me in the area I teach. Students need to know themselves as learners of Torah."

As the school year unfolds, the focus shifts to teachers as facilitators of learning, Jewish role models, partners with parents, classroom researchers, and members of a distinctive school community. By the spring and second summer, the curriculum broadens out to consider the larger purposes of day schools in American society and zeroes in on helping students

TABLE 3.1   The MAT DeLeT program at a glance (2008–2009)

	Classroom teaching	Clinical studies	Subject matter pedagogy	Learners and learning	Jewish literacy and identity
Summer I	Foundations of Teaching	Reading practicum	Teaching Reading; Teaching Math; Art Workshop		Studying the Bible; Beit Midrash for Teachers
Fall	Funda-mentals of Teaching	Internship	Teaching Bible; Teaching Jewish Holidays	Psychology of Student Learning (child study)	Jewish Educator Seminar
Winter/ Spring	Funda-mentals of Teaching	Internship	Teaching Science; Teaching Israel		Jewish Educator Seminar
Summer II	Making Classroom Culture	Teacher research	Teaching Jewish Holidays; Art Workshop	Teaching Diverse Learners	Philosophy of Jewish Education; Prayer and Praying

plan for the start of a new school year as teachers of record in their own classroom.

A signature feature of the program is the yearlong internship. DeLeT partners with eight day schools in the greater Boston area representing a spectrum of Jewish life, from Reform and Conservative sponsorship to modern Orthodox and community day schools. Each school hosts one to three interns a year. Mentor teachers attend a summer institute and a monthly study group during the school year where they learn about the work DeLeT students are doing on campus, develop their mentoring skills, and address emergent questions and problems.[23] Interns also have a clinical instructor who helps them connect what they are learning at the university with what they are doing and learning in their internship placement.

Learning the Contexts of Jewish Day Schools

The DeLeT program attends to three layers of context: the classroom as the main locus of the teacher's responsibility; the school as an arena of parental partnership, professional collaboration, and teacher leadership; and the broader society with its civic and global values and tensions. Each layer presents the day school teacher with opportunities for inquiry, integration, and community building, and each has implications for the teacher's stance, identity, and practice.

DeLeT concentrates on nested layers of context *internal* to the school, specifically the classroom and school. As the main arenas of teaching, they are logical foci for initial teacher preparation. Across these layers of context, day school teachers are shapers and participants in multiple communities, including a classroom learning community, a professional community of practice, and a schoolwide community of parents and families whose influence looms large. In Jewish day schools, community is both a quality of the learning environment and a valued outcome of that environment.[24]

Jewish day schools are also situated in multiple *external* communities. Most prominent in the DeLeT program are ideological communities—religious, civic, cultural, and global, including Israel and the Jewish people worldwide. Issues related to these external communities come up organically in response to local, national, and international events and in several assigned places in the curriculum. Compared to the internal layers of context, however, they receive much less explicit attention.

Classroom as Community

Creating a classroom learning community is a central task of teaching and learning to teach.[25] DeLeT frames this task through a Jewish lens, expressing it prominently in the second of its seven teaching standards: "Day school teachers create classroom learning communities rooted in Jewish experiences and values." A teacher who enacts this standard "build[s] Jewish values and experiences into classroom life, use[s] Jewish texts and rituals to shape classroom culture, and connect[s] students' personal and social responsibilities to specific Jewish values."[26]

DeLeT students experience firsthand what it means to create and be part of a professional learning community through their participation in a unique structure, the Beit Midrash for Teachers, or "house of study."[27]

The Beit Midrash meets full time for one week during orientation week in the first summer of the program. DeLeT students study rabbinic texts about teaching and learning with a *havruta*, or study partner, and reflect on their experience as learners in partnership with text and other.[28] In this intensive, introductory, Jewish learning experience, Delet students are expected to take responsibility for their own and their partner's learning as they actively listen, ask clarifying questions, generate interpretations, look for textual evidence, and support and challenge their partner's ideas. By naming these practices and inviting students to practice them and reflect on the experience, the Beit Midrash begins to cultivate the skills and stance DeLeT students will need to study teaching and learning in a disciplined way and to engage in professional discourse as "critical colleagues."[29] In this way the Beit Midrash serves as a microcosm of and incubator for the Jewish professional learning community that the program aims to foster.[30]

Having experienced and analyzed the formation of a learning relationship with their havruta and considered the implications for their own professional learning community, DeLeT students turn their attention to the formation of a classroom learning community. In late August–early September, they interview their mentor teacher about her goals and plans for the year, then observe how she begins the school year with a new group of students. To inform this inquiry, students discuss relevant chapters in *Teaching Children to Care* by Ruth Charney, a publication based on the "responsive classroom" model. Their classroom inquiry focuses on both general and Jewish aspects of the second teaching standard, creating classroom learning communities infused with Jewish values and experiences. Examples of the former include setting up the physical environment, communicating clear expectations, and building relationships with students. Examples of the latter might include using Jewish texts to introduce classroom norms and values about how to treat others, establishing a "sacred space" for class prayer, and ending the week with a ritual that establishes a Sabbath mood.[31]

Across the internship, DeLeT students assume increasing responsibility for maintaining and enriching their mentor's classroom learning community. In the spring, DeLeT students visit the third grade classroom of an alumna (or study a Web case of this classroom) to observe how the teacher uses Jewish texts and havruta learning practices to teach language arts skills and foster community.[32] Finally, in the second summer of the program, DeLeT students begin planning for their own classroom community in a course called Creating Classroom Culture, where they clarify the kind of classroom culture they want to foster and how they will launch it during the opening weeks of school. Many consider how to use themes from the fall Jewish holidays, such as beginnings, reconciliation, and personal relationships, to create their classroom community.[33]

Curricular Integration

Another central task of teaching and learning to teach is instructional planning. DeLeT students learn an approach called "backward mapping" that emphasizes teaching for understanding and the close alignment of goals, assessments, and learning activities.[34] Students are expected to use this approach in planning lessons and units. In the early years of the program, they were also required to design an "integrated" unit based around "some meaningful connections between general and Judaic subject matter."[35]

DeLeT students have created integrated units in science, language arts, and social studies. One of the most successful units, taught to first and second graders by a succession of DeLeT interns, was a unit on generations and the handing down of tradition. Pupils interviewed an elder in their family, shared family artifacts, studied Jewish texts about treating elders with respect, and made time lines of key world events experienced by the elders, all the while practicing language arts skills of listening, speaking, reading, and writing.

Early DeLeT documents imply that curricular integration relates in some way to the larger goals of day school education: helping students "see the world whole" or "make sense of the world in an integrated fashion" or "strengthen their dual identities as Americans and Jews."[36] However, as Jon Levisohn argues, this conflates a practical strategy with broader ideological, sociological, or theological concerns. In his Philosophy of Jewish Education course, Levisohn introduces DeLeT students to definitions and conceptual confusions surrounding the term "integration" and recommends instead a "pedagogy of integrity" that fosters the habit of seeing connections.

Do students celebrating Chanukah recognize the complex interaction of Greek and Jewish culture? Have they considered the relationship between 19th century colonialism and the development of Zionism? Are they thinking about the similarities and differences between ancient Mesopotamia and ancient Israel? Raising and exploring such questions are central to a pedagogy of integrity.[37]

While curricular integration remains an aspirational goal, DeLeT students are no longer required to design and teach an integrated unit.[38] Still, they are strongly encouraged to "bring Jewish content into their teaching of general studies" and to help students make such connections.[39]

Learning and Serving a Day School Community

Only a third of the DeLeT students attended a Jewish day school during their elementary years, so, for most, day schools are unfamiliar settings. The yearlong internship enables each DeLeT student to experience the professional and communal activities and relationships that are part of being a day school teacher. These include faculty meetings, schoolwide holiday celebrations, parent-teacher conferences, school fund-raisers, prayer and life cycle events for staff and families, and professional development opportunities. Because the program partners with a variety of day schools, DeLeT students learn how different day schools organize and enact their Jewish and secular agendas. Partner schools include a pluralistic community school with Hebrew immersion, a Reform day school with a strong emphasis on social justice, two schools sponsored by the Conservative movement with robust but separate general and Jewish studies curricula, and a small modern Orthodox day school with a palpable sense of family. By hearing about the experiences of their peers, DeLeT students learn about the similarities and differences across a range of Jewish day schools.

Over the year, questions about activities and events within and beyond the school community arise, like: How do different schools handle prayer? What and how do they teach about Israel? How do administrators and teachers respond to major national and global events (e.g., 9/11, presidential elections, Katrina, Sandy Hook)? How do they deal with death and sickness on the part of teachers, parents, children? Sometimes these discussions happen informally; often they take place in a class or seminar where the examples help illuminate different orientations, guiding principles, and animating ideas.

DeLeT graduates are expected to serve as role models of Jewish learning and contribute to the Jewish life of the school. To prepare for these responsibilities, students explore their evolving Jewish identity and consider what this means for their personal and professional lives.

The Teacher as Textperson

The main locus of this identity work is the Jewish Educator Seminar, which provides a supportive context for students to question, clarify, and refine their theological and ideological positions on a range of Jewish issues and practices (e.g., God, Israel, keeping kosher, prayer). The program regards teachers' Jewish identity as work in progress and believes that day school teachers need to think about where they stand and why and what they are uncertain about in order to respond to children in authentic ways. As Judy Elkin, the first program director, explained, "Self-knowledge and self-awareness are really important in negotiating issues around identity. If you haven't dealt with the stuff yourself, you won't be able to help your students."[40]

Students encounter this idea in a text by Abraham Joshua Heschel that is a core reading in the program. Heschel writes, "When asking: Do I stand for what I teach? Do I believe what I say?, the teacher must be able to answer in the affirmative. *What we need more than anything else is not textbooks, but textpeople. It is the personality of the teacher which is the text that the pupils read: the text that they will never forget.*"[41] One project that stirs strong feelings and promotes identity exploration and development is called Jewish Journeys. Students are invited to bring some new aspect of Judaism into their lives and explore what it feels like, where it takes them, what questions it raises. Examples of practices that students have experimented with include lighting Sabbath candles on a regular basis, saying the *Shema* (a traditional prayer) at bedtime, and studying the weekly Torah portion themselves or talking about it with their own children.[42]

Students write about the experience of taking on a new Jewish practice in journal entries that they share with the instructor and another student in the cohort. Elkin, who pioneered this inquiry, explained the vision behind the project and how it relates to being a day school teacher:

> I've asked them to look at their Jewish lives, starting with the journey that has brought them to DeLeT and to think about the next steps on their journey. As Jewish educators who will be influencing the Jewish lives of children, they need to be aware of their growth as Jews not only as Jewish teachers. I'm particularly interested in the intersection between the Jewish personal and professional identities of Jewish educators. If we're to meaningfully influence the journeys our students will take, it won't be because we only care about Jewish life intellectually or pedagogically. It will happen because we also care about our own personal Jewish lives, take that seriously, and are actively involved in and curious about the way we continue to live our Judaism . . . None of us is "done" growing as Jews . . . Rather, Judaism, like life itself, is dynamic, challenging us to question, grow, change, reflect, act, and sometimes pause before once again jumping in.[43]

At the end of the program, faculty and mentors help graduates find a school community where they can succeed as teachers and feel comfortable Jewishly. Sometimes graduates end up teaching in schools they might never have considered but that now seem accessible or appropriate based on greater openness or clarity about their Jewish identity and their sense of themselves as a Jewish educator. Again, Elkin explained: "We spend time doing environmental scans and suggest they go to the head and ask what the stance of the school is toward sacred texts or tradition . . . They have to go through the process of saying, 'Where can I be myself as a Jew in a way that works for me?'"[44]

Parents as Partners

One element in the day school context that looms large for DeLeT teachers, especially in their early years of teaching, are parents. Jewish day schools are private or independent schools, and most parents have high expectations for a strong academic program along with rich opportunities for Jewish learning and socialization. As one faculty member put it,

> These are private schools with paying customers. The schools will not survive if our graduates cannot communicate well with parents, if they cannot handle a parent/teacher conference, if they can't write a newsletter to send home. Those are all things they have to be alerted to in the political context and they have to have the capacity to deal with that political context.[45]

In her interview, Elkin explained the reasons why parents send their children to elementary day schools: "Some want a good social group for their kids. Some think it's a better education. Some think the values are good . . . Lots and lots of reasons." To counter the myth that all parents want the same thing, the program regularly organizes a panel of parents who talk about what they want from a day school education and why they have chosen to send their children to a Jewish day school. But the program relies heavily on the school—mentor teachers, heads, and others—to help DeLeT fellows learn the ropes when it comes to working with parents, as the following excerpts from interviews with DeLeT graduates reveal.

> *Alum 1:* In DeLeT we went over how to talk to parents but . . . because you are in the field, you are talking to parents all the time.
>
> *Alum 2:* Some of my parents push their kids really hard . . . A lot are pushy, especially when they're paying for private school . . . My mentor always told me to be confidant and that's something I worked on.
>
> *Alum 3:* DeLeT forced me to do it, like last year we had to lead a parent conference with our mentor there.
>
> *Interviewer:* Did you learn anything from that?
>
> *Alum 3:* Yeah, because I had to say, "What are we going to do? You know, this is the kid, what are we going to say about him, what kinds of things do we have to get across, how do you start, how do you set up a conference . . . like a great anecdote at the beginning, then the meat of the issues, then like a good feeling to wrap it up.

Situating Day Schools in a Broader Social Context

A third layer of the day school context that DeLeT wants its teacher candidates to think about concerns the broader social milieu in which day schools are situated. This includes the Jewish and American communities as well as the broader society. Consistent with the program's inquiry stance, the desired outcome seems to be a greater openness to alternative perspectives and a greater sensitivity to the possibilities and tensions inherent in the idea of liberal day schools.

DeLeT students come from families spanning the Jewish denominational spectrum. By the end of the program, the largest percentages still identify with the Conservative (22 percent) and Reform (22 percent) movements, with a smaller number identifying as Orthodox (5 percent) or Modern Orthodox (10 percent). Still, many more respondents (39 percent) describe their religious affiliation as "conservadox," "postdenominational," "nonpracticing" and "Jewish"—terms that challenge traditional categories.[46]

The program affirms these differences as learning opportunities, as one faculty member explained: "Pluralism is part of the Jewish self conception of the program . . . The students are coming from lots of different places . . . and there is value in engagement across those differences." While the diversity varies from cohort to cohort, each year students have to learn about each other's Jewish orientations and figure out how they will eat, pray, study, and celebrate together. In the summer, for example, the outgoing cohort plans a welcome picnic and a Sabbath experience for the incoming cohort and a pregraduation ceremony (*tekkes ha-siyum*) for their family and friends. These occasions require DeLeT students to think through how their community, composed of Jews with different practices and needs, can come together in ways that work for everyone.

The experience raises awareness about the range of ways to be Jewish and sensitizes students to the religious and cultural diversity that exists among the families in their schools and within the larger Jewish community. As one intern in a Reform day school observed, "Everyone here is Jewish but the way they practice Judaism is so different. To be able to talk about that is really important to me so that the kids can see how different people approach things in different ways."

One might expect that everyone who comes to the DeLeT program embraces the idea of day schools without ambivalence. This is not the case, especially once teacher candidates spend time in their internship placements. By now the faculty members anticipate this reaction and are ready to explore the issues and tensions that accompany what they have come to call "the bubble conversation." Based on her six years of directing DeLeT, Judy Elkin was ready when the issue came up: "We had a really big conversation . . . about day schools being a bubble and is this a good idea, to raise Jewish children who don't know about the real world?"

On the one hand, DeLeT students recognize the value of educating children within a shared tradition and forming strong affective ties as a foundation for group loyalty and identity, as one student reflected: "There's a value for children to live in a bubble before they go out into the world, and there's no other way to learn who you are and what you believe." On the other hand, as another student indicated, they wonder whether or how children will learn to appreciate ethnic and racial diversity:

> Can you learn anything about tolerance when everyone is just like you, more or less? In a community day school, you're Orthodox, I'm Reform, you're unaffiliated, you're richer than I am. There's a kid here whose parents just came from Mexico and who knows nothing about America or English. Is that diversity? Can you learn what you need to learn in that kind of diverse setting, or do you need to be in public school where you're talking real diversity?

Some students struggle with their decision to become a day school teacher. One student began the program with some ambivalence, but she came to embrace the choice of teaching in a Jewish day school because of the opportunities to nurture students' spiritual growth and be herself:

> I actually struggle a lot with the decision because I went to public schools and my parents are big believers in public schools. But I feel there is an aspect of the spiritual growth of a child that could be missing when you're not allowed to talk about anything religious . . . Because who I am as a Jew is so important to me, I want to be able to share that with the kids I teach. To be in a school where it's very important to the parents also—the

Jewish identity of their children—allows me to have conversations with the kids that I wouldn't be able to have otherwise.

The conversation about "Why day schools?" continues in Philosophy of Jewish Education, where the syllabus outlines the purposes of the course:

> As Jewish educators and teacher/leaders, it is vitally important to think about the ultimate purposes of education in general and Jewish education specifically, as well as such related issues as the role that day schools play in the educational process (and the justice of promoting private schools for the Jewish community,) the nature of religious education (and whether it is possible to educate for religious commitment without falling into indoctrination,) and the question of the limitations of educational and religious pluralism.[47]

One assignment has students comparing two books about vision-guided schools: Deborah Meir's *The Power of Their Ideas* and Daniel Pekarsky's *Vision at Work: The Theory and Practice of Beit Raban.*[48] The schools, one public and the other a Jewish day school, have many similarities—strong leaders, a commitment to student autonomy, a democratic spirit, elements of progressive education. But Meier's book makes a strong argument for public schools and their centrality in a democracy, while Pekarsky's book describes a school deeply committed to teaching classical Jewish texts and traditional academic subjects in ways that value and encourage student thinking and questioning. When the students find Meier's vision compelling, the instructor raises the question, "Why send children to a Jewish day school?

Often the answers tend to go in the direction of comfort for both students and teachers, which has both a positive and a negative valence. It's good for young children to be in a nurturing environment where they can explore and grow and feel known and understood. And it's good for teachers to work in schools where they feel comfortable being who they are. At the same time, one can be too comfortable, too satisfied, not sufficiently challenged. The instructor does not feel responsible for resolving this tension, only for raising questions and fostering sensitivity to the costs and benefits of being separate.

But, as Noreen Leibson, the current director, explained, DeLeT assumes that those who apply to the program value the idea of a school as a Jewish community, even if they have some conflicts and ambivalences: "It's okay if students are wondering, 'How will this play out for me?' But if you are really fighting with yourself about your Jewish identity, this probably is not a good place to work that out. We have a responsibility to prepare teachers who will be Jewish role models." By engaging students in these deliberations, the program hopes it is preparing teachers who can help their school continually re-examine how it is carrying out its Jewish mission.

Cross-Cutting Themes

In preparing teachers for liberal Jewish day schools, the DeLeT program combines features of reform-minded university teacher education with features of urban residency programs. The practice-centered orientation of the program is reflected in the heavy emphasis on pedagogy and in the yearlong mentored internship in a local day school. In many ways, the program relies on the internship to help aspiring teachers learn what it means and what it takes to teach successfully in a Jewish day school.

The program attends to three layers of the day school context: the classroom, the school, and the broader society. As the main arena of the teacher's work, the classroom receives the most attention. DeLeT students devote most of their time to developing the knowledge, skills, and dispositions they will need to be effective classroom teachers. The multisubject nature of the elementary school curriculum, the day school's dual curriculum of general and Jewish studies, and the program's vision of DeLeT graduates as teacher leaders and Jewish role models make this a challenging goal for a preservice program.

The focus on the classroom and school contexts makes sense. Many day schools are reluctant to hire beginning teachers. Given the cost of day school tuition, some parents resent having their child taught by a new teacher, and day schools are just beginning to take new teacher induction seriously. These aspects of the day school environment place tremendous pressure on new teachers who are still learning to teach.

DeLeT supports graduates in their first two years of teaching and offers continuing professional development to all alumni in keeping with the program's view that learning to teach well happens over time in a community of practice.[49] Novices teaching in the greater Boston area can participate in monthly dinner meetings at Brandeis that provide a forum for problem solving, support, and professional development. After three years of day school teaching, alumni may be considered for the role of mentor teacher, which the program regards as a form of teacher leadership. An annual, week-long summer institute enables interested alumni to work on curriculum projects with like-minded colleagues and faculty. DAN, the national DeLeT Alumni Network, sponsors regional and national conferences, online networking, and other opportunities for professional growth.

The DeLeT program aims to help day school teachers learn what they need to know to fit into their day school community, be successful in their classroom, and relate well to parents, colleagues, and administrators. At the same time, the program wants its graduates to become teacher leaders who strengthen the professional culture of the school, promote the ongoing improvement of teaching, and learning and contribute to the Jewish mission. Three themes unify the DeLeT curriculum across the different layers of context and help prepare DeLeT students for these varied roles.

The theme of inquiry plays out across the three layers of context. DeLeT students conduct a series of individual classroom inquiries, including a study of how their mentor begins the year with a group of pupils, a study of a child who puzzles or intrigues them, and a piece of classroom research based on a question or problem that has arisen in the course of their internship.[50] As a cohort, DeLeT students investigate various issues that affect day schools and their relationship to the broader world, such as how different day schools handle prayer, teach Israel, or respond to pressing national and international events. These investigations help foster a reflective, inquiry-oriented stance toward teaching and learning to teach in a Jewish day school.

The same inquiry stance is extended to the study of Jewish beliefs and practices. Across the program, DeLeT students explore, question, and strengthen their Jewish identity as they deepen their Jewish literacy. The guiding assumption is that teachers must be thoughtful about their own evolving Jewish identity in order to relate to their students with authenticity and integrity. A related theme, integration, further unifies the work of becoming a day school teacher. The program's embrace of curricular integration has come to mean making connections across different domains of knowledge, including secular and Jewish studies. DeLeT students are encouraged to make connections between their personal and professional identities as they explore the opportunities and challenges that day school teaching entails and seek a school where they can be comfortable Jewish.

A related theme of community shapes the DeLeT experience and links the different layers of context through its dual role as end and means. Students form a strong personal and professional learning community with their cohort, beginning with their early experience studying Jewish texts with a partner in the Beit Midrash for Teacher. They learn to create classroom communities infused with Jewish values and experiences and to participate in a schoolwide community of families and colleagues. They think about the broader implications of a day school education for children's understanding of and sense of responsibility for local, national, and global communities, both Jewish and non-Jewish. In all these cases, community is both an outcome of learning and a way to get there.

CHAPTER 4

Choosing to Teach

Identity and Agency among Beginning Teachers

BETHAMIE HOROWITZ

The foregoing chapters have emphasized the programs and how they pre-pared new teachers for their work contexts. This chapter turns to the thirty people the Choosing to Teach Study followed from the start of their teacher preparation through three or four years of working and learning in their schools. Here the beginning teachers take center stage in an investigation of what led them to these particular programs and how their experiences there shaped their professional lives going forward. How did they come to choose teaching? How did they come to see themselves as Catholic, urban public, or Jewish day school teachers? How they were able to mobilize themselves effectively in the early years of teaching? This is a tale about their evolving identities and their emerging sense of agency, and how both of these elements play a role in their ability to feel capable and effective as teachers.

Identity has gained considerable traction in the study of teachers, although the concept remains slippery.[1] As a concept, identity is needed to move beyond the idea of a person simply fulfilling a role. Becoming an effec-tive teacher involves not only learning a complex craft but also coming to inhabit and enact the role of teacher in the face of a complex array of expec-tations, demands, and requirements that vary by setting.[2] This conception of the individualized and internalized aspect of teacher identity suggests the importance of attending to the ways that teachers draw on broader personal capacities and resources beyond the specifics of teaching. For the most part, the research examines teachers' evolving professional identity as a distinct domain without explicitly linking the teaching self to other parts of the person. At the same time, scholars have employed the concept of teacher identity as the personal "glue" needed to integrate the knowledge and skills teachers need to be effective.[3]

The three teacher education programs in the Choosing to Teach Study explicitly focused on connecting teacher candidates' emerging sense of themselves as teachers to their existing sense of themselves as Catholics, Jews, or people committed to social justice because they viewed cultivating these connections as a particularly powerful way to prepare teachers for their respective schools. Likewise, the programs sought participants who were committed to their particular cultural/religious world (Catholic, Jewish, or social justice oriented) and expected them to work subsequently in those settings.

In studying participants from these programs, I used a wider aperture than is typically used in studying the identities of new teachers, one that allowed me to include their religious, cultural, and ideological backgrounds and attendant identities.[4] This strategy helps to connect the study of new teachers to the broader sociological investigation of emerging adults facing the challenges of determining their professional direction. For them the issues of identity formation, self-organization, and agency are shaping concerns.[5]

The juxtaposition of professional and religious or ideological identities in these programs created a rich opportunity to connect two domains that have typically been studied in isolation. Scholars studying religious identities have investigated the relationship between individuals' upbringings and their subsequent choices, while those who study teachers have focused on identity formation in the context of the teacher education programs and then in their work.[6] In bridging these domains, it is important to think about what people bring with them from earlier in their lives and how these ideas inform subsequent choices.

In the case of both religious identity and teacher identity, there is an involuntary aspect that stems from early upbringing, education, and schooling. Growing up within a particular milieu, individuals imbibe various images of what it means to be a Catholic or a Jew. This basic patterning creates familiarity, routine, and, ultimately, a disposition, sensibility, or outlook that shapes one's sense of place in the world, or habitus.[7] The process of becoming a teacher is similar. The long "apprenticeship of observation" that future teachers spend as pupils in elementary and secondary school results in deeply embedded preconceptions of teaching and learning.[8] These internalized images and ideas shape new teachers' beliefs and often form the default response in their work.

In the realms of both religion and profession, past experience, familiarity, immersion, and identity play roles in shaping, but not determining, a new teacher's future choices. Emerging adults are not shaped solely by their origins or by their aspirations for the future; often there is an interaction between chance, arising from circumstances of upbringing over which they have no control, and choice, the voluntary, deliberate things they seek to do.

In this regard, there has been a growing recognition that attending to identity alone is not sufficient in accounting for people's ability to navigate effectively in the complex, changing circumstances of their work lives. In addition to developing a sense of oneself as a Jewish or Catholic or urban public educator, a new teacher must also develop a capability to exercise judgment about what one needs to do and to make that happen. Social theorists call this *agency*.

Agency, or the ability to function effectively and creatively in an environment, involves three related elements: being sufficiently immersed in the context to operate fluently in it, taking stock of the conditions, and having a direction or purpose going forward.[9] Here I explore the interplay of identity and agency, chance and choice in the lives of thirty people who elected to pursue professional preparation for teaching. The data come from two in-depth interviews, the first conducted after a year of teacher preparation and the second two years later, plus a short background questionnaire that the teaching candidates filled out at the time of the first interview.[10] The longitudinal design allowed me to trace the participants' accounts of themselves at three points in time: during their upbringing, soon after they had commenced the teacher education program, and several years after they had been working as teachers, after they had moved out of the supportive orbit of the teacher education programs into the world of teaching. In particular, my analysis focuses on their *entrance accounts*, points in the interviews where they discuss how they ended up in teaching and in the particular program.

I begin with a brief socio-demographic overview introducing the thirty teachers, followed by a description of their connections to being Jewish, Catholic, or committed to social justice and to teaching before they entered the programs. After looking at the ways teachers' backgrounds aligned with the purposes of the programs, I turn more directly to learn about the participants in the process of making a life choice, analyzing how they spoke about their decision to embark on the program and grouping them based on how they spoke about this process—as chance or as choice. Finally, looking in greater depth at the cases of six candidates who came to the programs with more tentative commitments to teaching, I trace how their identities and sense of agency were affected by their particular work circumstances. I conclude with some reflections on why attending to agency matters in studying the preparation of teachers.

Introducing the Teachers and Their Initial Alignments with the Programs

Roughly two-thirds of the 30 teachers in our sample were female, and nearly all (27) indicated they were white, and most (25) were American born (see table 4.1). Nearly every participant (29) had recently completed a four-year college, which meant they were classified as "emerging adults."[11] All of the UTEP teachers graduated from the University of Chicago, the main source of candidates in the early years of the program. Both ACE and DeLeT drew from a wider array of four-year colleges.

One other thing characterized the people in this study: all of them expressed strongly the importance to their lives of being Jewish, Catholic, or committed to social justice. This should come as no surprise, given that all three programs recruit participants with strong Catholic, Jewish, or social justice commitments or identities. These commitments were mirrored in the kinds of upbringing people brought with them as they entered these programs.

Digging a bit deeper into their histories, I found a bit more variation in what each participant brought by way of background and prior involvement related to the cultural and teaching foci of the programs. The vast majority (27) of these ACE, DeLeT, and UTEP candidates came to their teacher

TABLE 4.1   Sex, race, and birthplace of participants by program

		UTEP	ACE	DeLeT	Total
Sex	Female	8	6	8	22
	Male	2	4	2	8
Race	White	7	10	10	27
	Person of color	3			3
Birthplace	United States	6	9	10	25
	Elsewhere	4	1		5

education programs from schooling experiences that were generally aligned with the cultural orientation or larger purposes of their teacher education program (see table 4.2). All of the ACE participants were raised Catholic and had attended at least some Catholic school prior to college, most of which were Catholic-affiliated institutions. Likewise, nine DeLeT participants were raised Jewish, six had attended Jewish schools, and three of the remaining four who went to public schools went to Jewish summer camps. Thus, both ACE and DeLeT attracted applicants from networks of schools, churches/synagogues, camps, youth groups, and so on that constitute (in part) the American Catholic and American Jewish social worlds.

In contrast, the world of social justice does not have that kind of long-standing institutional character. Seven of the UTEP participants attended public school, although this by itself is not indicative of their subjective, internal connections to either *urban* public schooling or to social justice.[12] In their in-depth interviews, however, eight described situations from their own backgrounds that revealed a visceral, emotional correspondence with UTEP's aims. For example, Lara linked her interest in urban public education to her own experiences growing up on a farm in rural Wyoming:

> A lot of [UTEP's philosophy and vision] matched with my own, which is kind of strange because I came from a rural background. I grew up on a farm. My dad was a farmer for thirty-five years. But I think just living in the city and for some reason, I always recognized; even before even living in Wyoming, I recognized the need and the inequality that existed in, not

TABLE 4.2   Participants' backgrounds: Religion and schooling

Connections to the program's cultural orientation	UTEP	ACE	DeLeT	Total
Current religion				
Jewish	*		10	10
Catholic	3	10		13
Lutheran	2			2
None	5			5
Religion of upbringing				
Jewish			9	9
Catholic	5	10		15
Other Christian	4			4
Jewish and Christian			1**	1
None	1			1
Type of schooling during upbringing				
Public	7	4	4	15
Any Catholic	2	6		8
Any Jewish			6	6
Other private	1			1
Summary: Participants with experiences during upbringing that aligned with the social justice, Catholic, or Jewish orientation of the teacher education program	8	10	9	27

*One UTEP teacher described his religion as "none" in the summary questionnaire completed at the time of the first interview but indicated that he was Jewish in his second interview, signaling the complexity of studying identity and also the difficulty of categorizing "Jewishness" in terms of religion, ethnicity, heritage, etc.

**One DeLeT teacher whose mother was Jewish and father was Quaker described her upbringing as "85 percent Jewish and 15 percent Protestant."

just urban schools, but rural schools too. So there were a lot of parallels and I think that's how it became more and more important to me.

Similarly, Sylvia attended Catholic schools but described her dawning awareness of being at the wrong end of the status hierarchy when she moved from a poorer inner-city neighborhood to her new white, middle-class, suburban neighborhood where she was the lone Hispanic child in her class.

The thirty participants came to these programs with backgrounds and

TABLE 4.3 Participants' backgrounds: Connections to teaching

Connections to teaching in participants' entrance accounts	UTEP	ACE	DeLeT	Total
Indicates a close relative is a teacher	1	4	6	11
Mentions an influential or memorable teacher	1	5	2	8
Mentions a bad teacher or lousy schooling	5	2	2	9
Had some teaching experience prior to applying to teacher education program	6	2	6	14
Loves working with kids	4	6	5	15

espoused identities that dovetailed well with the cultural foci of the programs. But what were their prior connections to *teaching?* In interviews they linked their current interest in teaching to three kinds of earlier experiences: significant relationships with teachers, moments of dawning awareness about problematic school experiences, and their own work experiences as teachers or in related roles, recently or in the past (see table 4.3). Nearly two-thirds (nineteen) of the participants explained their decision to enter a teacher education program by referring to at least one of these features of their own educational autobiography.

Eleven mentioned close relatives who were teachers, a fact that may have normalized teaching for some, although two participants said that having a close-up view of the lives of teachers led them to resist teaching as a career possibility. Additionally, eight spoke of favorite teachers influencing their decision to enter the teaching programs. For example, Erin, an ACE teacher educated entirely in Catholic schools, spoke about a particularly significant relationship with one of her teachers and how this figured into her choice of a career.

I had a teacher in fourth grade who I still keep in touch with. She lives in Massachusetts now, but we write back and forth and I think it's funny. I don't even remember anything specific about her. I just remember that I really loved her and that year was the greatest year. It was funny. I taught fourth grade in Oklahoma and so I would email her and tell her how I was teaching fourth grade now and she's just always kind of been in the back of my head as—like I want a child to feel the way I felt about her about me . . . I loved her and I wanted the children I now teach to feel that way about me.

In contrast, nine participants credited their experiences with "poor" teachers or "bad" schools as something that sparked their appreciation for the importance of better teaching. This was especially true for UTEP people; fully half the participants spoke about becoming aware of how poor their earlier schooling had been. Tran noted the extreme poverty his family faced coming to the United States as refugees from Vietnam. He went through public schools and did very well, but later, at the University of Chicago, he realized, "I went through school and I thought it was great until I went to college and I realized it sucked!" Mary's interest in ACE grew because she "had such bad teachers in grade school and high school, too, and I remember always talking about it, [wondering] would it have been different if there had been good teachers and things like that. And talking with other friends once I got to college about [their] teachers that had been so influential and things like that." Similarly, a DeLeT participant who went to an Orthodox Jewish school lamented, "I never felt that I had that one Judaic teacher who inspired me to become more Orthodox, and I thought that was sad, because I went to an excellent high school. So since then, I sort of always wanted to be in that position to inspire my students." These kinds of "bad schooling" stories underscored the narrators' deep familiarity with and commitment to the cultural field and their reasons for going into teaching.

Finally, fourteen of the participants entered the teacher education programs with prior teaching experience, which contributed to their belief that they could plausibly see themselves doing this kind of work. Half of them spoke about their long-standing love of working with children as motivating their choice to enter the field.

In sum, at the outset of the programs all 30 participants portrayed themselves as being wholeheartedly identified with the broader Jewish, Catholic, or social justice purposes of the program, what might be called their *cultural frame*; nearly all (27) came with extensive prior cultural involvement; but fewer (19) mentioned analogous linkages between their current interest in teaching and earlier experiences from their upbringing related to school or teachers.

Indeed, the accounts of how they decided to join their program revealed that only thirteen of the participants entered the programs with a commitment to teaching as a career. The others had a more provisional, exploratory attitude and were drawn as much by the program's Jewish/Catholic/social justice commitment as by its specific attention to teaching. And a few said that they got there by accident.

The contrast between the clarity and deliberateness of some of the participants' entrance accounts and the more accidental, serendipitous quality of others' raised the question of how much these candidates owned their decisions to embark on these programs. For example, John comes across as having made a very deliberate choice to enroll in ACE:

> I had spent a lot of time with the Jesuits. In Jesuit Volunteer Corps, I taught GED and ESL for two years, and I really, really enjoyed that experience. And then from there I opted into taking a job at [a Catholic private school in Texas], and there I was Campus Minister. But I had a strong desire to teach as well. And so I taught a year of government economics, and then from there I realized how much I loved it and I wanted to continue on, and I knew ACE was really the way to do that.

He described a connection between his different work experiences as a minister and as a teacher that led directly into his applying to ACE; he portrays himself as an active and planful chooser, deciding on a purpose and then working to make that a reality. He exhibited an interest in teaching and a sense of agency in deciding how to purse that interest.

In contrast, Tran described how he ended up in UTEP: "I was tutoring students in my four years when I was in college, and I just heard about the program through the university. I was in my third year, and I was looking for a job, and it was part of the job search. It just kind of fell into my lap." His account locates himself in the present, first working, then job hunting, and somehow chancing on UTEP. He did not express an interest in teaching as a career. Moreover, his account includes no internal process; he did not portray himself as deciding anything.

A third example is Lauren, who said,

> I resisted teaching actually, or going into education, because my [older] sister is a teacher . . . She knew she was going to be a teacher from day one . . . And I never really saw myself as anywhere similar to her, you know, and as patient as her and as knowledgeable as her. But then, on a different note, I was a camp counselor, very confident in my abilities in that area. I always felt like I was a really good counselor, and I loved it. I wanted to be a camp counselor for the rest of my life, but I did not know if I could get a job like that that paid any money.

In her account, Lauren differentiates her passion about being a camp counselor from the work of teaching exemplified by her sister. For her, the choice to try out teaching was neither deliberate nor haphazard. She saw DeLeT as a promising possibility.

The motivation to become a teacher and the sense of agency in pursuing that interest were closely associated for only thirteen of the participants. Given this, I examined all thirty participants' entrance accounts for their commitment to going into teaching as a career and for their planfulness and sense of agency in deciding to enter a program.[13]

This coding yielded three groups of cases (see table 4.4). The *early deciders* exhibited a great deal of agency; they deliberately chose to become teachers working in Jewish, Catholic, or urban public schools and sought out these programs as part of this pursuit. The *explorers* opted for the programs in light of their larger goals and constraints and were willing to explore teaching, or teaching in these settings, even though it may not have been their first choice. They, too, exhibited agency in choosing but without the commitment to teaching. This cluster included those ACE students who wanted to do teaching as a period of service or those in DeLeT or UTEP who were committed to at least five years of teaching but who intended to eventually move on to something else. The *accidentals* described themselves as serendipitously "falling into" these programs. All heard about the programs because of their cultural-religious involvements, but they did not portray themselves as actively seeking out this kind of opportunity. Instead, they said that it "fell into their laps." They lacked both agency and an explicit interest in teaching.

TABLE 4.4   Teachers' sense of agency across the three programs

Sense of agency	Program			Total
	ACE	DeLeT	UTEP	
Low	6	4	2	12
High	4	6	8	18
Total	10	10	10	30

For the early deciders, who expressed the most agency as well as prior commitment to going into teaching, the programs enabled them to learn their chosen craft, deepening and strengthening their view of themselves as able teachers.[14] For the accidentals and explorers, who entered the programs with a provisional rather than a full-blown interest in teaching, the programs played a formative role in shaping their sense of themselves as teachers.

Because the programs played a role in this process, here I focus on people who came to their program with less clear commitments to teaching but with different degrees of agency about their decision to embark on this path—the explorers and accidentals. I look more deeply at six cases in order to trace the ways in which teachers' views of themselves and their sense of agency changed over time as they entered and completed their teacher education programs and then went on to teach in their subsequent school sector. In selecting teachers to profile, I made an effort to focus on individuals who the program identified as exemplary teachers.[15]

UTEP: Sylvia (Accidental) and Allison (Explorer)

Sylvia (Accidental)

Sylvia came to UTEP with a hazier sense of purpose than many others. Although she had loved playing teacher when she was younger and viewed school as a place where she excelled, she didn't seriously consider teaching as a career, even when she worked as a public school tutor during college. Instead, having majored in sociology, she became passionate about the causes of inequality in the United States and imagined going into the nonprofit world or social work.

Then I received [another] e-mail about UTEP . . . and I really looked at it. "You know, [this is] something I've always wanted to do, and I've always been interested in teaching, and I feel that this is kind of the perfect opportunity because I know the college, I know what kind of rigor it would be expecting." And I was also drawn to the idea that it would only be one year after I graduated from college. So it was a mixture of all those different factors at work.

She entered UTEP believing that she needed "to be part of the solution and not part of the problem . . . my commitment to feeling like there needs to be action taken and you've got to start small in some ways and education is so important for civic skills and everything."

In describing her own background, Sylvia highlighted the fact that she grew up in Chicago attending Catholic schools "in a Hispanic neighborhood, and then I moved to the suburbs, so my school was mainly Caucasian, but there were some Hispanic children." Her commitment to urban public education developed through her experiences in UTEP.

We had done a field visit in Winnetka, which is like a super-wealthy suburb, and then the previous day . . . [a visit] in one of the poorest areas in Chicago . . . So what really then cemented my commitment to urban teaching was seeing the contrast . . . Just seeing the glaring disparity between the two it made me so mad, and so just frustrated, the fact that there are equally talented children and in one community their talents are allowed to flourish and in another community I feel like they're being squashed.

UTEP intensified Sylvia's initial passion about injustice in America and galvanized her belief about the importance of working with the children in the poorest neighborhoods. It gave her a concrete way of enacting "social justice" in a particular context where she could make a difference. Her commitment to working in urban schools solidified.

People have asked me a lot, "Why don't you teach in the suburbs, why are you doing that to yourself?" . . . I don't know any other way. I wouldn't even know how to teach in a suburban setting, and I don't want to teach in a suburban setting. I feel there's just a joy you get in the urban setting, and it's so hard to explain. But just the kids keep you on your toes and the questions they ask, they're not afraid to ask certain. It's a different ball-game, and I would not teach anywhere else.

After UTEP, Sylvia took a job in a newly established charter school "where social justice [was] the social studies theme" and where teachers were working through the question, "What does social justice look like in the primary grades of the startup charter schools?" She appreciated how unusual her school was, compared to other Chicago schools:

I wonder how I would feel about my commitment to social justice as a teacher if, in the school, there was that sort of "these kids are dumb, these kids are going nowhere," you know, where the teacher is looked at as like all you need to be is breathing, where there's really not the celebration of student identity. So that's why I feel . . . as a teacher I'm actually making change, because the school I'm at is supporting that change. And they're pushing me to think about teachers as agents of social change, that we are giving students the skills they need to become political leaders and activists and reflect upon their place in the world. And so I'm not sure how I would feel if I felt that I was being beaten down, or in a very negative environment, or not feeling like my colleagues were on the same page as me, where maybe they would feel like I was the idealistic young one who in ten years will be dragging my feet just like them.

She felt her teaching not only benefited her students but also contributed more broadly to the school's overall functioning and effectiveness, which, in turn, underscored her own sense of herself as an effective teacher helping to change urban public education.

When we interviewed Sylvia a second time, she was still teaching in the same school, mainly because the faculty was all "on the same page."

[In] my school all the teachers are really smart, and there's a lot of collaboration, lot of professional development. But the one thing I like knowing is that every teacher in the school is on the same page. So, you know, in some schools, like in a CPS school, you may feel like you're the only teacher trying to teach the social emotional skills for children, or you're the only teacher trying to work for social justice. And then when you pass your kids on to the next level you feel like "Oh, man. They're going to get that teacher, and they're going to erase all the work I've done this whole year." Whereas at my school it's like I feel confident passing my kids on to the other teachers.

Sylvia's sense of competence and agency as an urban public school teacher were closely intertwined with her sense that the work of teaching was broadly shared and that teachers were able to build on one another's work with the children over the years. In this way her professional identity and sense of agency and the school context reinforced one another.

Allison (Explorer)

Allison opted for UTEP once she realized that becoming a child psychiatrist was out of reach. She wanted a break from academia before embarking on medical school, but with her heavy college debt she couldn't afford to "just travel" or "do the Peace Corps." She loved working with children—"volunteering, teaching, tutoring and mentoring since [she] was a kid"—so when she learned about UTEP, it seemed to be a good opportunity. At least she'd be working with children, she thought, and, on the financial side, she would be eligible for federal loan forgiveness if she stayed in the field for five years. All in all, she wholeheartedly embarked on a teaching career as a next step after college. Her account reveals her planfulness and sense of agency in making this decision.

Allison's interest in urban public schools grew out of her experience tutoring in local public schools during college, where she came to understand the "real need for committed, enthusiastic teachers." She also found parallels between her own rural upbringing and the lives of inner-city children.

I feel like the schooling that I received when I was in elementary, middle, high school was pretty shoddy. I went to a public school in a really small rural town, and there weren't a lot of opportunities for kids who were smart. Mostly what I learned came from my family—my own love of learning, my motivation to learn about things . . . My mom and dad are pretty curious, self-improving people. So I kind of had those values instilled, which make you love learning. I feel like I didn't really get that from my schooling until I went to college. And so I would like to be able to instill that love of learning in my students, although I don't know how to do it yet.

She loved the UTEP program and immersed herself completely in it.

I *am* the job. I was just in Philadelphia visiting a friend and we were walking around to all these different stores and she just kept laughing at me because . . . we would go into a bookstore and immediately I would go to the children's section. We would go into . . . some cutesy store and immediately I would be thinking about what kind of art project I could do with my kids.

When she finished UTEP, Allison felt that teaching was her "dream." She took a position in a school where she was the sole teacher of thirty first graders: "Nine had IEPs [Individualized Educational Plans] for their behavior, not for academic issues. And this was in first grade! So in order for children to already have IEPs written up for them, their behavior has to be pretty atrocious. And it was." The challenges were even more daunting because Allison received no support from the school administration. Also, the school's expectations about teachers and their work diverged dramatically from her UTEP preparation: "As long as your students are quiet in the hallways and as long as they look like they're doing something in the classroom, then you're okay." While she did find some support from a like-minded veteran teacher in her school, Allison's situation was extremely demoralizing, which was made worse because of her tenuous job status: "Right now, actually, I'm not getting paid as a full-time teacher by my school. Technically my status is a long-term sub . . . And I'm the lowest person on the seniority totem pole, so I kind of got screwed over. So I'm not going to be paid this summer." She was so disheartened and overwhelmed by these circumstances that she wondered, "What was I thinking? Like, was I really making a good choice? . . . Is this really how it's going to be? You doubt to the core whether or not you're cut out for what you think is your dream. So, you know, that's definitely been rough." She ended the school year feeling unnerved and altogether doubtful about her career choice. But she noted, "I'm not a quitter."

Two years later, in 2008, Allison had a very different outlook. "These last couple of years have been very transitional," she said. "I finally kind of feel like I have something set up for myself that will be a little bit more long term." After her first school Allison switched to a more supportive school headed by a principal affiliated with UTEP. She stayed for one year and might have stayed longer if her UTEP mentor hadn't invited her to become her partner teacher at the same school where she had done her student teaching.

Not surprisingly, Allison saw herself as highly aligned with her new school's philosophy and practice. She also expressed a great deal of personal agency: "I also feel like if I wanted to do something that was a little different or new or not something that had been tried in the school before that I would have the license to do that and that they would be accepting of it. And probably other teachers would want to see how it goes and try to use it in their classroom as well." At the end of her second interview, Allison reflected, "Being a teacher was not my first career choice, but now I'm not so sure if I ever want to be a doctor. I really enjoy teaching, I really like it a lot . . . I'm not really sure when or if I will ever stop being a teacher."

ACE: Mark (Accidental) and Tammy (Explorer)

Mark (Accidental)

Mark grew up in Texas, where he attended Catholic schools from kindergarten through college. He majored in biology and was thinking of going on to medical school, like his older sister, but at the end of college he didn't feel "ready for it."

> My mother's a Catholic school educator. She's a phenomenal principal. And so a lot of my decision came from her . . . She won the Catholic Educator of the Year award in [Texas]. [At a reception] there was this small group of people at the front that led the prayer that evening and that were having a fun time and enjoying themselves at the dinner . . . And it was a group of [local] ACE teachers that had come and joined the archdiocese in honoring my mom that night. Then later on that evening, I talked to [a girl] . . . who did ACE and who went to [my college] and was a biology major also, and she had told me two years before that I should apply and that it's an awesome teaching experience and it would be for me. And so

it kind of started rolling that night. The deadline was kind of right there, and I got in. And that's it.

Although Mark came from a background that seemed to lay the groundwork for his eventual choices, to him it was by no means a given that he would opt for a career in education. Instead, his entrance account highlighted a serendipitous encounter with his "near peers" from ACE who made the idea of going into Catholic education seem both attractive and within reach. He found his own way in a world where he was already deeply immersed because peers made it attractive or acceptable.

Mark portrayed himself as an educator who was attracted by the possibility of reaching out to all kinds of students: "I don't think that being Catholic necessarily led to my decision [to go into teaching] but maybe, it sounds weird, but *being inclusive* kind of led to my decision. I had this feeling I wanted to include people in education." He saw his work with middle school children as centering on "the opportunity to have not just a *Catholic* conversation but some *moral* conversation at a Catholic school . . . Like that's an incredible opportunity that . . . you can't get at a public school." Getting his students involved in their own decision making, as distinct from preaching at them, was central to his sense of his work as a Catholic educator.

> Not because you got on some pulpit, but because you shared with them some teaching of the church. You gave them some moral scenario and they had to work through something, and you got to talk about something that was real and made sense to them. And the feeling I have at the end of that conversation's awesome. And I don't think I would feel that comfortable at a [school] where I couldn't have [this kind of conversation], because morality and decision making is just something that you have to discuss.

His convictions about the importance of reaching out to a wide range of people distinguished him from some of his more conservative ACE counterparts.

> It's like Peter being this cast-out, horrible fisherman, mired on the rocks, and *he* was selected to *lead* a church. He was selected to lead, to start this thing out. And this [is the] idea we have to include everyone. You know,

what are you doing right now to include the lowliest of His people? If your faith is strong enough and if you're comfortable, you don't fear those other things and you invite that conversation of, "Hey, let's consider if we brought, I don't know, this non-Catholic and this sinner, this person who is having premarital sex or this homosexual over here."

I think that in general the type of cohort that ACE provides kind of gets clannish, like, "Let's not include those people because we've *got* it. We know what it is and let's keep it within here." When, in fact, how are we supposed to spread the message if we do that?

Mark comes across as solidly grounded and confident about the merits of his own views in the face of contrasting ideas among his peers. But how much was Mark able to carry this sense of purpose and self-understanding into the field?

His initial school placement was in a school with a large Hispanic population in a low-income neighborhood in Los Angeles.[16]

Our school's image of Catholicism is really influenced a lot by our pastor, who is an ultra-conservative Catholic, who is sixty-five years old and just recently suffered a stroke. And it's not exactly about inclusiveness . . . Case in point is last semester. It was the first time that I set out a reconciliation service for middle school. It hadn't been done before because Father was the only pastor that had been there for like thirteen years. And Father said, "There will be no reconciliation services held for the school! I listen to confessions on Saturday and that's the day that the parents will bring the students to me."

Okay. First off, these parents don't even care enough to bring their kids to mass on Sunday much less a special reconciliation service on Saturday where Father, honestly, is going to . . . get mad at them for what they've done. So that's not really in tune with my idea of inclusiveness.

But Father Arturo (who is kind of . . . this priest working his way into the parish) and I kind of snuck underneath the radar last semester and held a special reconciliation service for the middle schoolers . . . It was a powerful and moving experience for these eighth graders who hadn't been to reconciliation since second grade, who had been either doing drugs or having sex or drinking or involved in gangs. All twenty-seven people confessed and shared something about it, even before or after, in stories. That was aimed at getting them more involved and including them more as a Catholic community, like the Holy Spirit working through the Sacraments. I believe that's possible in my own faith, and I saw it happen there.

This incident illustrated Mark's dedication to his students and their well-being and his sense of agency as a Catholic teacher and role model. He was committed to connecting with his students' lives through religious practice, an idea that he and Father Arturo were able to enact on their own. But Mark's way of working put him on a collision course with the principal, who fired him after three years.

Two years later, at age twenty-seven, after he completed ACE, Mark moved to another inner-city Catholic school with an entirely different ethos. The principal worked collaboratively with the teachers, and the school culture was much more progressive and in tune with Mark's own ideas. In the second interview Mark said that he would become the vice principal the following year and eventually go on for his doctorate in educational psychology in order to work in the Catholic school system.

Mark's initial account of how he came to ACE emphasized the *chance* aspect, suggesting that he was not making a deliberate choice to go into Catholic education. But his own background in Catholic schools and having a mother who was a successful Catholic educator made him receptive to ACE once he learned about it from admired peers. Despite some trying years in his first school, while still in the program he found ways to assert his own ideas about what his students needed, which made him come across as more agentic and self-confident in portraying his professional choices during that period. With advice from his mother and from a network of contacts in the world of Catholic education, he was able to find his way through some trying circumstances and to advance professionally, especially once he changed schools.

Tammy (Explorer)

Raised in Washington, DC, Tammy attended Catholic schools through college, where she majored in human services. In her senior year she knew she wanted to "do service" before embarking on a career: "I didn't know exactly what I wanted to do, whether it was counseling or social work, but I knew I needed a master's . . . Also I knew I wanted to spend some time doing service. I didn't really care where I went, but I knew I wanted to spend a year in service."[17]

Tammy heard about ACE from a campus minister who noted that she would be able to do service and get a master's degree. Then her brother, an undergraduate at Notre Dame, spoke enthusiastically about the ACE people he knew on campus. She took a pragmatic view: "It was just service and master's in one. I said, 'All right, I'll give it a shot.' I didn't know if I wanted to teach when I signed on. I knew that I needed a master's. I knew I wanted to do service, and I said, 'I'll try teaching for two years. If I don't like it, whatever, but now I have a master's.'"

Once in the field as part of her ACE placement, Tammy became committed to working with inner-city children:

> I don't know if I necessarily love teaching, but I love being with the inner-city kids. I think it's more of the mission that I'm doing out here that's important. When I think of teaching these kids, [I think of] so many other life lessons that these kids need to be taught . . . it's very fulfilling for me internally. I get peace from it and I think they feel good about it or rewarded as well, so I hope.

She credited ACE for helping her discover a passion for working with children in inner-city schools. "I don't think I would be at a school like this necessarily if the ACE program hadn't opened my eyes to it. Next year I'm applying to inner city in DC, the same kind of schools."

ACE also had a profound effect on Tammy's sense of herself as a Catholic:

> The program has actually deepened my spirituality a lot . . . Coming into the program, I would not say I was very religious. But I was surrounded by people that were very spiritual and openly religious, which I had never seen before in young Catholic adults. So that was kind of new and eye-opening for me and it took me a while to get used to it, but then I began to embrace kind of my own Catholic identity, to deepen my faith by being surrounded by others who have such a deep faith and who challenged me so.

At the same time, her encounters with some of her Catholic peers at ACE forced her to assert her own sense of what mattered to her personally as Catholic: "[ACE] doesn't [fit my view], because I think a lot is imparted on us as far as *teaching* goes but not as far as *doing* goes. I think that people know you're a Catholic by how you *act* and by what you're *doing* and I don't know if the program stressed that enough . . . Just because I don't know everything you're supposed to do with the rosary, I'm not a bad Catholic; I'm not a bad person."

Tammy taught in two different Los Angeles schools in two years. In speaking about her personal learning curve, she said:

> I think the ACE program helped me understand more about myself by putting me in this situation. I think it pushed me to go outside my comfort zone, outside my boundary, daily try new things in the class-room, at home, with the community, a new route going to school because you're sitting in traffic. It forced you to do new things, so I think I've learned a lot more and broadened my horizons by being pushed outside my comfort zone.

She found her first school in Los Angeles to be difficult. "Everyone was on their own," she said. "We had no community at our school . . . I didn't know any other teachers on a personal level and didn't communicate with any other teachers at the school. It was kind of survival." At the same time, she had a good relationship with the school's pastor. She introduced him to an ACE alumnus who was a principal who joined the board at Tammy's school and advised them on finding a new principal. The next year she moved to a second school where the faculty was "a more close-knit community" and where she felt better prepared professionally: "I was able to look at kids differently and understand who they are and how to reach them instead of having them meet me."

By the time of our second interview, Tammy had moved to back to DC. She first worked in a bilingual Catholic school, which was not a good fit since she didn't speak Spanish, and then she ended up in a school with a student body that was "100 percent African American." There her own biracial back-ground served as a bridge between herself and her students. Her pleasure at working in this K–8 school was evident, though she was concerned about the pedagogic level of her peers. She was teaching reading and had continued to build her own professional practice by enrolling in education courses at a local college. Throughout both interviews Tammy portrayed herself as a capable and effective person who is eager to grow and learn. She planned to go on for a PhD in education and to work with teachers. Regarding her commitment to staying in Catholic schools, she said:

> I think I like being able to teach the faith right now. I also am considering upward mobility, kind of, administration. I think I can move up faster in the Catholic school system than in the public school, so I think I want to kind of feel out what I want to do in the Catholic school system. Right now, yes, I think I'm here in the Catholic school system for a while. If I go into school counseling, I might have to move to the public school system just because Catholic schools don't necessarily have it all. So I think it would depend kind of, my career path with the future.

This statement shows her sense of agency in thinking about her career goals going forward. Tammy's professional self was not entirely bound up in her Catholic faith, although that remained an important part of her life.

DeLeT: Noa (Accidental) and Aliza (Explorer)

Noa (Accidental)

Noa "fell into" DeLeT without having explicitly considered teaching as a career. She majored in fashion in college and was working at a mortgage company in New York City.

> I was just living, enjoying, but I didn't have any direction and I knew that's not something I wanted to do for the rest of my life. I was just trying to figure it out. And then I went to this Shabbat lunch and met this girl who did this program called DeLeT, and she told me about this amazing fellowship in Boston through Brandeis University that she thinks I'd be qualified for.

The serendipitous way that Noa portrays her entrance into DeLeT conveys a submerged sense of personal agency. As she investigated the program, she saw how DeLeT could make sense for her: "I had always been involved in camp and have always—I've nannied and I've babysat, and my parents have always told me to be a teacher." Her mother worked as a teacher, "So education has always been talked about, like how wonderful of a profession it is. But I kind of put it out of my head because you don't want to do what your parents tell you to do." And she recalled how "school was hard for me." Noa attended a Jewish school through grade 5 but didn't liked it, although in retrospect she felt she "took a lot more with me than I thought I did, like Hebrew and the holidays." But she always loved "being with children," and Judaism had always been "a predominant part" of her life.

Through DeLeT, Noa came to see that teaching was a great way to bring together her many facets.

It's a part of who I am as a person. You have to like kids . . . you have to have patience . . . and you have to enjoy learning and be open-minded. And then in some ways, since I was interested in business and marketing and creativity—I feel like I run my own business half the time . . . I can have the walls the way I want them. [There's] such a creative element to teaching, and I love that. So that's definitely a huge part of it. So I look at it as my own company.

DeLeT continued to influence Noa's teaching: "When I get frustrated with a student, I stop and say to myself, 'Noa, see them as a learner. What is this child good at and what are their strengths?' And I go from there."

After DeLeT, Noa went on to teach second grade in a new Jewish school, and there she was entirely engaged: "I love the people I work with. The school is wonderful. It just happens to be Jewish. I like the Jewish stuff because it's warm and fuzzy, and Shabbat is nice, and I love the Israeli dancing on Friday afternoons, and I love working with Israelis and speaking Hebrew." In her second interview, she described the advantages and limitations of the school where she continued to teach.

My school is very small. It's a start-up school, and because of that there are a lot of advantages. You know all of the students, you see everybody. The faculty is like a family; we're very close, comfortable. But on the other side, I'm the only third grade teacher. There isn't that much professional development . . . And I feel like we do a lot more work than maybe other teachers do because we're so small that we have so much more responsibility.

Still, she expressed a great deal of pride in her work. "There's a lot of creative freedom because it's so new. So the third grade curriculum I developed; it didn't exist . . . The administration, they trust me. I have a good reputation . . . It wouldn't be like that in a different school or public school, maybe a bigger private school. So it's comfortable here."

Compared to her self-portrayal at the time she entered DeLeT, Noa's sense of herself as a teacher and her agency in that role had been transformed.

Aliza (Explorer)

Aliza came from a family with extensive, positive ties to Jewish life. She attended an Orthodox Jewish day school and a Jewish summer camp, which she "loves to this day" and where she and her husband continued to work. During her undergraduate years at a "prestigious" college, Aliza tutored in an inner-city program and read to children in the hospital. On graduating, she wanted to join Teach For America and teach in an urban public school.

Aliza began her account by saying, "I'm never going to work in a Jewish school!" and then went on to describe how she ended up teaching in a Jewish day school after all. First, her husband got a job in Boston, and "there wasn't a Teach For America in Boston." Then she investigated various teacher preparation options before deciding that DeLeT was her best opportunity because it offered excellent pedagogic training and allowed her to begin full-time teaching in a classroom, albeit in a Jewish school setting. She said to herself, "Fine, but I'm never going to teach in a private Jewish day school. I'll do my internship and then I'll leave."

Then she came to the dénouement of her "choosing to teach" story:

Up until last year I was thinking of leaving. I mean, I was going to teach, but I wanted to teach in a *public* school. And then I got a lecture about how I can never do that. Well, Vivian was like, "You can't do that to the Jewish people . . . You can't leave Jewish education, you have so much to offer". . . I have a wealth of Jewish knowledge that just wouldn't be used if I was in a public school setting. So she kind of lectured me.

   And I thought about it for a while, and I think that it's been like more influential that I'm in a Jewish school rather than just a regular school

. . . I definitely find it more . . . fulfilling to know that I'm not only a role model, a teaching role model, and I'm not only a teacher to these kids, but they look up to me as a person, and they come over to my house on Shabbat, which is so cool to me.

Vivian was a charismatic master teacher in DeLeT who had taught in public schools for much of her career prior to DeLeT, which may have lent particular authority to her advice. In light of Vivian's own biography of successfully combining a career in both general and Jewish education over the years, perhaps Aliza could see that one need not preclude the other over the longer haul.

Later in her first interview Aliza described the way her educator self and Jewish self had become comfortably intertwined:

I'm definitely a Jewish educator. I mean, I'm always thinking about Judaism, and I'm sure that comes across. I mean, even in math my examples are always, you know, "You're baking Challah," things like that. I just feel like there are so many missed opportunities that why not seize them with. I mean, by no means am I saying they don't live other lives, but I think that they're one and the same, and it's very easy to make those connections and help students from a young age to realize how those connections can be made so easily. I consider myself a Jewish person, you know, a Jew before anything else, and I think that that's an important value to instill.

In that first interview, Aliza came across as a person who very much wanted to be a teacher—originally in a public school but who fell into teaching in a Jewish day school initially out of expedience and then due to a more deliberate choice. Aliza's experience teaching in a Jewish day school had been positive, reinforced by the quality of her relations with significant others in her world. She had become comfortable viewing herself as a Jewish educator.

When we interviewed her two years later, we learned of some noteworthy changes in her life. She accepted a full-time teaching position in the same school where she interned. Also, around that time she and her husband bought a house in the town where the school is located and she became a mother (so there was another self—and a very demanding one—

that needed to be accommodated).[18] At that point in her life, Aliza came across as more fully committed to her work, more immersed, confident, and professionally grounded than she did at the start of the study. But she made a point of stating that it would not be out of the question for her to move to another kind of school or another role in the field of education in the future, depending on the circumstances.

Choosing to Teach as an Ongoing Process

Choosing to become a teacher is an ongoing, constant process of evaluating one's past, hopes for the future, significant others, and social settings, and that process changes partly in response to one's own agency. In a sense, in a healthy person, choosing is never over.

In addition to being an ongoing process, more than a single event, choosing to teach is complicated by many different factors—not only for the six people profiled here but also for all thirty teachers in the Choosing to Teach Study. Candidates arrived in their programs with whatever background experiences they had accrued in their lives up to that point, which shaped the ways they envisioned themselves as teachers. Moreover, they came with different expectations about whether or not to make a career of teaching.

The three teacher education programs presented participants with ways of working that in turn shaped people's ideas about teaching and fired them up about their work as Jewish, Catholic, or urban educators. In their subsequent positions, these new teachers encountered varied circumstances that in some cases aligned well with their formal preparation and in other cases presented obstacles.

The reason agency mattered for the teachers is that unless they were able to *enact* that kind of self-understanding as Jewish/Catholic/urban teachers in the particular school setting, the "identity work" alone was not sufficient to make them effective. Being able to navigate an environment effectively was essential.

The likelihood that these participants would come to feel a strong sense of agency as teachers was related to the circumstances they faced in their work environments. Sylvia was able to flourish when she began working in a school that was strongly aligned with the approach to teaching she had absorbed from UTEP. Allison faced more severe obstacles until she found a more congenial school setting. In the end, both Allison and Sylvia exuded a sense of confidence and agency as teachers once they found compatible school contexts.

Mark and Tammy were able to experience themselves as effective teachers in some ways despite their difficult school contexts because they got support from their ACE peers and the program's advising system and, in Mark's case, his mother's expertise as a Catholic educator. By going up against the authority of the school's pastor and the ingrained patterns at his school, Mark managed to enact some of his own ideas about how to reach his students, but it also cost him his job. Once he began working in a more compatible school, he thrived. Tammy moved schools almost every year. Since her account did not explain what led to those changes, we do not know about her own initiative in the matter. Still, her self-portrayal conveyed a sense of personal agency bolstered by a strong relationship she developed with one of her ACE mentors.

Inspired by the powerful advice of an admired DeLeT mentor, Aliza came to view and value herself as a Jewish educator rather than as just marking time until she could escape from Jewish schools to the public system. After DeLeT, Aliza landed a job in a setting where she flourished professionally, one that also worked well in the context of her changing family life. Noa entered DeLeT tentatively with a view of herself as a mediocre student who was willing to explore the possibility of teaching. She blossomed in DeLeT and became a teacher in a new, small school where she thrived. Noa eventually began to feel that the school might not provide sufficient professional development opportunities going forward.

All in all, when these new teachers were able see themselves as having a stake in the broader ethos and functioning of their school, this contributed to their sense that their work was both aligned with and valued by the school as a whole. This increased their sense of agency as teachers and reinforced the rightness of their career choice. Note the important methodological lesson here: if the study had relied on data gathered from only a single moment in time, we would not have seen this dynamic process.

These case analyses focus on those people who were not wholly committed to becoming teachers at the outset—explorers and accidentals whose psychological paths into teaching differed from the more direct pattern of the early deciders. That so many became committed teachers speaks to the power of their teacher education programs and to the wellspring of commitments and experiences they brought to teaching from their religious and cultural backgrounds and upbringing. Studying the cases of those who entered the programs without full commitment to teaching as a career lets us see that agency is not a dimension of character or personality. Rather, it emerges from the interaction of person and setting. By keeping the focus on the importance of the interface of person and setting, this analysis underscores the importance of attending to the contextual (i.e., program and school-level) features that need to be in place to enable agency in the teachers.

CHAPTER 5

Visions of Good Teaching

Variation, Coherence, and Opportunity to Learn

KAREN HAMMERNESS

What kind of teacher do teacher educators aim to prepare, and why? What kind of teaching do they hope their graduates will practice after they complete their preparation? What do teacher educators most hope their teachers will accomplish in schools? In short, what difference do they hope to make through the work they do in their teacher education programs? These questions about the nature of our vision(s) sit at the center of teacher education. For many of us teacher educators, answers to these questions about aims and goals are deeply important, providing a sense of purpose and guiding program design and implementation.

Using vision as the conceptual lens, I offer in this chapter a cross-program view of the University of Notre Dame's Alliance for Catholic Education, Brandeis University's Day School Leadership Through Teaching Program, and the University of Chicago's Urban Teacher Education Program by sharing the visions of good teaching of the three programs, digging into the relationship of vision to each program's coherence and opportunities to learn, and discussing implications for program design.

Unpacking Program Visions

Four themes emerged from an examination of the visions of each of the three teacher education programs studied in the Choosing to Teach Study. First, each program had a clearly articulated overarching vision of teaching that was elaborated in different materials, consistent across documents, and could easily be identified. The continual presence of such statements suggested that, for these programs, vision served as a key motivating and unifying force. Discussions by faculty also revealed a strong sense of purpose and a shared understanding of the program vision, suggesting coherence around the visions. Faculty and staff did not feel that their vision was simply produced for external review; rather, it was an expression of their personal and programmatic commitments, was integral to the program and the reason for their work.

Second, perhaps not surprisingly, the content of the program visions differed, echoing what others have argued regarding the considerable variation in conceptions of good teaching across U.S. teacher preparation programs.[1] The programs reflected three visions, each related to quite different views about the nature of good teaching and the role of teachers:

- *Teaching as service,* which conceives of teaching as only one of many opportunities to "give back" or contribute to society
- *Teaching as social justice,* which conceives of teaching as a direct means of addressing social inequities
- *Teaching as a practice,* which focuses on teaching as a profession with a knowledge base and set of practices that can be learned and developed over time.

Third, each of the programs emphasized one or more of these different visions of good teaching; the emphasis was distinctive and seemed to have a consistent relationship with the visions, career plans, and even the classroom practices of its graduates. These programs offered very different opportunities to learn that were clearly aligned with the program visions, suggesting the presence of coherence in these programs as well. Finally, programs varied in the extent to which they linked vision and practice and in the degree to which they provided opportunities to enact aspects of the program visions of good teaching.

Three Distinct Visions

In determining what visions of good teaching the three programs emphasized and the leaders' and faculties' aims and goals for good teaching, I relied heavily on faculty interviews and focus groups as well as printed and online materials from each of the programs.

Alliance for Catholic Education—A Vision of Teaching as Service. The program vision of ACE focuses clearly on a vision of teaching as service. The program director emphasized the idea that ACE students should think about the program not exclusively as a "teacher formation" program but more broadly as contributing to the Catholic community through education. As one faculty member explained, "When [our students] enter, we don't say, 'You're entering this to become a Catholic school teacher.'" She noted that they wanted their graduates to excel at teaching, "[but] for those two years, we want you to be the best Catholic school teacher you can." Another faculty member expressed the hope that, after teaching, ACE graduates remain interested in and invested in Catholic schools: "The [program] is working hard . . . to get the people who go on to law school and who go into areas outside of education to stay involved in some way . . . we need lawyers who are interested in working for urban Catholic schools and who are going to help us raise money and to do pro bono work for schools and regions." As another faculty member reflected, "When we look back on our graduates, we would hope . . . that they would stay in Catholic education or be involved through further graduate studies," concluding that there were many "different ways" for ACE graduates to serve the Catholic community.

Many faculty members talked about constructivist, student-centered pedagogy as the focus of their vision of good teaching, but they did not voice a shared understanding of specific practices they envisioned graduates enacting in the classroom. While they talked about wanting to prepare ACE graduates to be "master teachers," faculty descriptions of what that kind of practice would look like in the classroom differed. Rather, when talking about the kind of teaching practices they hoped their graduates would enact, each faculty member emphasized different strategies or approaches. For instance, one instructor talked about classroom management, while another described the importance of being a reflective teacher, and a third highlighted the ability to question students and to understand the role of good questions in the classroom. All the faculty members agreed that their program planning template, a rubric for lesson planning used in multiple courses, was a good representation of the kinds of teaching they hoped their graduates would enact. While the template focused on curriculum planning, it did not specify particular instructional practices. And while the program does specify some performance indicators to guide feedback and evaluation (see table 2.3), the indicators are not subject specific and represent fairly generic teaching practices. Indeed, the indicators could be enacted in quite different ways depending on the teacher. For instance, "Establishes a culture for learning" could be enacted in quite different ways, from enforcing a rigid, militaristic culture to a student-centered, community-based environment. And similarly, "Selects instructional outcomes/goals" could range from the setting of technical, narrow learning goals to the development of deep disciplinary and generative questions that might undergird a lesson or unit.

Yet, the faculty agreed that that its ideal graduate would embody the "image of Christ the teacher as kind of a model." Over and over, faculty underscored the personal characteristics of the ideal graduates as involving "compassion and being a role model of the Gospel values." As one member concluded, "Being that ethical role model is something that I think is fair to say is [integrated] across all courses . . . I think that's something that we all share and holds us together as a community." In general, the faculty members interviewed and materials analyzed suggested that ACE conceives of teaching as an important way to serve the Catholic community and, in particular, to work with underresourced Catholic schools. ACE promotes a vision of candidates developing a long-term commitment to the Catholic community with an understanding that students will either aim for eventual leadership in education or become advocates for Catholic education in other fields. As one faculty member concluded, "When [prospective teachers are] in ACE, they are not pushed to stay. It happens because of what the program is, and we encourage them, [but the overall vision of the program is] to help sustain and strengthen Catholic schools."

Day School Leadership Through Teaching—A Vision of Teaching as a Professional Practice and a Form of Service. DeLeT's vision of good teaching in Jewish day schools is that it is a professional practice that should improve student learning as well as a service to the Jewish community. When asked about the ideal graduate, faculty members were careful to point out that the program did not graduate teachers who were "finished products." Rather, its aim was to create "well-launched beginning teachers who have a lot to learn and hopefully have developed the capacity to learn those things from their positions." Another added that graduates should have confidence in their early abilities to realize that "I know more about how to set up a classroom than I did a year ago. I know more about how to plan and how to think about assessment and goal setting and making sure that the way that I'm planning supports students and really learning something that matters."

DeLeT faculty also described the aim that graduates integrate Jewish content with general studies and contribute more broadly to the Jewish mission of the school. One faculty member commented that they hoped to prepare teachers who would be "looking for opportunities to bring in Jewish content. Looking for opportunities to be a member of the faculty and talk about . . . the Jewish mission of the school in a way that benefits the entire faculty." Another described in detail how the program helped support the integration of Jewish and general studies by helping students first think about their own Jewish identity and then move on to think about their students' Jewish identities.

> Students need to know themselves as learners of Torah and as actually celebrators of the Jewish holidays. And I often find we need to do a little unlearning for [the] stereotypical, "Let's teach about how to light the candles" and the big idea. Being able to take the big idea and say, "What's underneath this? Why are we doing this?" We're looking to develop lifelong Jewish . . . practice and curiosity in students. So being able to work on what that means; . . . how to be sure to first understand their own stance to the text and their own issues, . . . [then] to move that aside so that they can see their students a little more clearly. So I work on this framework with them, "What's your relationship to this piece of text or to this holiday? What interests you? What are you passionate about? What do you think your students will be passionate about? And where do those two meet?"

Faculty also consistently talked about the idea of creating Jewish community as both a means and an end of teaching. One member described helping students learn a model of text study that promoted classroom community: "[We are using] a Jewish study model in the general studies classroom for creating classroom community where students study specific

Jewish texts that are related to certain classroom values that they're trying to cultivate and study that in pairs where they really are taking responsibility for each other." Important, too, was the value of community within the cohort itself as part of the vision. One instructor described how DeLeT students came together as "a Jewish community by virtue of certain of the activities that they participate in and because of the orientation towards their goal of teaching in Jewish day schools."

Finally, faculty emphasized the importance of understanding the nature of student learning to the program's vision. As one member noted, "[Our graduates] ought to be committed to and thoughtful about student learning ... that ... is a quality that ought to be visible in our ideal graduate." Similarly, another member talked about the role of understanding child development in the DeLeT vision and learning to observe children and evaluate their thinking in a way that reflected a broader conception of assessment:

> I'm thinking about child study. So in that [assignment] there's a way of paying attention to what's happening with students' learning and the kinds of things that teachers can do, like the kinds of questions one can ask, the kinds of different tasks one can provide, that both allow the teacher to have insight into what does this child know and also helps move this child where one would want the child to go. So that is, in a sense, a form of assessment, but thinking about assessment perhaps more broadly than people might come into the program thinking about it.

They also felt that the vision of teaching involved thinking about curricular planning as informed by assessment and an emphasis on "big" generative ideas:

> We think about unit development in a particular way. We have a stance on how we teach students ... that has a strong role for assessment. So thinking about the entire year, thinking about segments of the year, and then thinking about the particular lesson ... all of those pieces. But beginning with big ideas and going to the smaller; as opposed to from the small to the big.

Finally, faculty saw the ability to know students as learners as deeply connected to building community. As one described that connection: "Part of what we want students to start unpacking is [that] the way you call on a student is connected to the way your classroom community is established, the way you're teaching for understanding . . . all of these different bigger ideas are then embodied in the smaller decisions that you make around planning and enacting your plans in the classroom."

Urban Teacher Education Program—A Vision of Teaching as Social Justice and as a Professional Practice. UTEP, which was created to prepare teachers for urban schools, promotes a vision of teaching that fosters greater equity and opportunity for all students, especially those in the Chicago Public Schools. The program's Web site captures its emphasis on a vision of social justice in a quote from Gandhi: "Be the change you wish to see in the world." Interviews with faculty and program directors also revealed a conception of good teaching in urban schools as a professional practice that is culturally relevant and informed by specific, practical teaching strategies such as learning to ask thoughtful questions and balanced literacy.

When faculty members spoke about their ideal graduate, they said they wanted their graduates to have "a commitment to social justice" and an understanding "that race and class play a role in the lives of their students and in their own lives." One faculty member emphasized, "We certainly want all graduates to believe that all children can learn," and another spoke of graduates who were "always positioning themselves as learners, not just two or four years out, but always." Faculty also noted the importance of being able to work productively with all members of a community, including all "stakeholders, parents, community members, all members of school staff, administration, whether or not you agree or disagree." One member added that UTEP graduates should have a strong sense of purpose that drives their work with different members of the community, enabling them to remain committed to their own aims and goals: "I think an ideal graduate is somebody that has a really strong sense of what they believe in terms of an educational philosophy, but also having the ability to represent that differently with different stakeholders . . . So an ability to work well with people who don't always agree with them while still holding fast to their core beliefs."

While emphasizing a set of broad goals, program faculty also described specific practices and routines they imagined graduates enacting in the classroom. One instructor described how this would play out in the teaching of reading, noting that she wanted their graduates to be cognizant of students' unique needs and strengths in their planning and teaching.

> They understand their students as readers, each student in a different way, and have a drive to work toward each student's strengths and support them in their areas of need. So really to continue to put a lot of thought into that work on a daily basis, to not hopefully go to a place where they are given a curriculum and they execute that curriculum without really thinking about their students as individual readers . . . If a student is not reading fluently, rather than saying, "Read faster," you are helping them understand what it means to coach a student to read more fluently [and] how they can model reading assistance and having the student read after they have read it. I think once those things become more practiced, then they become instinctual.

Faculty also emphasized the centrality of children's prior knowledge and cultural background in their vision:

> I think we really emphasize getting to know what the prior knowledge of the students is and understanding the culture of the students and using that as part of the context that teachers design and plan for. Again, I can't imagine a school or teacher not doing that to some degree, but I think it clashes in contrast to the notion of a canon or a sort of standard curriculum that I feel like suburban or other schools outside the urban context might subscribe to. We don't espouse that. We want teachers to find out what kids are interested in and tailor the curriculum to meet those interests.

They were quite clear about their vision of good teaching and how they would help new teachers learn about it.

> I would say that some of the kinds of things that we talk about with reference to our vision of good teaching have to do with *teaching with purpose*. I think the way that we try to "park" that idea is through our work on unit design and planning. We work a lot with the Wiggins and McTighe backwards design model in getting our interns to really think about, "What

are your goals first? What is the kind of evidence that you're going to want of understanding? How will you know if students understand it?"[2] So starting with that purpose. It is interesting to think about that with reference to this idea of practices becoming habitual.

When asked if they had a specific set of classroom practices that they wanted graduates to develop—and to become "habitual," as one faculty member described it—the program director affirmed that "on any very specific concrete level, clearly there are particular practices in literacy [or mathematics], being able to lead an effective guided reading group, to do interactive read-alouds, delivering meaningful mini-lessons."

UTEP's teacher educators also envisioned graduates teaching for the long haul: "They believe in this work wholeheartedly, that this isn't a phase of something to do for three years and then try something else . . . This is really something that is so important to them that they are *in* this." As one faculty member contended, the program is "preparing students to be effective in the context of *what is* while preparing them also to think about what *could and should be.*" He concluded, "The reality of urban education is that we have to produce students who are capable of functioning in this environment of urgency, but we also want them to come away with a larger vision of what is possible."

While all three of the programs have a broad vision that emphasizes their graduates' impact on society, the coherence and specificity of the visions of good teaching vary. The personal visions of the teachers in these programs illustrate how this variation interacts with graduates' personal visions and affects their career plans and own images of ideal teaching practice.

Coherence of Teachers' Visions and Program Visions

Perhaps not surprisingly, the personal visions of graduates were consistent with the content of the program visions. Of course, this kind of alignment likely reflects the programs' selection process; all three programs deliberately recruit and select student candidates who share some of the key program commitments. It is also likely that some students selected their program because it was consistent with their own conceptions of teaching and their own personal aims and goals for education (although, as detailed in chapter 4, a subset of teachers "fell into" programs without choosing them in an intentional way).

For instance, in keeping with the aims and goals of their program, virtually every ACE teacher emphasized a commitment to serve the Catholic community as a central element of their work in schools. John remarked that he had gone into teaching as a way to help advance the Catholic community: "It advances our community, it advances our society, and those are all things that are really important to me." When asked about their overall aims and goals, ACE teachers often spoke about influencing the spiritual and personal lives of their students. As Mary explained, "I felt like I was going to be someone in these kids' lives who they could learn from, that they could see was trying to be a good Catholic, trying to make moral decisions, and trying to do the best that she could and that they could learn from that." In keeping with the program vision, the ACE teachers described good teaching as a process by which one influences and molds children—helping young people lead moral, spiritually guided lives. They envisioned good teachers as modeling the process of leading good Catholic lives.

Consistent with the program vision of teaching as service, all but one of the DeLeT teachers interviewed talked about wanting to serve the Jewish community. David said, "I partly want to do this [for] the Jewish community . . . It is where I want to put my effort and where I hope that a lot of the benefit will accrue to the Jewish community." Related, some DeLeT teachers talked about being "role models" in the Jewish community: "Kids need strong role models in order to grow up into the kind of human beings that we want them to be, and . . . as a teacher you can have incredible influence . . . so it's pretty fulfilling."

The same consistency between program and individual visions was evident in interviews with UTEP teachers. Reflective of that program's vision of teaching as a form of social justice, all of the UTEP teachers we interviewed described visions of more equitable schooling and social change. For instance, Lara explained how she "recognized the need and the inequality that existed in not just urban schools, but rural schools too. As the type of person I am, I just can't sit back and let it happen."

But how do these visions shape learning opportunities in the different programs and to what extent and in what ways do programs help teachers not only learn about the guiding vision but also how to enact it in practice? And how does this relate to graduates' descriptions of their own classroom practice? To address these questions, I turn to the relationship between opportunities to learn and the program visions and look at ways in which the students are not only learning about the content of the vision but also learning how to enact it in the classroom.

Opportunities to Learn

An evaluation of documents, syllabi, and interviews with faculty revealed very different kinds of learning opportunities across the three programs, but all were consistent with the visions of good teaching. For instance, ACE student teachers had substantial opportunities to explore the concept of teacher as moral agent and to reflect on and pursue their own spiritual growth. They participated in a strand of courses and in experiences that supported them in thinking about their own development as Catholics and their role in helping form and develop future Catholics. Almost every syllabus addressed the formative and spiritual role of the teacher in a number of ways, suggesting that this topic received strong emphasis in the program as implemented.

At the same time, ACE offered fewer opportunities to think about the development of learners. Even the course on child development focused heavily on the role of the teacher. For instance, the first topic for a writing assignment asked, "How is the teacher a moral agent in the classroom?" The course syllabi stated that the purpose was to help students learn the importance of developmental theory and research for effective teaching as well as to integrate moral issues into classroom planning. While the course placed some emphasis on learners and learning, no assignments required ACE teachers to follow a student throughout the course of a day, to write a case study about a student, to interview a student, or to use pedagogical strategies that may help prospective teachers understand the perspectives and lives of children.[3] Few assignments appeared to be grounded in practice or in concrete teaching experiences.

Yet, these opportunities to learn are consistent with the program's vision of teaching as service, which focuses squarely on the role of the teacher and the opportunity for teachers to serve their community. Thus, while the ACE syllabi and assignments reflected structural coherence around a vision of teaching as service, they also revealed fewer opportunities to learn to enact this vision in the context of university courses. Even though ACE candidates were plunged into teaching after their first summer in the program, course assignments during the school year and second summer rarely drew on their classroom experiences.

In fact, all three programs exhibited coherence—a consistency of learning opportunities with the program vision of good teaching. Each program offered a set of courses designed to address and "form" teacher identity in relationship to the program vision. For instance, the director of the DeLeT program taught a course called the Jewish Journey in which novice teachers had opportunities to explore and reflect on their growth as Jews and as Jewish teachers. The UTEP soul strand asked students to focus on their cultural identities in relationship to that of their students. In terms of the vision of social justice, UTEP students had multiple opportunities to consider what it means to be an urban teacher as well as to affirm their commitment to urban schooling.

Both DeLeT and UTEP offered students substantial opportunities to learn about learners and their development and repeated opportunities to learn about particular classroom strategies and practices in keeping with their vision of teaching as a professional practice. For example, in DeLeT's Language Arts Methods course, students practiced using a number of assessments of students' reading and writing abilities, such as spelling inventories and running records. This course, offered during the first summer, had a practicum in which student teachers worked with small groups of elementary school pupils in a summer school program for three hours a week. In this context, they had opportunities to try out these assessment strategies. Then, in the class, they reflected on the use of the strategies and wrote progress reports for the children. These activities resemble the kinds of work teachers do in their classrooms as full-time teachers and are consistent with the program's vision of good teaching as a professional practice.[4]

In their course on human development and learning, UTEP students wrote a child case study.[5] They spent the first part of the course preparing to conduct observations and learning how to look at student work in nonjudgmental ways and how to capitalize on student strengths. Sessions addressed how such observations can feed into one's teaching practice: the syllabus noted that student teachers "will make use of observations and understandings of child development and student learning to brainstorm about effective practices for students."

As these assignments suggest, teacher candidates in both the DeLeT program and the UTEP program had opportunities to try out the kinds of practices and strategies they would eventually use as teachers. UTEP also provided opportunities for students to reflect on and develop an understanding of what it means to teach for social justice. And in DeLeT, teacher candidates considered teaching as a way to express one's commitment to the Jewish community. In short, students in these two programs had opportunities to learn about *both* program visions.

This cross-program view suggests that program visions can be traced to program learning opportunities and even to specific assignments, indicating some aspect of coherence in these programs. Yet, across the three programs there are considerable differences in the ways these opportunities are (or are not) grounded in the actual practices of classroom teaching. DeLeT and UTEP provide such opportunities to rehearse in some university classes, but in ACE mainly they learn to practice in the internship. Perhaps the kinds of learning experiences offered in DeLeT and UTEP reflect the specificity of the programs' visions in terms of teaching practice. A well-elaborated vision of good teaching may enable faculty to identify specific instructional practices that novices need to learn and to design opportunities outside the real world of the classroom to analyze and rehearse those practices.[6]

Coherence in Graduates' Teaching Visions

When program graduates described their teaching in the classroom and talked about their goals and ideal classroom practices, differences across the three programs were once again evident. The variation seemed related to substantive differences in program visions and the extent to which students had opportunities to practice enacting those visions.

While ACE teachers were very articulate about their visions of teaching as service and their role in the Catholic community, some struggled to describe their goals for classroom teaching. This was surprising, since the ACE teachers provided thoughtful and specific responses to questions about their commitment and work. Still, some seemed unsure about what to say in response to a question about their aims as teachers, as did Mary, who said, "Oh, boy. I don't know. I guess, I hope to, like, make a difference for these kids somehow." The ACE teachers, consistent with the program vision, described clear goals for children's personal growth and development and for the support and guidance they would provide as teachers; however, they did not emphasize particular curricular, intellectual, or learning goals.

In contrast, the visions of teaching practice articulated by graduates of DeLeT and UTEP were very specific, concrete, and detailed regarding their goals for classroom teaching and learning. Nathan, for example, described his vision of good teaching as being informed by careful observation of children paired with purposeful curriculum planning:

> Listening to the children, watching the children, and comparing my observations of the children with my co-teacher . . . To try to really understand what's going on with each individual child and then thinking about what needs to be done to meet their needs and challenge their interests. And then I think also in terms of planning teaching around goals . . . I think it's also important for the children to know [the goals as well].

UTEP graduates talked about visions of teaching in ways that were consistent with the program's vision of teaching as a professional practice, emphasizing practical strategies for teaching urban children. For instance, they provided detailed descriptions of the teaching they envisioned being most effective in supporting children's literacy development. Ella's description of a typical day suggests multiple strategies to help children learn to read:

> You would see many lessons that are about twenty minutes . . . where there is a concept that's taught and modeled. So I would show the students what they needed to do or the elements of the skill or the concept and then they would practice it with partners or in groups. And as they would be doing that, I would be going around and sort of checking in with the groups [asking,] "Can you two work together to see if you can explain it to one another?"

UTEP and DeLeT teachers' discussions underscored the clarity of their aims and goals for teaching. Their descriptions of their classroom practices were consistent with their program visions of good teaching as social justice and service, respectively. Furthermore, their aims and descriptions of what they wanted to accomplish also reflected an understanding of pedagogies consistent with their programs' visions of good teaching as a practice. Indeed, in both DeLeT and UTEP, student teachers not only had opportunities to learn about a vision of social justice or service as well as a vision of teaching as a professional practice, but they also had opportunities to learn to enact those visions. Yet, the future plans of the ACE graduates—in which they did not see themselves as continuing to teach long term—reflected opportunities in their program to learn about (and come to see) good teaching as a form of service.

Variations in Program Vision and Teacher Visions

Three key features of teacher education programs may differ quite considerably and may help account for variation in teachers' visions of good teaching, as well as in their career commitments and classroom practices. Far from being empty statements, the visions of teaching that undergird teacher education programs can have substantial impact and import. There is evidence of these visions on multiple levels: in the shape and design of the curricula and learning opportunities, in descriptions of classroom practice on the part of graduates, and, later, in the student teachers' future plans. For these three programs, visions of teaching are embedded in the programs, influencing them in deeply meaningful ways.

The ways in which these visions were emphasized in program materials and embodied in learning opportunities contributed to program coherence. Each of the three programs appeared to have a shared vision that came through in faculty discussions of aims and goals, suggesting a kind of shared understanding of a set of clear ideas about good teaching. And because the visions are evident in the courses, assignments, and learning opportunities, the programs appear to have a kind of intellectual or conceptual coherence around a shared set of ideas.[7]

Yet, coherence is not all that matters. The content of the vision of good teaching also has an impact. All of the ACE teachers had a strong vision of themselves as a moral and spiritual guide in the classroom, one consistent with the program's vision of good teaching as a form of service. At the same time, a number of them were much less detailed and specific about their classroom practices. Indeed, ACE teachers' plans to leave classroom teaching and go into administration fit with the ACE vision. A vision of good teaching as a form of service can, in fact, be enacted in a number of settings, not just in classrooms. Furthermore, if a vision of good teaching is not specific and developed—or if faculty do not share a conception of the teaching practices that are involved in that vision—then they may not design coursework and assignments that provide specific opportunities to practice or rehearse elements of that vision. In turn, novices may not be able to learn to enact it.

DeLeT and UTEP teachers expressed strong visions of good teaching as a professional practice, ones consistent with the visions of their respective programs. More of these graduates had a well-articulated sense of the aims of their classroom teaching and of the concrete and specific practices they would be using in their classrooms. Many imagined themselves remaining in teaching for the long term. Having prepared to teach in programs with a strong vision of practice and regular opportunities to learn that practice, these new teachers could envision the kinds of practices they wanted to enact based on their own emerging vision of good teaching. Their ability to translate vision into practice may help explain why they could imagine a long teaching career.

Indeed, the degree to which professional learning opportunities are related to real teaching practice seemed to matter in these three programs. DeLeT and UTEP teachers had consistent learning opportunities grounded in real teaching practice. They also had opportunities to rehearse aspects of classroom teaching in their professional coursework—again, consistent with their programs' visions of teaching as a professional practice. These teachers could describe in detail the kinds of classroom practices they were using as teachers and the impact those practices could have on pupils.

Implications for Teacher Education Programs

Because of the multiple ways in which vision informs and guides the three programs in the study, it important for programs to pay greater attention to the role that visions of good teaching may play in contributing to program coherence and guiding program design. While ACE, DeLeT, and UTEP may be unique in terms of the definition and focus of their visions, the potential value in articulating program visions as part of general program design and structure seems clear. Each of the programs had a clear vision of good teaching, as reflected in the aims and goals stated by faculty and graduates as well as the learning opportunities available to student teachers. Because research suggests that students learn better and develop more expertise when learning experiences cohere, it is particularly important to pay greater attention to the ways that programs are (or are not) coherent around a set of shared images of good teaching and practices that help enact it. Of course, the vision has to be not only compelling but also defensible and robust.

Furthermore, the content of the programs' visions seemed to either aid or impede the candidates' growing sense of identity as classroom teachers. This suggests teacher education programs may not only need to have a clear and coherent vision, but they must also consider the kind of teaching they wish to promote. Three very different visions of good teaching underlie these programs:

- A *vision of service* that conceives of teaching as only one of many opportunities to give back or contribute to society
- A *vision of social justice* that conceives of teaching as a direct means of addressing social inequities
- A *vision of practice* that focuses on teaching as a profession which has a knowledge base and set of practices that can be learned and developed over time.

If programs have a strong vision of service, graduates may conclude that they can fulfill that vision in a variety of ways—not all of which involve classroom teaching. In fact, a teacher can have a vision of service and still accomplish that vision even if she switches careers. These findings affirm the need for programs to articulate—and for new teachers to develop—a vision of practice as part of developing an identity as a classroom teacher.[8] Graduates of programs with well-specified visions of practice could imagine themselves enacting their visions as classroom teachers for the long term.

Finally, varieties of opportunities to learn *in practice* also correlate with graduates' plans to stay in teaching. It follows that programs must address what Mary Kennedy has called the "problem of enactment" and consider how to help student teachers learn to *do* teaching practice.[9] Having a vision of good teaching as a professional practice may be an important aspect of a strong teacher education program, but student teachers also need opportunities to learn to actually carry out the vision. These assignments, or experiences, must be tightly connected to real classroom practice so that prospective teachers will be able not only to envision but also to practice them in their future classrooms. At the same time, being grounded in practice does not need to be literally "in the field." Both UTEP and DeLeT offered a number of the practice-centered learning opportunities in various university courses. For instance, when students at the University of Chicago learn to teach the "read-aloud," they design and rehearse a read-aloud with their peers in the context of their methods class first before actually teaching a read-aloud with real elementary school children.

A Balance of Visions

A vision is, at heart, an expression of commitment. These programs exemplify three quite different visions of good teaching, each of which is based on a particular conception of teaching. The nature of those visions of teaching—and the commitments they express—have important implications for how teachers think about their work, their aims and goals, and their careers. This examination underscores the necessity of articulating visions, but it also illuminates the value of interrogating program visions of good teaching to be sure that they fully capture *all* the aspects of teaching that the programs value and wish to support.

Because this research reveals the importance of connecting vision to practice, it highlights the need to consider the degree to which a program's vision of good teaching has a well-articulated connection to classroom practice. Given the vibrant conversation in teacher education about developing more opportunities to learn that are tightly connected to real classroom practice, efforts to clarify the specific kinds of practices that embody and enact those visions seem particularly timely and important.[10] A vision of good teaching can not only promote alignment in a program around a set of core practices that reflect specific kinds of teaching, but it can also give direction to the design of specific learning opportunities to develop those practices.

Finally, this examination also shows that a program can have a vision of teaching as a professional practice which embodies central moral, ethical, or even religious values. Our study of UTEP, for instance, found that having a strong vision of good teaching as a professional practice did not preclude the program's commitment to social justice.

Indeed, having this particular combination of visions may be particularly powerful for the development of new teachers. If a program only promotes a vision of teaching as a professional practice, it runs the risk of supporting a view of teaching as narrow and technical work. Or, if programs invest solely in a social or moral vision, graduates' understanding of teaching might remain at the level of ideology and rhetoric. However, if a program promotes a vision of good teaching that captures broader social values along with a vision of the professional practices that are required to enact that vision, student teachers not only garner some protection against a technical view of teaching but also gain the potential to be the kind of teachers we hope they can be.

CHAPTER 6

Exemplary Teaching

Putting Principles into Practice

ERAN TAMIR AND KAREN HAMMERNESS

In exploring how programs prepare teachers to learn about the specific and local contexts of their teaching, this volume has also begun to hone in on the particular challenge of learning to *practice* in those settings. Teaching is, after all, a professional practice. From our perspective, learning to teach means learning to enact a principled teaching practice in a particular context.

Recent research has drawn renewed attention to the importance of centering teacher education on core practices of teaching.[1] This work raises concerns about the emphasis of university-based teacher preparation on theory and the lack of targeted opportunities to learn teaching practices. Indeed, although practice-centered teacher education has a long history, teacher candidates do not uniformly have opportunities to see and practice the kind of teaching advocated by their program, which contributes to the persistence of what has been called the "problem of enactment."[2] While teacher educators often provide substantial opportunities for students to learn *about* education, schools, teaching, and learning, they offer far fewer chances for students to implement what they have learned and to practice teaching.[3]

A renewed interest in teaching practice is also reflected in teacher education policy. For instance, federal investments in programs that provide extensive clinical experiences, such as urban teacher residencies, are growing. A recent blue ribbon panel urged that teacher education be "turned on its head" by giving greater emphasis to clinical studies and practical experience.[4] A growing scholarship on "high-leverage teaching practices" or "core practices" in teacher education is investigating what it takes to center teacher education around a set of specific teaching practices. Some teacher educators are designing opportunities for teacher candidates to learn to enact these core practices in context in relation to relevant understandings of learners, teaching, and learning.[5]

At the same time, a focus on practice-centered teacher education runs the risk of reducing teaching to a set of techniques and strategies. As Ken Zeichner points out, "There is a danger of narrowing the role of teachers to that of technicians who are able to implement a particular set of strategies but who do not develop the broad professional vision (deep knowledge of their students and of the cultural contexts in which their work is situated) and the relational skills they need to be successful in the complex institutional settings in which they will work."[6]

In this chapter we look at select program graduates five to seven years after graduation, examining whether (and how) the different program emphases on visions of teaching, social and/or religious missions, teaching practices, and the contexts of teaching are reflected in their actual teaching practices. We also consider how teachers' reasoning and pedagogical choices might reflect their preparation and how teachers themselves discuss the roots of their pedagogic strategies and practices. We consider whether central aspects of the programs' missions, visions of good teaching, and key program themes are enacted in these teachers' classrooms and teaching practices and the ways in which these graduates reflect the school settings in which they were prepared to teach in their current classrooms.

The teachers we observed had been in their schools for five to seven years (including the programs' internship or service periods), which meant they had multiple learning experiences and opportunities that either constrained their development or helped them to grow professionally and build on their teacher preparation. We do not suggest that the pedagogies the teachers enact or the ways in which they teach are entirely shaped by their teacher preparation. Rather, we focus on the fundamental question of how teacher preparation affects teacher practice.

To that end, we followed a sample of teachers from ACE, DeLeT, and UTEP into the classroom.[7] Program leaders helped us choose teachers from each program based on their ability to embody the commitments and pedagogical practices advocated by their program. We observed each teacher for a full day and conducted interviews before and after the lessons in order to obtain additional insight into teachers' goals for student learning, pedagogical reasoning, and rationale for curricular choices. In providing these snapshots of teachers in action, we aim to illustrate some of the distinctive pedagogies promoted by each of the programs as they are enacted in the classroom. In each of the cases, we demonstrate some of the ways that the teachers in these different settings brought to bear local and contextual understandings on their teaching practice as well as how they shaped their contexts by reflecting on what they know and have learned about the settings in which they were prepared to teach.[8]

DeLeT Teachers

In observing the DeLeT teachers, we looked for key elements of the program vision, such as an emphasis on building community both as an end and a means. We wondered if we would see any evidence of efforts to integrate Jewish and general studies and, in light of the program's emphasis on attending to children's specific strengths, needs, and abilities, if we might see this stance played out in the classroom in teachers being particularly attuned to children's thinking.

The two teachers we observed, Nathan and Linda, both taught in Kadimah, a K–8 Jewish day school in the Boston area. The school served primarily middle- and upper-middle-class Jewish families from neighboring cities. In 2012 the school charged annual tuition of more than $25,000 and described itself as having a progressive, child-centered approach coupled with an embrace of pluralism. The school's stated goals were to

- Nurture each student's capacity for intellectual discovery and decision-making within a respectful, pluralist, bilingual Hebrew-English environment
- Give our graduates the ability to create their futures informed by Jewish values, texts and culture, and to make a difference in their communities and in the world
- Kindle the flame of life-long learning in all its constituencies and serve as an inspirational model of innovative, effective and joyful teaching and learning beyond the school.[9]

Nathan

In his sixth year of teaching, Nathan was teaching the kindergarten class, which consisted of sixteen students (approximately half boys and half girls). He was co-teaching with another faculty member, Mica, who taught in Hebrew. (All classes in the lower school of Kadimah were staffed by one English-speaking and one Hebrew-speaking teacher). We spent a full day with Nathan observing him teaching both mathematics and language arts as well as attending to the regular routines at play in his classroom.

Entering Nathan's classroom, we were struck by the amount of children's work on the walls. One wall displayed students' illustrations of shapes; children had taken a basic shape and added features that transformed the shapes into pictures. For instance, one child had transformed a triangle into a sailboat; another began with a circle, added hands and feet and a hat, and labeled the picture "Haman."[10] Another wall featured a large, multicolored apple made of puzzle-piece-shaped papers, each with a photograph of a child in the class illustrated with designs or phrases like "I love monkey bars" or "I learned how to ride a bike without wheels." Next to the apple was a poster titled "The Gan Haviv Community," which explained in a teacher's neat handwriting:

> Just look at what we can all accomplish when we contribute and work together! Before school began, each of us received a cut-out "shape" in the mail. We were instructed to decorate it, each of us in his or her own special way. When we played a game to put the pieces together as a puzzle, we discovered that together we made a big apple, just like for Rosh Hashanah . . . We are all starting a new year together, new in Gan Haviv, new in our school. When we all work together, we can create something that is bigger and even more special than any one person alone!

The artwork on the walls reflected some of the themes we saw illustrated throughout the day in Nathan's classroom teaching. In it we saw the same attention to community and understanding as well as to individual student thinking and needs. Nathan's teaching also reflected a strong commitment to integrating Jewish values with general studies while developing understanding of the subject, whether math or literature.

On the day we observed Nathan, his class began with a morning ritual: the students recited the Pledge of Allegiance and then sang a Hebrew prayer from the traditional morning service, during which two students holding a Torah book circled their seated classmates. Next, Nathan called the students to order and asked them to work with someone seated nearby. He gave each pair several paper dice with different-colored shapes on each side. After students had a short time to talk about what they noticed about the shapes, he asked, "Who can share one interesting thing that their partner told them?" He turned to Abigail: "Who was your partner? What did they notice?" The girl responded, "That it was cut out from paper and taped together." Nathan asked, "Okay. Anyone have a different observation?" Another student responded, "Mica told me it was a square." Nathan remarked, "Okay, that the shape was a square, or a cube." Ari raised his hand and said, "My partner was Mica and he noticed the colors." Nathan nodded, adding, "The colors." Another student raised his hand and spoke in Hebrew, and Nathan listened and then told the class, "Assa said he noticed the shapes."

In this brief interaction, Nathan drew out students' observations by asking questions and revoicing their comments—all strategies taught in DeLeT that reflect close attention to student thinking and uncovering student ideas and understandings. In addition, Nathan's move to translate Assa's comment into English so that non-Hebrew-speaking children might understand also allowed Assa to participate and feel part of the discussion. Such strategies, widely advocated in the literature on teaching multilingual students, enable children who might otherwise be marginalized to feel included.[11]

Next, Nathan gave all the students a set of pattern blocks, dice, and an outline of six large hexagons. He instructed them to play the game Fill the Hexagon in groups by rolling dice, selecting pattern blocks, and making hexagons from the shapes. He explained that the intent of the lesson—which comes from the Technical Education Research Centers (TERC) Investigations mathematics curriculum adopted by the school—is for children to learn and understand all the different and possible combinations of shapes that might together produce the shape of a hexagon.[12] The children were not only supposed to name and categorize shapes (including more complex ones, like trapezoid or hexagon) but also to understand visually how such shapes fit together and to begin to see spatial relationships among geometric shapes.

Before students moved into groups, Nathan demonstrated how the activity was to work by showing an outline of a hexagon on the overhead and illustrating how they were to roll dice and what shapes they might need to fill the hexagon. This kind of modeling, regarded as a move of expert teachers, gives students a picture of what good work looks like before they undertake it themselves.[13] Before they got to work, Nathan reminded the students that they were supposed to be "helping one another."

Throughout the remainder of the lesson, Nathan moved from group to group asking questions and observing conversations. When some of the groups completed the activity quickly, he asked them, "What is the way to fill the hexagon with the *most* shapes?" and "How many does it take?"—pushing them to think harder about alternatives and other combinations. When one student responded that you could use "triangles," Nathan responded with another question, one that required that the student do the thinking, rather than providing an immediate answer of wrong or right: "How many does it take?" One group called Nathan over to say that they were "done." He came over, looked at their work, and asked them if they could complete the activity using even more shapes: "Can you make a hexagon with eight shapes?" When the students said they had, he said, "I didn't see that. Will you show me?" Each time Nathan interacted with students, he asked questions that required students to think and to show their work.

When two girls disagreed about whose turn it was to roll the dice and came to Nathan for help, he asked them to solve the problem: "What is the reasonable way you can solve this problem?" It was evident that students had experience working together and talking together about their work—with comments such as "I can help you," "Let's roll the dice at the same time," or "Let's roll, we need to roll," and when one student sought a shape, another said, "I can find you one." This suggested that Nathan had done substantial work throughout the year to help students learn how to work and talk together in productive ways—again, important work that experienced teachers do to set up a classroom environment where children learn how to work together. Further, it illustrates a key thread of the DeLeT program that emphasizes classroom learning communities where students learn how to work together and talk to one another and where, over time, because of prior scaffolding, they can do so without a teacher's direct guidance.

At the end of the class, Nathan brought the students back together on the rug. He asked, "So here is the question we are going to end thinking about: What do we know about hexagons?" "It has sides you can fill up with shapes," said one student. Another said, "It's in the shape of a cookie." Nathan followed up by focusing on the key attributes of the shape, an idea he wanted to make sure they understood: "So the first thing you said was how many sides it has?" One student called out, "Six." Nathan sought to find out what more students in the group understood by saying, "You have to tell me one thing about hexagons to get your pass for snack," to which students responded, "It has six sides!" or "It's made up of two trapezoids!" In these brief observations we saw Nathan's emphasis on informal assessment, how he determined quickly where at least most of the students were in terms of what they learned from the activity, as well as how he allowed students to hear one another's answers.

After the students returned from lunch and recess, Nathan did not immediately move on to the next activity. Rather, he asked the students "to debrief about recess." He asked students to hold up fingers to represent how well recess went for them. Most students held up four or five fingers. "So what was something that made it a five for you?" he asked. "We were playing nicely together," said Ella. To this Nathan said, "Give me a very specific example." Ari mentioned that they had been playing a soccer game and offered, "We were *passing* and playing together." Nathan then asked the class specifically about what had happened "on the swings." Mica raised her hand and explained, "Rachel dropped her headband and went to pick it up . . . but then Sam took her swing . . . but then we worked it out." Nathan turned to Sam and asked, "Sam, how do you feel about what happened?" He responded, "I got to swing later, so it was okay." The recess debrief ended with Nathan asking specifically about how "lining up" was going and pointing out that "we have another recess and a chance to try again." In this brief interaction, we again saw some central tenets of the DeLeT program emerging. The attention to a community of learners—the notion that children need opportunities to talk about, build, and reflect on what that community looks like and how it functions (both well and not so well).

Finally, another key aspect of Nathan's classroom implied in the artwork and wall displays, but not made explicit in this observation, were the ways in which the work reflected a commitment by him and his students to integrate general studies and Judaic studies. One of the projects students completed at the end of the school year was a video assignment that Nathan explained was designed to help the children reflect on their entire school year. The class made a timeline of all the activities they engaged in over the course of the year and illustrated it with photographs of their activities as well as drawings by the children. Then he asked the children to make an avatar or robot of themselves that stopped at three different points in the year's timeline, highlighting activities that were particularly meaningful or interesting to them. He also asked them to assign an action to the robot that reflected how they felt at that time (the robots could wiggle or jump or move from side to side, etc.). As Nathan explained it, this culminating assignment integrated Jewish and general studies by having students identify key learning moments that were part of both the Jewish and secular calendars.

These projects, which involved students reflecting on their learning over the course of the year, aligned with DeLeT's emphasis on observing and closely attending to children's thinking, providing children with opportunities to reflect and think about their learning, and creating opportunities for children to think about how their secular and Jewish lives are intertwined. Such metacognitive opportunities are not typical of kindergarten. Yet, Nathan's year-end project offered a unique and powerful glimpse into the ways that such strong teaching strategies can be used to help young children assess their own learning over the course of the year.

Linda

Linda, also in her sixth year of teaching, taught a third grade class of sixteen students. Hanging on the classroom walls were samples of student work, including class expectations in children's handwriting. A poster listed expectations such as "Be safe," "Be respectful," "Be responsible," "Be focused," "Take challenges," "Ask questions," and "Have fun!" in English and Hebrew. A poster labeled "Pack-Up Routine" listed in various children's handwriting (in Hebrew and English) such tasks as "Clean up your area,"

"Stack your chair," "Do your job," and "Put homework in backpack." And yet another displayed the message "Support each other!" These explicit expectations reflected DeLeT's emphasis on developing classroom community and revealed Linda's practice of making positive expectations clear for the children. The poster featuring a rainbow covered with photos of all the children in the class holding hands perhaps best captured the emphasis on classroom community.

Around the classroom, other materials revealed important themes consistent with DeLet's preparation. The program's focus on providing a rich literary environment was reflected in the poster titled "Genres We Like," which listed different literary genres—fiction, adventure, long books, how-to books, magic, mysteries, historical fiction, and pop-up detail. Posters from previous units decorated the walls as well. One, for a unit in which the children had read a book about homeless people, read "Initial Ideas" and listed impressions such as "no job; no home; orphaned; ragged, huddled on the street"; and a second poster, labeled "After Book," included a list of new ideas from the children, including "Have family; have friends; father works; buy food; don't steal." These visual aids indicated DeLeT's emphasis on eliciting children's thinking and revealed Linda's process of unearthing children's prior knowledge as well as making the process of learning explicit for children by recording prior ideas and new ideas and displaying the development of their learning in the classroom.

The class we observed began with a mathematics lesson aimed at helping children understand how to divide geometric shapes into equal parts and the relationships between dividing parts and numerical representations of those parts—an introduction to fractions. Linda started the lesson with an engaging idea:

> I've been visiting this new café. It's called Equal Pieces Café. They have new owners, and they are really friendly! And they really want to support new customers. I have been going there almost every day, getting coffee and brownies. But because they are just getting started they need some help with their bakery and business. I told them about you guys . . . you are all so creative, I thought you might be able to help with the Equal Pieces Café.

She noticed a student with a raised hand and asked him, "Carey, what are you thinking?" Carey answered, "That you are going to assign us to design a fancy design for their café?" Linda smiled, then called on another student raising her hand. Sarah said, "I think you are going to ask us to get equal pieces!" Linda responded, "Yes, why did you think that? By the name?" She then continued with the lesson: "So, they have this new concept—tell me what you think of this—to get more groups of people coming to their bakery, to figure out ways to have them buy more brownies and goodies. So, do you ever walk into a coffee shop and you see a big brownie calling your name?"

In this initial exchange, the DeLeT emphasis on eliciting student thinking came through in Linda's responses to her students—"What are you thinking?" and "Why did you think that?"—as well as in her drawing on common experiences her students might connect to, such as visiting a local bakery or a coffee shop.

Next, Linda held up a sheet with a set of eight large rectangles outlined in black and slowly showed it to all the students in the room. She continued to explain, "So, some people are health conscious. They need help cutting them up so two people can share it. So the first challenge for you is to cut the brownie up." She held up the brownie picture again. "But they don't want them cut up the same way; they are interested in having them cut up in all different ways." Then she added, "And another thing: I don't know about you, but if I had to share something like this with my brother, if he got even *one* extra piece or even a crumb, I would throw a fit . . . So for the bakery, it has to be equal! Sarah has figured this out. It is called Equal Pieces. So you guessed it: the pieces have to be *equal!*"

As she gave her explanation, Linda handed out sheets of paper with images of eight rectangular brownies on them to the groups of students sitting at their tables. One student stood up, walked to the front, and got a ruler. Linda affirmed, "That's a good idea, get a ruler!" As the groups of students started working, Linda circulated. She bent down to the different tables, confirming that they understood the task and asking, "Mary, do you understand what to do?" and "Silas, do you understand what we are doing?" The students responded by showing her what they were working on. She continued to walk around to the groups of students as they began to measure and draw lines on the brownies. As the students worked, she asked questions like, "What if you did that a different way?" and, when a student was using the millimeter ends to measure and was having trouble reading it, "How about if you try it with the inches side?" Each of her interactions revealed the kind of discussions emphasized by DeLeT—asking students if they understand and what would happen if they did it in a different way and making suggestions to try a different strategy.

After the students had worked together for about ten minutes to draw their lines, Linda told them to stop their individual work and said she would like to have some students come up and show their solutions. She called on one student, "Jesse, can you come up and show what you did?" Jesse stood in front of the group and showed his sheet, explaining, "I drew the line diagonally." Another student raised his hand and indicated, I did it the exact same way." Linda then pressed the discussion to the conception of fractions: "So you did it with a diagonal line? What would you call it when you divide it with this line? What would we call that fraction?" Jesse responded, "One half."

Next Linda asked, "Can I have someone come up and share another way to split the brownie in half?" Malia volunteered, walked to the front of the room and faced the class. Showing her work, she explained, "I did this [shows that she made an N-shaped line on the brownie]. I know it looks strange. I do this in my house sometimes . . . I like to figure out what interesting halves I can make. I came up with this one." Linda looked at the picture and asked, "How do you know these two parts are equal?" Malia responded, "If you cut them and turn them around, they are the same." Linda pressed with another question, "So what fraction would people have if they were to buy it?" The student pondered this and suggested, "A third?" Linda nodded and then asked for other students to bring up their solutions. She then told them to "start working together" to divide up the remaining brownies. At this point one of the students asked, "How do you write one quarter?" Instead of providing the answer, Linda asked the student, "What do you think?" The student responded, "One slash four?" Linda affirmed, "Yes."

Several features stood out in Linda's interactions with her students. Her move to have multiple students share their solutions with their classmates as opposed to the teacher sharing a solution reflects DeLeT's emphasis on engaging students actively in sharing their thinking. Also, her choice to invite a number of students to share reflected her appreciation and understanding of the importance of giving children opportunities to demonstrate what they know and describe their thinking. Furthermore, her efforts also communicated a central idea critical in mathematics teaching: mathematical problems can be solved in multiple ways. Her acknowledgment of the appropriateness of the different methods of solving the brownie division problem underscored for students the idea that different strategies can and should be applied. Finally, over and over she asked questions rather than telling students how to solve something—"Anyone else?" "How did you do that? Did anyone else do it the same way?" Even in this brief incident we saw her efforts to uncover student thinking and to make student's thinking explicit not only for other students in the classroom but for the individual learners themselves—all practices consistent with DeLeT's emphasis on attending to individual students and their thinking.

UTEP Teachers

When we visited Chicago to observe two UTEP graduates, we looked for the core practices, strategies, dispositions, and stances advocated by their program. We were interested in the ways teachers enacted culturally relevant teaching practices, how they built on children's strengths and knowledge, how they enacted balanced literacy, and whether they adopted a general stance that emphasized issues of equity and social justice as they might play out in everyday classroom life.

The teachers we observed taught in two charter schools located in two different neighborhoods on Chicago's South Side.

Allison

Allison had been teaching for six years at the time of our observation. She taught a first grade class with twenty-seven students, twenty-six of whom were black and one who was white. The school was made up of roughly 95 percent African American students primarily from households with median incomes of around $17,000. The charter school is located in a neighborhood shaped by a long history of racial segregation in close proximity to the University of Chicago.

One of the first things we noticed on entering Allison's classroom was the substantial number of books divided by such topics as "peace," "professional careers," and "public figures" (e.g., Michael Jackson). The updated technology included a SMART Board and computers, and posters on the walls emphasized routines and strategies. For example, near the bookshelves a poster titled "What can I do when I come to a tricky word?" explained strategies for identifying a new word in a text. Another poster illustrated the pillars of a strong classroom community by featuring pictures of children to illustrate concepts like "Listening," "Mutual Respect," "Participation and Right to Pass," and "Appreciation." These homemade posters reflected an emphasis on creating a rich, positive atmosphere in the classroom that is both culturally relevant and supportive of instruction, concepts staunchly advocated by UTEP.

We also noticed Allison's strong affection for each and every child. As each student entered the room, she greeted them with a smile and a hug. She then asked students to sit down on the rug, beginning the day with compliments: "I love how Susanna is sitting. Thank you, Jaden, for sitting so quietly and peacefully." She then said, "We will do yoga today because we are so wiggly. Pick a letter, Linda." Linda picked Y, and Allison asked the children to "do a Y shape" with their body. The children all participated and seemed cheerful as they were forming the letter Y. Her supportive comments to students illustrated the ways that a sense of trust, respect for children, and positive reinforcement for good behavior form the backbone of this classroom community, a central UTEP tenet.

After finishing the short yoga session, Allison and her students discussed the class's donation project: "Let's start with donations. So why are we collecting donations?" "We want to help hungry people," says Rasheed. Allison invited the children to come and put their donations in a jar. "Thank you for being so generous." In asking students to donate a few cents, Allison helped students think of themselves as contributors to noble causes that could make a difference in the world—a move aimed at empowering students that enacted the social justice core tenet of the program.

Caring for and empowering students are closely related to the building of a strong classroom community. When we asked Allison about the things she tried to achieve in her class, she noted,

I have the kids basically run morning meeting . . . when they're using the SMART Board, and they're giving compliments to other students, and they are trying to be positive, and so that's definitely something that I worked really hard on with them. That all takes time, too . . . The foundations for this are from UTEP. UTEP worked a lot with us on thinking about the classroom environment that you want to have . . . [Are] you going to speak to them in a positive way, or is it going to be mostly negative? Are you going to be the one that's putting down all of the judgments, or is it going to come from the children?

Throughout the day we observed numerous manifestations of Allison's thriving classroom community. Indeed, students took responsibility for facilitating and managing classroom discussions and activities, and Allison encouraged those who served as facilitators to exercise some of her teacher responsibilities. During meeting time, one of the students was responsible for inviting other students to share their stories. Later, two students were responsible for leading the reading aloud of the schedule and facts of the day (from the SMART Board). Before reading aloud the schedule, the student facilitator said, "I like how Rozana is sitting. I like how Nathan is sitting." Allison encouraged the student facilitators to provide specific feedback by prompting, "Why do you like how they sit?" "Because his eyes are on the board. Because he listens," the facilitator explained. Then the two students took turns reading out loud, "Today is Wednesday, May 4th. The temperature is 71 degrees. We have $64.83 in our donation box."

Plants were the topic of the day. Allison had designed multiple activities to help students gain basic knowledge about plants before moving to more advanced concepts like photosynthesis. She started by explaining basic facts about plants, introducing parts of plants on the SMART Board, and describing the process of photosynthesis. Then, in order to help children understand these complex issues, she showed them a short video about the parts of the plant. That same day students drew different parts of the plant and planted seeds, so they would be able to observe how plants grow. As Allison noted, she used these activities as "chances to talk about the different parts of the plants, and I [also] have a couple of plant part worksheets that they're going to be filling out, so there are going to be a lot of ways that we go over that." Her use of multiple approaches to learning reflected her understanding that helping children learn and keeping them engaged requires a curriculum designed for various students with different strengths or intelligences—another core concept emphasized by UTEP. When a child lost focus, Allison either gazed at or gently touched the child while continuing to talk. This ability to maintain a positive working environment without losing precious instructional time is one mark of a well-prepared teacher.

In keeping with research on the benefits of group work, Allison made extensive use of this learning format.[14] For this lesson, she divided students into groups and moved them between stations to carry out different tasks. Variously, she asked them to do individual work within the group; at other times she had them work in pairs, in groups, or with her. Although group work is a complex instructional arrangement that can be challenging and requires a great deal of scaffolding, Allison's students worked effectively doing what they were supposed to do—drawing, discussing, planting seeds, or working with the SMART Board.[15] For example, in a reading center assignment, Allison worked with the "Michael Jackson" group on English literacy reading and comprehension skills, focusing on strategies students could use during reading comprehension to decode unfamiliar words, such as using context clues or starting with familiar words.

Allison: "Today we are going to work on the first 5 pages of the book . . . On your papers you see the word 'habitat.' Now, whenever you see a word like 'habitat,' you would need to figure out what that word means. Now remember what we do when we try to figure out what a word means?"

Rob: "We can look at the dictionary."

Allison: "That's right, but what kind of things can we do with our book to figure out that word? Eli?"

Eli: "We can look at the picture."

Allison: "We can look at the picture. What else can you do, Mike?"

Mike: "You can find a word that you know."

Allison: "Yes. But if we read the word and are not sure what it means? Jenny?"

Jenny: "Read the page that it is in."

Allison: "The page that it is in, and then the page can give us a clue to what that word means, right? So, if we want to figure out the word 'habitat' . . . we would need to read the words around it and figure out what it means."

What stood out from this exchange was its explicit emphasis on learning specific reading strategies.[16] In addition, during her interactions with students, Allison not only included all the children in the conversation by asking each one to respond, but also skillfully took up or "revoiced" key ideas they shared and elaborated on their initially incomplete answers. All of these approaches were part of UTEP's curriculum and are also strategies researchers suggest as particularly critical for student learning in reading.[17]

We observed Allison working confidently with different groups of students using appropriate materials to stimulate students' curiosity and interest in nature and animals while helping them improve their reading skills. She attributed her inclination to use small groups to her UTEP training and noted that she used the skills she learned in the program as a springboard to innovate and improve her practice:

I was taught how to do guided reading for literacy, like how to work in small groups with kids at their level, so you're hitting specific skills for each group, and so I feel like that's a really good way to teach reading . . . I decided to use that to figure out how to teach math, so my teaching program taught me how to teach in the small group style, and I'm now using that for math as well.

Anne

Anne taught social studies to seventh graders at a renovated urban charter school. At the time of our observation, she had been teaching for six years. The school served a student population of almost 100 percent African American students from low-income families (roughly 80 percent of the school's families are described as low income by the Chicago Public Schools, with the median household income in the neighborhood at around $16,000).[18]

Anne's class was neatly organized with many posters and student work hanging on the walls. Curricular resources, like books divided by subject and a TV screen connected to a laptop, were accessible to the students.

Two wall posters featured events from recent U.S. history focusing on the experience of black Americans. One poster described the "push factors" in the South and "pull factors" in the North associated with the migration of African Americans. Another poster laid out key social studies vocabulary that students had been introduced to, including such words as "racism," "geography," "primary source," "upstander," "tyranny," "stereotype," and "federalism." These posters reflected UTEP's commitment to empower students through culturally relevant teaching about their history and were also evidence of the high-level thinking and expectations that Anne demanded from her students.

We observed Anne for an entire day, focusing on her teaching of social studies in two classes. Each class we observed was carefully designed and executed using multiple strategies to keep students focused and attentive. She gave clear instructions, set high expectations, and encouraged students to collaborate with peers.

An explicit commitment to social justice and student empowerment, both cornerstones of UTEP's mission, were apparent throughout Anne's classes. When students entered the class, they found a question posted on the TV screen: "What was the reality of life in Chicago for African Americans and how did they respond to it?" After greeting students, Anne asked, "What are some of the examples in which people responded to the reality around them?" A boy replied, "Shooting." Anne said, "Yes, using violence. Can you think about other responses people use?" A girl replied, "Demonstrating, making speeches." Anne said, "These are all great examples, thank you."

Anne used this introduction to delve into the main subject. "Our idea for today is to talk about resistance. How can we fight the way some people think or act against us?" In order to clarify her question she suggested an example: "You are resisting wearing your yellow school shirts by wearing something on them that we keep asking you to take off. How can the arts be used as a form of resistance? What do you think about this idea?"

She then assigned each group twelve photos of art works that could be interpreted as examples of resistance. "[I] want you to sort these works in your group. Think what do some works have in common and create a specific list of categories . . . I would like to see artworks divided into groups that you create. You have five minutes to do that. You may not write on your laptops today, only on a sheet of paper."[19] When she observed a group that started working, she was quick to say, "I really appreciate the groups that have started discussing the artworks so seriously." Such use of positive feedback is a powerful strategy to encourage learning as well as constructive student behavior.[20]

While student were working, Anne stopped by their tables, checking for understanding by asking questions such as, "Which categories have you noticed? What do you think about this work? What do you see here?" When the five minutes were up, Anne asked table representatives to report back on the categories they identified, and the students offered the following responses: "There were works about peace," "There were works about money and how government pays for wars instead of helping the poor," "Works about violence." Anne typed the responses on the TV screen so that everybody could see them.

When we asked about the unit's design, Anne explained that one intention was to enable students to bring to bear their various strengths and interests. She noted,

> All of our students have these talents and a lot of them are very artistic and creative. They don't get to show that very much in every day school life . . . So this unit, we thought would be a great way to . . . use those interests and energy . . . whether it be rap music or sketching in [a] notebook [and find a way to] use that and connect it to the history of [their neighborhood] or the concept that we're studying and then produce something that [students] are proud of at the end. So, the main thing about their own artwork is that somehow it expresses a part of their identity. And that, in itself, is an act of resistance, right?

Underlying Anne's curricular choice was a broader and more coherent vision of urban education and social justice. Her explanation of this vision shed light on how teacher preparation may help shape teachers' professional commitments and practice.

> Every year I have a unit at the end of the year about resistance that is taking everything that we've learned and applying it in their every-

day lives. And I think that's an important part of the year for whatever subject I teach. So it's how I teach it, what I decide to teach, and what I feel is important for students to know that UTEP has given me; that goes back to my philosophy of education and [UTEP's] philosophy of education and the values that they've instilled in me and having the high expectations [from] students . . . knowing [they can] grapple with it. And I mean, it's hard, like it's conceptual, like resistance. "What is that? How can art be a form of resistance?" It's hard for even us to answer . . . but we have those expectations that kids are able to understand that and start thinking about it at a young age.

Turning from a macro vision of purposes to a micro vision of classroom management, Anne carefully employed a variety of strategies. For example, she insisted on capturing student interest right from the beginning of the lesson: "The hook . . . this is how you connect it to what we've been learning so far, to what they're interested in . . . [Today] the hook was trying to get at the idea that they perform individual acts of resistance every day."

She also created various structures to facilitate learning for all her students, including opportunities for students to work in groups, so that students who still had difficulty reading, but had better listening or oral skills, could participate and contribute to the discussion. In addition, Anne made extensive use of the environment to support student learning, an approach that she saw as coming from her

> knowledge of balanced literacy and how literacy should be taught. So, for example, the word "wall" is one example of making sure that students understand the vocabulary that you're teaching. So, for example, they wrote down a definition of resistance today, so they should have that definition; it's going to go on the word wall. We can refer to it and use it in class.

Several features stand out in Anne's interactions with her students. Her classes were carefully planned and reflected her deep commitment to social justice and student empowerment. And her nonconfrontational approach and unruffled classroom management style encouraged student interactions and gained her the respect of students.

ACE Teachers

While ACE's student teachers were placed primarily in urban Catholic schools during their first two years, those who continued to teach after graduation worked in a variety of school settings, including suburban schools located in the Northeast. In observing the ACE teacher, we were curious whether we would see attempts to serve as role models, to exemplify or model processes of decision making in a moral or ethical way reflecting Catholic values, or to develop classroom instruction and community inspired by ACE's focus on subject matter and classroom management.

Thomas

At the time of our observation, Thomas, in his seventh year of teaching, was teaching history, geography, and French at St. Markus High School, located in the outskirts of a midsized city in the Northeast. The school tuition of approximately $12,000 per year likely drew students primarily from middle-class families. The school's student body consisted of 90 percent white students, 6 percent Asian students, and about 3 percent black and Latino students.

St. Markus's religiosity was not easily detected. Some of the school leaders still belonged to religious orders, and images of crosses appeared in every classroom. However, the school's focus on academics seemed paramount, and teaching was conducted mostly by lay teachers. Its suburban feel and focus on academics were reinforced by the school's Web site, which informed visitors about the percentage of students who took Advanced Placement classes and participated in extracurricular activities like sports, community service, music, arts, and politics. The site also reported that almost all school graduates attended college.

We observed Thomas teaching geography and history. On entering the class, we saw the roughly twenty students sitting in rows. Posters on the walls illustrated important events in U.S. history, and a large map detailed important developments in the occupation of the western frontier. The classroom had a projector connected to a laptop, and a designated area at the back of the room had several shelves filled with history books. All students had laptops they received from the school.

The first class, Geography of the Middle East, began with a quick quiz. Then Thomas asked students to investigate a country in that region using the Internet. He gave instructions for how to conduct the research as well as how the project would be graded and offered some specific guiding questions (which also appeared on a handout for students): "Try to find out who is the ruling party. Who is the opposition?" "You can make a PowerPoint if you like, but you don't have to. It will be good if at least you have a map of the country . . . If you want to ask your partner a question, that's fine, but most of the work should be yours." Thomas also identified potential resources: "Try broadcast news . . . Let me show you an example. I looked this morning on the BBC's Web site, which is an excellent source of information. So we have here information about each country's population, where it is located, who is the ruling party. I want you to have at least two sources in your report."

In this geography class, Thomas designed a learning environment that encouraged students to explore and construct their own ideas and content within a clear framework of expectations. When we asked what was he trying to accomplish and how it might be related to ACE, Thomas responded,

> One of the things I did learn from ACE that's taken me a few years to really work on (and I'm still working on it) is the idea that it's not all teacher centered, that I'm there to help instruct them, to set the parameters, and then the learning is something that they need to do. In geography today, climbing up that ladder, you've got your simple quiz-like identifications, but then we're going to apply things . . . The idea for today is that the Middle East is changing very rapidly . . . and we need to understand what's going on and what will the future of the Middle East be.[21]

Soon, after the students started delving into their research, a barrage of questions erupted. A student studying Syria asked, "What does it mean to be in a 'state of emergency'?" Thomas said, "That's a good question. This is something that varies across countries . . . it might mean a curfew from a certain hour. You need to look more into it." Another student asked, "It says here that there is a standoff between the president of Iran and its supreme leader. What does 'supreme leader' mean?" "This is part of your research,

Jim," Thomas reminded. "Try to read more and find out." These exchanges echo Thomas's comment that, as a teacher, he needed to facilitate learning and let students do the hard work. When we looked around, we saw students working independently, exploring the Internet, and visiting news Web sites, such as CNN, BBC, *New York Times,* and NPR. Some used Wikipedia to further explore names of leaders or political parties.

The second class we observed, a history class, explored the end of the western frontier and the establishment of the state of Oklahoma. Thomas began the class with a short activity: "Take out your notes. Open a clean page. Today we are going to talk about the American frontier. Put in the middle of your page the word 'frontier' and circle it. So, what comes up as you think about this word?" One student in the front responded, "Farming." Thomas pointed to another student, "Native American." A third student offered, "West." "These are all good examples," Thomas said. "Now take two minutes and write down these words . . . Here is your chance to have a word with a neighbor. Just one pair at a time. Do that. I encourage you to exchange ideas . . . When you have some ideas, come to the board and add some of your words."[22] We noticed at least fourteen students writing their words on the board. "Oh great!" commented Thomas. "We have a lot of volunteers." During the activity he walked around encouraging students to share their ideas: "Have you added a word? You have good stuff here. Go add it." He later explained, "I try to get everybody involved. There are a few kids who always have their hands raised . . . but one of the things I've been trying to work on is to try to call on some more kids."

Observing how Thomas framed and taught the fraught settling of Oklahoma was particularly interesting. We were curious to learn if and how he might invoke ACE's mission in this discussion, particularly in regards to social justice and compassion. In class, Thomas reminded students about the Dawes Allotment Act and various other steps that led to the establishment of Oklahoma. He also mentioned briefly the plight of Native American tribes, stating how their land rights in the area that became Oklahoma were violated.

Later we asked Thomas about the degree to which teaching history is linked (or not) to Catholic values. In response, he told us,

A couple of weeks ago, we talked about immigration, and . . . about Irish and German immigration . . . and a kid made a comment about immigrants today, Mexicans, and it just gave me an opportunity, and I stopped . . . So we talked about the idea of immigration and justice for immigrants . . . because the student was saying, "Immigrants take jobs." We just had to kind of realize that the stereotype of immigrants leeching from the system isn't true. And the term "illegal immigrants," I'll use the term "undocumented" . . . So we talked a lot about the Catholic ideas of justice and how they apply to these cases.

These examples illustrate Thomas's commitment to social justice and how it guided his approach to teaching in general and teaching history in particular. Apart from helping students make tangible connections between history and current social studies, he saw his role as helping students understand how history and politics are woven together and how Catholic principles could be relevant to and provide an important lens for understanding complex, politically charged issues like racism and immigration. These social justice commitments that stand at the core of Thomas's teaching are well aligned with those of the ACE program.

Linking Teacher Preparation to Teaching Practice

The observations of these five new teachers suggest that long after graduation their teacher practices clearly reflected many of the ideological commitments, religious and social values, and distinctive pedagogies advocated by their programs. UTEP teachers practiced and articulated a deep commitment to promoting social justice using specific practices like balanced literacy while being mindful of the context of the Chicago Public Schools. ACE teachers focused on building academically rigorous lessons, carefully planning and managing their classes, and trying to offer a moral reading of current events guided by Catholic values and beliefs. DeLeT teachers were committed to building a strong classroom community infused with Jewish values, asked many questions, and tried to stimulate learning through discussions.

All of the teachers we observed enacted many elements of strong teaching, like offering positive feedback to students, being clear and organized in their instruction, using multiple approaches to gain insights into students' thinking, and requiring students to do the intellectual work. The UTEP and DeLeT cases are particularly telling because we observed teachers implementing their programs' visions of good teaching and larger social and/or religious missions in the kind of schools for which they were prepared. In the ACE case, the teacher, like the rest of the ACE participants, had moved from his initial teaching placement in an urban Catholic school serving low-income, minority students to teach in a Catholic high school serving white middle-class students.[23] While the ACE teacher taught in ways that were consonant with the program's religious mission and general vision of good teaching, we do not know how these practices would have played out in a different and more challenging school setting.

Although these findings come from a small sample of teachers, they suggest that some types of teacher preparation can have a significant, positive impact on teachers' practice long after graduation. This challenges prior quantitative studies that used broad categories to distinguish teacher preparation pathways and programs and found only weak correlations between them and multiple teacher outcomes.[24] Instead, many educators believe that the work environment of schools shapes teachers' practices and commitments.[25] This chapter does not refute the important role that schools play in socializing teachers; it does, however, offer portraits of practice which suggest that programs resting on a compelling social/religious mission and a robust vision of good teaching that provide opportunities to enact that vision may also play a critical role in preparing strong teachers.

We suggest that mission-driven, context-specific preparation with a clear vision of good teaching and opportunities to enact practice, prepare teachers to teach effectively in both challenging and supportive school environments. Such teachers take the ideas and strengths of children seriously and challenge and strengthen their learning.

CHAPTER 7

Support for New Teachers

Principal Leadership and School Culture

ERAN TAMIR

An element of the story that has been largely missing from the discussion so far is how schools and principals perceived beginning teachers hired to teach at their schools. To bring in this school perspective, this chapter turns to the leaders of the participating schools who hired and supervised the teachers in the Choosing to Teach Study. In a series of interviews, principals explained how they understood and perceived the newly minted teachers, what they did to induct them into their schools, and what forms of support and guidance they provided to help them succeed in their work.

The urban schools on Chicago's South Side included traditional public schools, a magnet public school, and two charter schools started by the University of Chicago Urban Education Institute, the sponsor of the UTEP program. Except for the magnet public school, which served gifted African American students from low-, middle-, and high-income families, the other schools served low-income African American and/or Latino students.

The Catholic schools were mainly located in southeast Los Angeles and catered to low-income Latino students. These schools operated under extreme economic pressures and were dependent on the Catholic Church, parents, and private donations. Principals in these schools reported dwindling enrollments and concerns about the future. One Catholic school was located in an upper-class neighborhood, where it served mainly white upper-class families.

The Jewish day schools, located in the greater Boston area and serving white, primarily middle- and upper-class Jewish families, were either affiliated with a Jewish denomination (e.g., Reform or Conservative) or were community schools, serving families with diverse Jewish orientations from secular to Orthodox and everything in between. Amid the economic turmoil of 2009, some of these schools were struggling to stay afloat.

For the study, we interviewed nineteen principals and/or assistant principals who hired and/or supervised the work of the thirty participating teachers.[1] These interviews took place four years after the teachers were hired. In trying to locate these principals, we discovered that all the sectors had experienced considerable turnover in leadership, with only a quarter of the principals staying in their original school for more than five years.[2] These school leaders played a central role in shaping the professional culture and working conditions that influenced new teachers' practices and professional growth as well as how they felt about their work.

Principal Support for New Teachers in the Literature

Two lines of research focus on the contributions of school support to beginning teachers. One focuses on new teacher induction on the grounds that teachers, like other professionals, are more likely to feel committed, teach more effectively, and stay longer if given appropriate on-the-job support. Some studies show that different forms and combinations of support affect teacher retention.[3] For example, researchers have found that

> having common planning time with other teachers in their subject area . . . reduced the risk of leaving by about 44%, at a statistically significant level. Participating in regularly scheduled collaboration with other teachers on issues of instruction reduced the risk of leaving by 27%, at a statistically significant level. Participation in an external network of teachers (e.g., one organized by an outside agency or over the Internet) reduced the likelihood of leaving by about 44%, at a statistically significant level.[4]

School principals can encourage, strengthen, and institutionalize at least some of these induction structures and practices so that they become part of the professional culture in their schools. For this to work, more experienced teachers must take ownership and provide leadership in teacher collaboration and professional development. Susan Kardos and Susan Moore Johnson found that schools with strong professional cultures communicated clear expectations and had a supportive administration.[5] Principals can also offer teachers paid time to work on curriculum and other classroom tasks.[6]

A second line of research focuses on principals as instructional leaders, especially their role in promoting professional relationships among teachers, developing a shared vision of good teaching for the school, and creating the necessary structures to support a strong professional culture of learning. Researchers have found that principals can make a difference by developing strong professional communities and making schools hospitable to beginning teachers.[7]

A Wallace Foundation study suggests that successful principals exercise sets of practices related to "setting directions, developing people and redesigning the organization."[8] These core practices, or *leadership functions,* have been linked with improved school, teacher, and student outcomes.

The first leadership function, *setting directions,* concerns a leader's ability to identify, articulate, and communicate clear aims for the school. Looking at how principals set directions for their schools provides an opportunity to examine and compare how schools within and across sectors discuss their different priorities and goals. Understanding these priorities and goals reflects on the school's commitments and the type of teachers who would best carry out its goals.

The second leadership function, *developing people,* emphasizes the leader's commitment to ongoing professional support and development for the faculty. For novice teachers, this includes inducting them into the school mission, policies, and expectations and providing educative mentoring during their early years on the job. It also includes providing job-embedded professional learning opportunities for teachers at all career stages to sustain their engagement in the ongoing improvement of teaching and learning.

The third leadership function, *redesigning the organization,* focuses on the role of transformational leaders in motivating organizational learning and change, promoting a shared sense of purpose, and supporting a collaborative professional culture. Establishing a professional collaborative environment requires hard work and the building of trust among principals and teachers; it signals that a school is taking practice seriously and willing to invest the required resources to maintain it. These schools are likely to align well with the visions of teaching advocated in particular by UTEP and DeLeT.

I use this framework to examine how school leaders perceive their role vis-à-vis beginning teachers and what practice and policies they use to shape a school environment conductive to the professional growth of beginning teachers.

Leadership in Urban Public Schools

The urban principals interviewed in this study came from a diverse sample of schools on the South Side of Chicago. While the schools varied in their levels of autonomy, all were subject to ongoing pressure to meet the state's adequate yearly progress (AYP) requirements. That drove principals to use data as a key component in school-based professional development aimed at assisting teachers to help students improve their test scores. Overall, the schools adopted similar, but not identical, goals. There was more variation in how the urban principals responded to state and district pressures and enacted professional standards for instructional support of new teachers.

Setting Directions

The first thing the study asked was what the urban public school principals considered the primary aims of their schools. This question offered a window on school leaders' priorities and gave a sense of what kinds of school they hoped to create and what kinds of teachers they hoped to hire.

There are three recurring themes in the principals' responses. Almost all articulated the aim of *improving academic learning*. For some this meant providing students with the skills needed to attend college and get a paying job that would support a comfortable, healthy life. For others this meant meeting state standards and preparing students for middle school or high school.

Mr. Holbrook, the leader of an elementary charter school, took a career-oriented approach to academic improvement.

> We are drilling in our kids' minds that they have to go to college, so we try
> to give them all the training they are going to need when they go to high

school . . . We're teaching them note-taking skills, good habits, how to organize themselves, so that they will enjoy high school and go to college. Ultimately we want . . . our kids . . . to be either in college or to be working in a job that is legitimate, because the opposite is doing something that is not legitimate, which is very common around here. So our ultimate goal is, five years after eighth grade, the kid is either in college, or the kid is gainfully working, employed and paying taxes to society.

Other principals had more modest goals. For example, Mrs. Shire, a CPS principal, explained her school's aim as "mak[ing] sure that we prepare our students to be successful in middle school and to be able to get in to selective enrollment high schools here in Chicago. That's basically what we really want to do with our students."

Three of the eight urban principals mentioned social justice.[9] Some used the term to denote an overarching commitment to provide opportunities for social mobility to minority and low-income students. These principals developed and implemented a range of initiatives, including free breakfast and lunch, extended school day programs, educational programs for families, and curricula that addressed the particular history and inequities experienced by their students.[10] Some schools had most of these programs; others, just a few. Ms. Shelby, a passionate educator and founder of a charter school, articulated the social justice mission of her school and the range of commitments it entails.

We have a social justice mission and feel that it is our obligation to prepare children to be active, engaged participants . . . and positive leaders in [the] local and global communit[ies] . . . we are preparing scholars for success in college prep high schools. So that means developing pipelines to strong high schools and helping our families navigate the maze of selecting and enrolling in a high school. It also means helping our scholars develop habits of independence and self-advocacy and collaboration and all of the things that our scholars will need to be successful in high school and in college.

Another aim was *serving the community*, which more than half of the Chicago principals we interviewed saw as an important goal for their school.[11]

This aim acknowledged that schools can play a positive and important role in bringing together families across a neighborhood and helping them raise and educate responsible citizens, thereby improving the community as a whole. Ms. Shelby, a CPS principal, expressed her school's commitment:

> As a community school, we have extended services, hours and relationships. We work closely with our community. We are, what you call, a neighborhood school. We're not selective enrollment. It's open enrollment in terms of children from the community having access to the school. But also being that community school, we give some additional services. So our school day is longer for some of our children because they still have the option of staying for that extra hour for tutoring and for after school enrichment clubs. We are very, very committed to working with the community . . . We have a "no child left behind" advisory committee. We have a local school council. So all of these individuals participate in the decision-making process of the school. So as a principal it's not about what I do unilaterally. It's a group thing. It's consensus among all of the stakeholders.

Finally, three of the Chicago principals mentioned the goal of *developing children's character*.[12] This is especially noteworthy in Chicago, where leaders like Arne Duncan have for years forcefully implemented a reform agenda based on testing data and AYP reports. In contrast to this push, some principals in our sample argued that in order to help students improve academically, they first need to develop socioemotional habits and skills. Ms. Shelby was an enthusiastic advocate for expanding the narrow academic curriculum.

> We're constantly questioning ourselves and our scholars in terms of what learning opportunities provide the [best] chance to think critically and creatively. And one sees that in our integration of the arts. We have music, visual arts, dance, oratory. One sees that in the . . . biweekly public speaking and performance opportunities at the school. We have . . . a schoolwide assembly of performance and presentation. And, of course, [you see that] throughout the curriculum and instruction but also in some of our norms such as goal setting. We have goal setting conferences where schol-

ars are identifying their own goals. And that puts the emphasis on the learner leading the learning versus the traditional model of parents and teachers being in charge of that.

Overall, the goals and priorities of schools were somewhat similar, although we observed some differences between "regular" public and charter public schools. Having such different goals and priorities meant that schools offered different environments for teachers in terms of what they were expected to align with, commit to, and enact in class.

Developing People

In carrying out their responsibilities to develop people, especially the new teachers in their charge, school principals used a range of strategies. But there was considerable variation in the scope and quality of induction and mentoring provided to teachers. Some principals were careful and systematic about orienting new teachers to the school; others provided a haphazard introduction because they were overburdened with more immediate challenges or because they did not know how to design an effective induction program. In these schools, new teachers learned the ropes on their own.

Ms. Fluhr, a CPS principal, took an informal, almost intuitive approach to orienting new teachers.

> Whenever a new teacher [is hired], we have staff meetings any time that I feel we need to have them. We bring the new teacher probably into a leadership meeting . . . It's never been a problem here . . . The teachers really just kind of go up to a new teacher, and, even without having the assigned mentor, they just kind of go up, "I'm so and so. I'm the teacher. If you need anything." It's nice. The teachers kind of take care of each other.

In contrast, Ms. Shelby introduced new teachers to her school through a carefully planned orientation: when a new teacher is hired, a staff member welcomes her aboard and "starts talking, starts planning, starts thinking, starts sharing." The school also invested in "explicit team-building activities" devoted just to beginning teachers to help them develop a sense of belonging to the school.

So we'll do team building and learning. The new teachers will learn about each other as learners and their own experiences in school and what their hopes and dreams are for the school year. Then they'll learn about the philosophy, certainly about efficacy, our philosophy on instruction. They'll learn about the history of the school . . . about all of the different stakeholders and our very diverse community . . . It's beyond faculty and staff. It's families. It's community groups. It's funders. It's everyone.

Ms. Shelby ended the weeklong orientation by letting the new teachers know that "it's safe to ask. There's no shame in not knowing, but it's not okay to stay in that place of not knowing . . . So that to me is a very important invitation and authorization in joining the community." After making it clear that the new teachers were expected to ask questions, she invited the new teachers to join in the "schoolwide team building and cluster building" with all of the faculty and staff.

Two main elements affected the quality of new teacher orientation: the timing of hiring (before or after the school year began) and the amount of time and attention devoted to the orientation. Five of the seven urban public schools offered relatively short orientation programs. These schools often hired teachers late in the summer and sometimes after the beginning of the year.[13] Only two schools, both charters, offered a weeklong orientation, made possible because the school worked hard to hire early, where new teachers discussed school regulations, culture, and expectations with experienced peers and administrators.

Another key factor in shaping the experience of new teachers was the appropriateness of their assignment. Were assignments based on new teachers' training? Did they reflect their status as novices or were they based on seniority? When asked how they decided on classroom assignments for new teachers, the principals provided a wide range of responses. In some cases, they just shrugged their shoulders, saying that they assigned new teachers to whichever classroom needed a new teacher. Others said that they put a lot of thought into trying to select and assign teachers in ways that resulted in the best possible fit for the school and class.

In four of the seven schools, classroom assignment was based on *need*— that is, schools did not make any adjustments or shifts in classroom assignments but simply recruited a teacher who would be a good fit with the available classroom. This strategy made sense in small schools that had only one grade for each age cohort (although that still represented a challenge for many beginning teachers). We also heard the need argument from principals in larger schools that could have offered smaller and/or less challenging classes to beginning teachers. Ms. DeFazio, an assistant principal from one of the bigger middle schools in Chicago, was among those in a position to offer less challenging classes to new teachers. She explained how she assigned a new teacher to a class:

> [It] depends on their certification and where we have the need . . . For example, if we need a seventh grade person with a language arts and a science endorsement, we only interview people who have [such] middle school endorsements in language arts and science, and then we tell them, "This is what we have, do you want it?"

In three schools, the difficulty of the class and its fit with the candidate's skills were the prominent factors in the process of classroom assignment. This kind of professional commitment and understanding usually required consensus among veteran teachers who were willing to forgo their traditional seniority rights in favor of providing a nurturing professional environment for beginning teachers. In one of these schools, the principal told us about a different solution that her teachers proposed.

> We really don't have what you might call a "hard" class because generally when we divide our children we try to make sure that every class is balanced. That's something that [the teachers] did as a result of looking at the data . . . If they need to do some separation then that's okay because I trust their judgment . . . They know that those kids have to move. And, by the way, they came to me with that—"We need to do this"—so I trust it even more. [If] every classroom has a good balance, you're going to have some kids in there who are challenging, but you [also] have some kids in there who are not.

The most common approach to supporting new teachers was mentoring, typically offered during the first and sometimes second years of teaching.

While all the urban public principals in our sample claimed that mentoring was available to beginning teachers in their schools, the actual practice and implementation varied across schools. In order to highlight these variations, we asked principals to explain not only if they offered mentoring opportunities to beginning teachers but what kind of mentoring and how it worked (e.g., how often mentors met with their mentee, what they discussed, how mentors were chosen, whether mentors were compensated, whether they observed each other's classes, whether formal time was set aside to meet).[14] Knowing about the character and quality of this mentoring experience was important to the Choosing to Teach Study, since research shows that some mentoring forms and structures yield better results than others in improving teachers' practice, satisfaction, and retention.[15]

Of the seven urban school principals, two took a relatively unstructured and informal approach to mentoring. As Mr. Parker, a magnet school principal, explained:

> There's a mentoring program that you have to sign up for with [CPS] . . . We [also] have some teachers who are willing to help the younger teachers, to show them the ropes and stuff . . . [They meet] just maybe once a week, and then I always encourage them to ask—they can always come to me. My door is always open. If you have some issues or you need some questions answered, just come in and see me . . . If it's a primary teacher, then you're talking about kindergarten, first or second or maybe third grade, so you would assign someone to look out for them and help them out, show them what the schedule is like, the policies and stuff like that. I do give them a handbook, but it's better to have someone to actually talk to.

Principals from small schools, in particular, scrambled to offer appropriate mentoring and were forced to compromise and assign teachers who were not experienced and/or skilled enough to mentor novices. In addition, mentoring in these schools was often underfunded or not funded at all.

Only three schools built mentoring into the school's fabric and offered mentoring programs that were carefully designed, in which mentors and mentees had regularly assigned times to meet during school hours, and, in some cases, for which mentors received additional compensation. Administrators in these schools had high expectations for mentoring and were often able to match mentors and mentees according to grade, subject matter, and/or personality. Mrs. Shire described a thoughtful, comprehensive approach to mentoring based on her understanding of what the district offered beginning teachers and what other types of mentoring they needed.

> The second piece [of teacher education in addition to the UTEP and district coaching] is [to] assign a person to grade-level partner to be a mentor for them. If the grade-level partner is new, then my [assistant principal] and I will work more closely with that teacher . . . They also get their grade-level partner if that person is not new, at least has more than two years. And then the third piece is that we try to pay a little bit more attention to them. The principal and the assistant principal are also reading coaches, too, and so we'll . . . visit them much more to try to give them as much support as possible . . . But you kind of have to make it so that they can [succeed], because it's tough. No matter how good you are, it's still tough.

Redesigning the Organization

In examining the last leadership function, redesigning the organization, the study focused on the ways in which principals took responsibility for developing and fostering collaborative professional communities and for engaging staff, parents, and students in building a stronger sense of school community. We looked specifically at how principals perceived and promoted teacher collaboration and facilitated a shared approach to teaching as a means of gaining insight into the schools' organizational and professional cultures.

Classroom teaching is lonely work. Most teachers have few regular opportunities to observe and work with colleagues. More and more, however, researchers and school leaders recognize the power of productive collaboration to improve teaching and retain teachers.[16] Teacher collaboration varied in form and scope in the diverse urban public schools we sampled. In some schools it was nonexistent; in others there were small pockets of collaboration initiated by two or more teachers; in still other schools, critical colleagueship was the norm.

In five of the schools the administrations actively supported teacher collaboration and allocated free and paid time for teachers to meet and work on curriculum together. Still, not every one of these schools was able to make professional collaboration an integral part of the school's culture. In fact, in only one school, Ms. Shelby's charter school, did a notable professional community exist because the principal gave explicit attention to building a strong sense of togetherness among the faculty and enabling strong professional collaboration.

> Our retention is very high and I think that goes back to the fact that teachers of scholars have a strong voice, have participated very actively and passionately in developing curriculum in their . . . study groups and identifying areas for growth and change in terms of policy or structures in the school. My bias is one of collaboration always. So, when we opened the school seven years ago there were somewhere between twelve and fourteen adults and 100 children. And every morning we would stand in the lobby of the school at 7:50 and the adults . . . would hold hands, and I would give an affirmation or a thought for the day and everyone would go around, sort of like a morning meeting . . . and share thoughts and reflections. And then we'd start the school day. And often times . . . we'd all end up in my office, which has a big conference table, and sit and talk, cry, or be frustrated, whatever the experience was. And two days of the week, Wednesday and Friday afternoons, it was mandated that we all met together and reflected, et cetera.

Ms. Shelby articulated the hard work, emotional bonding, and trust required to build effective collaboration across the school and illustrated how collaboration needs to be nurtured as a dynamic feature of the school's culture. As she explained,

> One of the most challenging things to maintain . . . is to find ways to build structures so that we have authentic vibrant learning community of adults even at this size ["sixty-some adults"]. So how are teachers expected to live the mission? It starts, I mean, in every single way, building trust with families and with scholars, learning each parent, learning each scholar, learning colleagues. Once again, in the spirit of thinking as

one of our mission points, we do so much thinking and debate and there's so many disagreements at times it can be overwhelming. But it's not a top-down sort of school where I say, "Here's what we're doing" . . . And certainly I've continued to learn there are times when I just need to make an executive decision . . . But our school grows out of conversation and collaboration . . . There's a real sense of community.

The other charter school in our sample illustrated the opposite end of the collaboration continuum. No doubt, the principal, Mr. Nelson, faced a daunting task. He received a building, some funding, and limited time to rebuild a school from scratch. He sought to motivate teacher collaboration by having classrooms co-taught by two teachers, but, as he explained, that did not work well.

There were two teachers per classroom of twenty-five kids. In my mind, I want[ed] an experienced teacher and a rookie, which is where these teacher programs [e.g., UTEP] came in. That backfired [*laughs*] in a lot of ways. Turf wars. The kid who came from a teacher prep program who probably had state-of-the-art techniques, been taught to teach in a certain way, and then you had somebody who had been in the classroom for twenty years. "That kid can't tell me anything" . . . But my gut told me to go with the experienced teacher as the lead. And we had four out of the six [classrooms] that worked and two [where] it crashed and burned miserably.

Mr. Nelson learned that for teaching teams to function in productive ways, "a whole lot of relationship building" had to take place before the teachers entered their classrooms and started teaching together.

Another aspect of school culture that affects teachers' practice and their sense of community was the extent to which they shared an approach to teaching. Three of the seven principals interviewed believed that their teachers held and enacted the same approach to teaching. When we asked Ms. Fluhr whether teachers at her school held a similar approach to teaching, she responded:

Oh yeah, absolutely, because the teachers are constantly asking their coaches, "Well, I'm not comfortable" or "I don't understand this. Can you come in and model for me? Can you come in and do some team teaching with me? Can you come in and do some co-teaching with me?" We videotape and have teachers look at their lessons, not as a gotcha but as an instructional tool. Teacher and coach sit down and talk about the lesson . . . When we do a postconference with a teacher, we're looking at the rubric. But because we do the inter-rater reliability rarely does one person go into the classroom to observe the teacher. It's usually at least two people so that we can come back and have that conversation and make sure that we are only looking at the evidence of the lesson and not what we feel and what we thought, only the evidence . . . We never say, "So let's see how you scored." We always say, "Well, let's talk about your lesson. We're here . . . to help you make your practice more effective."

Three other principals believed that most, but not all, of the teachers in their schools held a similar view of teaching as their own. Only Mr. Nelson, head of the newly established charter school, admitted that a shared approach to teaching

was lacking because of the different places people were coming from . . . We had two African American ladies whose children were the best-behaved children in the building, but I wouldn't say they were nurtured or loved [laughs]. [And then we had] these kids [UTEP teachers] who tended to be . . . very idealistic, very earnest and sincere about what they were doing and yet getting frustrated . . . [One of the UTEP teachers] had issues with listening to co-teachers . . . and being able to see it from someone else's perspective.

The range of school environments illustrates how sensitive, divisive, and challenging teacher collaboration can be for principals and teachers and what it takes to build and maintain an effective collaborative culture.

Leadership in Catholic Schools

Our interviews with Catholic schools leaders suggest that most schools operated in a volatile environment with significant financial challenges. These schools were relatively small in size, and their principals reported dwindling enrollments and expressed concerns about the future. In general, the study found that Catholic principals emphasized somewhat similar goals for their schools, though there was larger variation across Catholic schools in how they developed teachers and shaped school culture.

Setting Directions

Unlike the urban public school principals who were primarily concerned with academics and in some cases with social justice and character education, all Catholic principals emphasized religious Catholic education, tying it to the mission of welcoming and serving minority students and underserved populations.[17] Often the aim of offering a solid academic program was revealed later in the interview, but in some instances it was connected to the main goal of Catholic education. Mr. McKee, a high school principal, expressed a comprehensive commitment to all four aims: providing Catholic education, addressing the needs of diverse student populations, promoting social justice, and offering a rigorous academic program.

> [The] school . . . serves a very diverse population in every sense of the word, very racially diverse, socially, economically diverse, and geographically diverse. It's a place that welcomes all students of all backgrounds and focuses on giving students a quality Catholic education that is centered in, obviously, the teachings of the Catholic Church, that celebrates diversity, and I think that really provides a safe and nurturing environment as well so that students can reach their full academic potential. Whereas, if they didn't have the opportunity to come here, I don't think that they necessarily would be afforded the same opportunities and find the same success.

Ms. Holbrook, principal of an all-girls high school, described a similar set of aims. She spoke with considerable passion of tying together Catholic education and a commitment to social justice through an academic program structured to meet the special needs of underserved minority girls.

> It's all about changing the world through education, justice, and peace and a mission of the Catholic Church. So a teacher that would be coming into that school needed to really understand the needs of those young

women . . . [and that their teaching should not be] disconnected from the understanding that this is all part of the human experience. To me education is a part of the understanding of human experience, how does it shape you as an individual, then to go forward and make a difference in the world for the better. Education is not just about a degree or a job or a career. To me, education is about shaping a person to be the best that they can be and use the gifts and talents that God's given them to really make a difference for the better in the world.

Another principal, Ms. Labara, emphasized the primacy of religious education to meet the needs of ethnically diverse student populations. She noted that "the mission of the school was to provide a Catholic education that was welcoming of all cultures. [It had] a large Hispanic and Filipino population, as well as African Americans and some whites. So [the] goal [was] to provide a Catholic education for all, welcoming everybody," not just one group. Finally, Ms. Belanda argued that her school offered a Catholic education, academic and spiritual, in collaboration with the students' parents: "Basically, the mission of the school for . . . almost 100 years . . . [has been to] serve the parish and the families here in East Los Angeles. And so, we partner . . . with the parents to provide a Catholic education for the children. Not just academically but also the spiritual part of their journey through Catholicism."

In short, the Catholic school principals interviewed for the study expressed largely the same goals for their schools and shared similar perceptions about education and schooling. Yet, there were some minor variations in the principals' statements, suggesting that they might prioritize differently the order in which they hoped to achieve certain goals.

Developing People

Urban Catholic principals implemented a range of strategies to promote induction and professional development of beginning teachers in their schools. By and large, they provided limited induction, including a modest orientation to the school. Only one principal in our sample seems to have thought carefully and systematically about how to design an effective induction process that addressed the concerns of new teachers and gave them necessary information to help integrate more easily in the school. The other schools had a modest orientation or relied on an informal, unsystematic process. As a result, new teachers often learned the ropes on their own.

This certainly does not mean that the other Catholic schools did not welcome new teachers. Take the case of Ms. Flanders, a principal of a small Catholic school, who described the warm welcome she offers to all new teachers.

> The first thing we would do is I would bring them for a faculty meeting to introduce them to all the teachers, and then we would have a formal introduction and a welcome, and probably before we did that we would've had coffee and donuts or something to welcome her. And I always had gifts on her table. I'd have an apple, I'd have some little goodie that I always had as a welcome, and a sign that said, "Welcome to St. Lukas School" But there would always be a personal touch there for her. I would give her a mug with her name. Everybody had a mug with their name and that was filled with candy or something. And then the children would say, "Welcome," and I would say [to the children], "When you meet Miss so-and-so or Mr. so-and-so at recess today, please give them a special welcome," and the kids would do that. They'd go up there and say, "Thank you" and "Welcome," and they would introduce themselves. "My name is so-and-so." Even the little ones. "Hi, my name is Mark. I'm in first grade. Welcome." So we had them trained that way.

While this "orientation" was well planned and consistent, it did not include any professional content, such as a review of the curriculum, school policies and procedures, or a discussion about the makeup of the community or persistent challenges.

In only one school did the principal and his staff provide a carefully organized, professionally executed orientation. The principal, Mr. McKee, explained:

> There's often . . . a really good sharing of information and lessons from one teacher to another . . . In terms of the noncurricular pieces, the classroom management, expectations, those things are discussed at our pre–school faculty meetings. We meet for a week in August before the school

year starts, and we talk about a lot of those things that we expect. Some being things going back to teacher programs [regarding] classroom management. We talk about expectations of when you would send a student out of a room and the consequences of that . . . the expectation that it is their responsibility to manage the behavior and the learning environment . . . [how to] communicate . . . [with] the parents . . . So I think those expectations are pretty clearly communicated to the teachers, and a lot of it is ongoing discussions . . . of different techniques that they may utilize and talking that over with a more veteran teacher or with one of the deans or myself about different approaches . . . We [also] have them on a separate day go over more in depth a lot of the school policies and procedures and basic things, like how to use the copy machine, and to ask some of those questions that they may not be comfortable asking in front of the entire staff.

In terms of teacher assignments, some principals hired beginners and tried to adjust their classroom assignments based on the teacher's needs; others hired a teacher for a particular classroom assignment. In two of the schools a teacher's fit with the classroom was a prominent consideration. Ms. Labara told us that she moved teachers around to find the class that would best fit them.

Possibly something that would be easier for them. If, for whatever reason, maybe being in the higher grade isn't helpful, then bring them down. [If] the teacher has the potential . . . because they already have that dedication and that love for teaching, it's just kind of putting them in the right spot . . . [For example, if] in this grade they're going to be even better because the kids are going to be more tame—comparing a junior high student with an attitude versus a little first grader that only wants love— well, then let's put that teacher there and see how that works . . . There might be the time you want to give them another year, see how they do, but at the same time always providing them with the support they might need. When you observe them you see what their strengths are, you see what their weaknesses are. If a weakness could be something like classroom management, maybe during that year you can provide them with either more help with that, some professional development with that, something that would be able to help them.

At least three of the principals told us they made teaching assignments based on need. Ms. Belanda explained, "It's usually whatever's available. If a teacher leaves, then that grade level is available." Ms. Flanders gave teachers who were already in the school priority in applying for new openings. For the most part, principals who thought hard about how to match teachers with classes appropriate to their skills were also likely to be sensitive and responsive to the professional development needs of their teachers.

All the Catholic principals in our sample reported that mentoring was available to beginning teachers in their schools. Yet, the type of mentoring varied across schools. The Los Angeles archdiocese did not offer its own mentorship program, but ACE had regional supervisors who visited teachers several times a year to offer support. ACE also required the schools that hired its teachers to assign a staff member to mentor them. This requirement set a high professional bar for some schools. Ms. Sweeland, an elementary school principal, admitted that mentoring at her school was highly informal. She found ACE's systematic and standardized approach "helpful."

> There was an idea [in our school] of a mentor, but it wasn't as formalized . . . The ACE program had a terrifically formalized mentoring process that provided evaluation tools, provided for a schedule . . . of turning in . . . things that they were supposed to be doing toward the meeting. So it was a lot more structured. And it was helpful. In our own school's background . . . [it was,] "Come to me any time you have any questions." And maybe they'd meet over coffee, or if the teachers really sort it out and if it clicked in terms of personalities, they could become the best of friends and it worked great. But it was much more informal in the tradition of the school.

There was only one school where mentoring was carefully designed and professionally conducted and integrated into the school's culture. Mr. McKee gave careful consideration to matching teachers and offering them shared office space, which contributed to effective mentoring.

All new teachers have a mentor teacher, and usually we try to have that be someone within their discipline, and it's usually the person they—or it always has been—that they share their office space with. And I think, again, that's been really helpful in having a point person that you share a professional space with, too, that can ask a lot of those questions. And I would say those are some of the big ways that we introduce new teachers. Especially that mentor teacher, I think, is really the key person. And again, they would have a shared planning period with their mentor teacher that they share the office space with.

Redesigning the Organization

Catholic principals' perceptions of their schools' professional cultures and teacher collaboration parallel what we found about their approach to teacher assignments. Two principals, Ms. Holbrook and Mr. McKee, made systematic attempts to formalize teacher collaborations at their schools. They actively supported teacher collaboration by allocating free time, designing the space (in Mr. McKee's school), and creating organizational structures and policies that encouraged teachers to meet regularly to discuss student work and develop curriculum together. When asked about the opportunities his teachers had for working together, Mr. McKee noted,

That's an important piece for us. We approach that . . . with the layout of the building. We created teacher offices . . . that are separate from the classroom . . . and they share that office with somebody else in their discipline. So it's a place where there's often very organic collaboration going on with another teacher. We, as much as possible, try to allow those teachers to have a common planning period as well, so they have time where they can discuss lessons with each other. I think that's where a lot happens . . . We also have, because we are a small school, instead of being broken down traditionally into departments, we're broken down into three divisions, which we call Humanities, English and Arts, and Math and Science . . . Those groups meet regularly to discuss curriculum, lessons, anything else going on in the classroom . . . Over the past few years, too, we've also required teachers, at certain points of the year, to observe another teacher so they have been partnered up with teachers and have to go observe another teacher and . . . discuss what they see with each other.

In three other schools, the principals worked hard to create a sense of collaboration and collegiality among the teachers. They described their school as a family and their relationship with teachers as personal, informal, and caring. Ms. Labara's description of her school is a good example: "It felt like a family. It felt like a home . . . I think once ACE program got in, I think that's the feel they got. [I think] they liked the support they got . . . from the administration, and . . . from each other, and everybody felt very close to each other." In another school, which was on the brink of closure, the principal told me that she and the few remaining teachers are doing everything in the school, so they have no time to plan together. In order to cut costs, the principal herself teaches full time.

When asked if their school had a shared approach to teaching, each principal's response aligned with their perceptions of collaboration. The two schools with a thriving professional community also had a shared approach to teaching. The principals who relied on warm, familial relationships among the staff believed that teachers who "know what they are doing" should have the autonomy to teach as they see fit and were therefore less concerned about having a shared approach to teaching in the school.

In the Catholic schools, we observed a divide between principals who strove to organize their schools as a family and principals who chose to organize their schools as a professional community. Teacher may feel comfortable and emotionally supported in familial schools, but research clearly suggests that schools with strong professional communities are more likely to help teachers grow and become more effective.

Leadership in Jewish Day Schools

By and large, Jewish heads of schools emphasized relatively similar goals and reported having strong collaborative cultures and shared approaches to teaching. Nevertheless, they held different approaches and implemented different structures to induct, orient, and mentor their beginning teachers.

Setting Directions

The most salient aim that Jewish day school leaders mentioned was to provide rigorous academic training that could compete with the best schools in the area. Leaders were also quick to identify their school's commitment to offer a rich Jewish environment and opportunities for students to develop, strengthen, and deepen their Jewish identity. A third goal was to meet the special and diverse needs of particular students.

While all six Jewish day schools in our sample embraced these three goals, they emphasized different aspects. Ms. Allen, principal of a small day school, emphasized her school's commitment to meeting the needs of every student.

> We are very focused on differentiated instruction and on full inclusion . . . We expect the teachers to really, really get to know the children in a very in-depth way, because if you don't do that then you can't possibly do differentiated instruction. The first step is that you have to really know the kids. And I think that especially novice teachers often are focusing on content and curriculum and materials, and we have to try to help them . . . to shift some of their focus [to] kids.

Her school offered teachers practical tools to improve their teaching skills. All teachers were sent to responsive teaching workshops, and the school was a part of "the Hidden Sparks Project," where teachers learned "how to really look at . . . children's strengths and . . . challenges according to how the brain works."

Another principal, Mr. Sweitzer, felt that parents treated the school's academic rigor as a given and reported making an intentional decision to rebrand the school as a beacon of excellence, while placing the Jewish educational mission on the back burner.

> We actually just changed our mission statement to reflect . . . [a growing] emphasis on the academic excellence that we promise to deliver. It's not to say that we have in any way changed our mission Judaically, but I think the way we present it to the community deemphasizes the Jewish educational piece, and that has really more to do with the change in the community. Twenty years ago [the] first priority was . . . to [create] a Jewish

day school . . . [where kids can] be with Jewish kids . . . who also observe the same traditions . . . We felt that people focused . . . too much about the "Jewish day school" part, and so the mission really reflects our desire to be an excellent, excellent academic institution based in Judaism with an integrated curriculum and a pluralism in which all denominations and all beliefs and all family structures are accepted.

The Jewish day schools in the Boston area operated in a competitive environment struggling to recruit (and retain) middle- and upper-class students away from suburban public and private schools. In order to succeed, these schools emphasized a commitment to excellence and rigor, small class size, whole-child development, and Jewish traditions and values. These aims suggest that in order to achieve their mission, Jewish day schools sought to hire teachers who could differentiate instruction to help individual students grow, integrate Jewish values with subject matter knowledge, and communicate effectively with demanding parents.

Developing People

Like the urban and Catholic schools in the study, the Jewish day schools differed in the kind and quality of orientation they offered beginning teachers. Two of the six schools seemed better organized to provide an orientation, while the other four day schools relied on a more limited and informal process in which teachers were welcomed briefly but then were expected to find things out on their own. Ms. Vishniak described one of the limited orientation plans.[18]

Everyone gets invited to our annual meeting if they're hired, so that's at the end of June, and they sort of sense the culture. We have staff time at the beginning of the summer, and because there's been so much turnover . . . I thought the new teachers should be having their own orientation in a way, but not a formal one-on-one for new teachers.

Ms. Allen's school offered a somewhat more organized and formal orientation with some important elements.

There's a weeklong summer orientation for all the faculty that takes place a week before school starts. And then in the week before that we do . . .

one day of orientation for the new people . . . and then we . . . introduce them to everybody. We do on the first day a type of ice breaker, and the faculty are very friendly, so that's not a problem usually. So we try to let them know at the time that they're hired the grade that they're going to teach . . . and then in the beginning of the summer try to make sure that they have already been assigned a mentor to work with and that they've been given materials: their curriculum in writing and then materials that they can start preparing. In some cases they're also going to be sent for training in the summer.

In one of the two schools with a strong orientation, the most important issue was to start the hiring process early so that new teachers had an opportunity to get involved in the life of the school as an observer. In addition, the school required new teachers to meet over the summer with other teachers in the same grade and with their mentor and supervisor. Ms. Feldman noted,

We're very aggressive in our hiring. We try to identify the positions that we know will be open for the following year in December. We start listing them in January. We try to have everything wrapped up by [April]. Usually we're done before that, so we start early and then invite the people that we hire to come back and be with that grade level . . . for a couple of days or however much time they can spend without having to be in charge so they can sort of get the flow. We invite them for special events for that grade level . . . so they can see the event before they have to run the event. We also invite them for all of our faculty meetings (if they can come). Then there's an over-the-summer mentoring process.

When asked whether and how they might accommodate the needs of new teachers when assigning classes, all the day school principals, with the exception of one, were willing to adjust the difficulty of classroom assignments for new teachers. Ms. Feldman articulated the most new-teacher-friendly policy, noting,

The way we do things is we make sure that a new teacher always has an assistant teacher . . . that's unusual [in] Jewish day schools at least . . . And the harder one, which is we don't . . . place students that we think might provide an out-of-the-box challenge in that class or a parent who we think would provide an out-of-the-box challenge. We only do it for the first year because it puts a lot of weight on the other teachers at that grade level, because it means that they have everybody like that. So let's say that there are five kids like that or parents like that, we might put four in the other room and one in theirs, or something like that. On a few occasions, like with teachers who are new to teaching, we might put everybody in the other class.

While not every school can find the resources to assign assistant teachers, almost all the day school principals reported a willingness to rearrange classes so that beginning teachers got the least-challenging class during their first year on the job. Ms. Vishniak, the only dissenting voice among day school principals, did not believe that beginning teachers require special treatment:

I don't think I've done that nurturing. Not really. I try to be nicer to new teachers in the sense of, like, I can be a little bit [pushy in] delegation of extra responsibilities, [so] I have that in mind, you know, how many extra activities they have to work on for the school . . . But you can see some people can carry a lot even though they're beginning teachers. It depends on who they are. Depends on their personality.

All the day schools provided mentoring to beginning teachers, but, consistent with the other sectors, the quality varied across schools. Some day schools developed rigorous standards and expectations, tailoring an individualized mentoring program for all new teachers. Ms. Shuster, who built and supervised the mentoring program of her school before becoming a principal, noted, "So, any teacher coming to the school gets a mentor, whether you've taught for twenty years or whether you are a new teacher. And then we adjust what it is that you really need support in. And a lot . . . [is] about [the school] culture and what do we do [and] how do we do [it specifically here]."

Ms. Feldman approached mentoring in a systematic manner. She had clear and high expectations about how often a mentor and mentee should meet, what areas and subjects should typically be covered in a weekly mentoring session, and what kind of crises and challenges mentors are expected to help new teachers resolve.

> Formally they meet every week, informally they meet a lot more. It's passing them in the hallway, and, I mean, we're not so big a school that you don't see them all the time. And I would say probably the most important meetings are the crisis, running up to your mentor in tears, and [saying,] "Oh my God, this parent just said something awful to me" or "Oh my God, this kid is failing and I don't know what to do." And that's where [mentors are] critical.

Ms. Jacoby, a veteran principal, provided a sober account about the principal's role as a buffer between parents' demands and pressures and beginning teachers who needed time to make mistakes and grow with the guidance of an experienced mentor.

> I don't expect [teachers] to be perfect because they don't have experience yet, right? So I'm willing to match them with a . . . mentor when they come here . . . we'll do whatever we need to do over the summer. Not enough, there's never enough, and the first year is so hard. And the other thing is that I'm willing to fight . . . for a teacher, willing to fight for a new teacher, too. Because so many times parents say, "This teacher is terrible" the first year, but [I] know the teacher is gonna be great. And the next year they are saying, "This is the greatest teacher," because that second year is when it all comes together. And the more support we can give them the first year, the better off they will be.

Redesigning the Organization

We found that teacher collaboration in the Jewish day schools was pervasive, taking place not only between co-teachers or mentors/mentees but also among many teachers across the school. Ms. Vishniak's school illustrated schoolwide collaboration among teachers, a practice that she fervently supported.

> It's a very small school, so people here have to be team players. I've met people who I think are very capable but I didn't think their personality . . . would fit in. You know, because you can't really have outliers; it's really

tough in a small system . . . My teachers want someone who pulls their weight, who's equally dedicated to excellence. And they know it about each other, you know, if you see someone's who's slacking, the other ones don't like it because they're really working hard.

Ms. Vishniak's school not only offered many opportunities for teachers to work together, but collaboration was seemingly the norm.

[Teachers] have a lot of opportunities to [collaborate]. Often they are in the rooms at the same time, so they are watching each other, so they have built relationships over time . . . Two years ago one of my teachers initiated lead teacher meetings. So every Monday they . . . have their own meeting where they can talk about best practice, can talk about a problem, talk about things they're concerned about, their report cards . . . So it is sort of their place where they get to vet some of the challenges and then they come to me in a respectful way. So they have initiated it, and I've given them carte blanche to do it even though it's a little bit nerve racking, you know. They could be talking about anything. They could be unionizing for all I know . . . But they need [to] feel they're supported, and they support each other . . . So we aspire for people to work together in every possible way, and that's why I say I look for that element of team. There's only a certain amount of outlying behavior I can tolerate.

In one of the day schools, teacher collaboration was less prominent. The principal, Ms. Allen, told us that the school was slowly trying to adopt a more collaborative approach to teaching, but the transition was taking time.

In the elementary school, teachers don't have enough opportunities to work together. We don't do team teaching, but we needed to really think about it . . . I think a lot [about this] since we've been in DeLeT and the [Mandel Center]. One of the biggest problems with the profession of teaching is that it's isolating. The teacher's alone in the classroom. So some teachers like it because they think they could do whatever they want, but a lot of teachers really want input and want to collaborate.

The study's findings suggest relatively little variation in the level and quality of support available to beginning teachers after the initial orientation, which did vary greatly. Most day school principals were skilled in using the small school environment to build trust, establish professional standards and expectations, and create opportunities for teacher collaboration.

The Significance of Sector Affiliation for School Principals

The Choosing to Teach Study found that sector affiliation was a significant factor in shaping the direction of schools. In all the urban public schools, preparing children academically was a primary goal. The somewhat narrow emphasis on academics was understandable given the persistent pressure coming from No Child Left Behind, Race to the Top, and district-related policies regarding AYP requirements. Yet, even in this harsh environment, some principals, particularly those in charter schools, tried to promote other goals related to social justice and character education. While the focus on academics was very strong in Jewish day schools, principals also sought to emphasize Jewish values, traditions, and texts and to focus on the whole child as well as the Jewish community. Some of these goals may have reflected a response to market demands and fierce competition from private and suburban public schools. The Catholic schools' principals were also committed to providing a strong academic preparation, which was often tied to ideas of social justice and cultural diversity.

We found greater variation in the kinds of goals principals set for their schools between sectors than within sectors. This suggests the presence of some significant structural forces pushing schools within a given sector to adopt similar, though not identical, goals and shaping demands for a particular type of teacher who can best meet the goals and challenges of schools in the sector.

This study also found substantial variation in the quality and scope of support available to new teachers, particularly among the urban public and Catholic schools. In each of these sectors we identified schools with visionary principals (or heads of school) who provided impressive support systems (orientation, induction, mentoring) for all teachers and helped establish a schoolwide professional culture of collaboration. We also met principals with more limited, traditional perceptions of what new teachers should be able to do and what principals could do to help them. Some of these principals tried to offer new teachers a warm and caring environment; others had a hands-off policy, expecting beginning teachers to do a good job from day one. In contrast, we found that principals in Jewish day schools, despite variation in school size, financial stability, and religious affiliation, tended to create conditions and opportunities to help new teachers develop and improve their practice and become active members of the school's professional community.

Sector affiliation was less powerful in shaping principals' perceptions and actions regarding new teacher induction and school culture. The variation in how principals developed teachers and reorganized schools was substantial, particularly in the urban public and Catholic sectors. We observed similar variation across Jewish day schools when we looked at orientation, induction, and mentoring; but when we mapped issues related to collaborative culture and a shared approach to teaching, we saw a convergence among Jewish day schools with almost all the schools offering opportunities for teacher collaboration. This means that schools in each sector varied significantly in the conditions they offered teachers.

CHAPTER 8

Teacher Retention and Career Commitment

Staying, Moving, or Leaving

ERAN TAMIR

This chapter situates the thirty teachers in the Choosing to Teach Study within the larger trends shaping their respective school environments. Here the spotlight is on the interaction between teachers' personal convictions and pedagogical preparation within the working environments that teachers encountered in their schools.

There is a broad consensus that teacher quality is the most important school factor affecting student learning outcomes. Research has shown that it takes time to become an effective teacher. And while not all those who leave early on would develop into great teachers, evidence suggests that when beginning teachers leave teaching early on and before mastering their skills and are constantly being replaced by new cohorts of beginning teachers, the level of teacher quality is not likely to improve.[1] Specifically, teacher attrition among beginning teachers has harmful effects on districts, schools, and students. Short-term employment of teachers forces districts and schools to invest scarce resources on recruitment and induction of new teachers instead of focusing on the long-term development of existing teachers.[2] Moreover, research suggests that high attrition undermines teachers' sense of trust, belonging, and collaboration, which are cornerstones of a strong professional culture.[3] Finally teacher turnover has direct and harmful effects on student achievement because it involves more experienced teachers leaving the classroom and being replaced by novice teachers who need time to become effective.[4]

The scope of teacher attrition is considerable. Estimates in 2001 put the annual rate among public and private school teachers at 13–17 percent.[5] According to more recent data, about 15.5 percent of teachers moved from one school to another or left teaching entirely, and about 21 percent moved or left their private schools.[6] Longitudinal studies of beginning teachers from 2000–2001 data suggest that 33 percent of all new teachers leave within the first three years, and up to 50 percent leave within five years.[7] Current data suggest that attrition among beginning teachers has not changed and may be inching up. A 2013 report by the National Center for Education Statistics found that roughly 45 percent of those who started a teaching career left the profession or moved from their original school within their first four years.[8]

These averages do not reveal the full scope of the problem as it affects different school sectors. Teachers in urban public and Catholic schools and in Jewish day schools are more likely to leave or move from their schools than are teachers in suburban public schools located in wealthy enclaves.[9] The problem is particularly severe in urban schools with high percentages of low-income, minority students. In such schools, the annual rate of teacher attrition is considerably higher than the national average and hovers around 20 percent.[10]

Teachers move or leave urban public schools for many reasons, including lack of administrative support, lack of adequate funding, inadequate planning time, poor discipline, and large class sizes.[11] Federal legislation (NCLB and Race to the Top) and state policies aimed at increasingly scrutinizing teachers' work were a relatively new factor cited by teachers who left teaching in search of a less punitive working environment.[12]

The results are very troubling. The Philadelphia public school district in a period of six years lost 70.1 percent of those who began their teaching careers in the city's schools. This does not include an additional 13.6 percent of the teachers who moved from their initial placement to another school in the district.[13]

Urban Catholic schools, the largest segment of private schools serving low-income and minority families, face some of the same challenges as urban public schools but often in more extreme versions. For example, Catholic urban schools face an uphill battle for funding because of low tuition, community donations, and, in some cases, diocese support. With the loss of a ready supply of teachers from the ranks of nuns, brothers, and priests, Catholic schools now struggle to recruit lay teachers.[14] Convincing these teachers to stay is an even greater challenge, given the general lack of resources and the higher salaries and benefits available in neighboring public schools (urban and suburban). According to Stephen Provasnik and Scott Dorfman, more than one-fifth of Catholic teachers leave the profession every year.[15]

Unlike most urban public and Catholic schools, Jewish day schools cater to middle- and upper-class families. Compared to their public school colleagues, teachers in these schools often teach smaller classes and are not subject to intense testing and narrow curriculum requirements. Yet, day school administrators and teachers often mention communication with parents as very challenging, particularly for beginning teachers. In addition, and like the Catholic schools, most day schools cannot match the salary and benefits available to teachers at public schools. As a result, recruiting and retaining high-quality teachers are ongoing challenges for many Jewish day schools.[16]

Choosing to Teach Teachers' Careers

When we interviewed teachers during their first year of teaching (second for ACE) and asked where they saw themselves in five years, they uniformly expressed high motivation to serve as teachers or leaders in their particular schools and communities. Eighty percent said they were confident they would teach for more than five years, which contrasts sharply with national teaching force data showing roughly a 50 percent retention rate among beginning teachers.[17] This level of commitment to teaching is even more notable when we consider the fact that two-thirds of the teachers (from UTEP and ACE) were teaching in schools serving low-income minorities in urban settings, and all were teaching in hard-to-staff schools, including schools where salaries and benefits were substantially lower than in suburban public schools.

When we asked the same teachers two years later (during their third year in teaching for DeLeT and UTEP and fourth year for ACE) whether they intended to stay in teaching for at least five years, we received an almost unanimous response: 83 percent said they were likely to stay in the classroom beyond their fifth year.

In that second interview we also tried to determine whether the teachers had stayed in their original schools, moved to new schools, or left teaching altogether. We found that most teachers had either stayed in their first school (14) or moved to another school (13); only 3 had left the profession altogether. Looking more closely at teachers from each program, we found that 8 DeLeT teachers stayed at their schools, 1 moved to a different school, and 1 left teaching. Six UTEP teachers stayed at their schools, while 4 moved to new schools. None of the ACE teachers in our sample stayed; 8 moved to new schools, and 2 left teaching.

We also looked at whether teachers showed a strong commitment to teach in the school context for which they were prepared. We learned that all UTEP teachers were teaching in urban public schools: 7 in regular urban public schools, 2 in charter schools, and 1 in a different type of urban school.[18] Situated on Chicago's South Side, these schools served African American or Latino students from low-income families. Some of the schools

FIGURE 8.1 Teacher retention across programs, 2006 vs. 2008

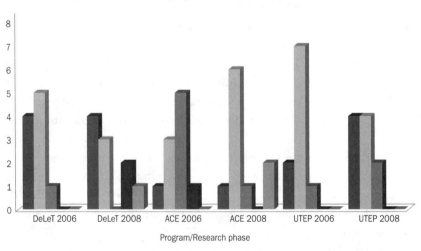

TABLE 8.1   Summary of teachers characteristics (N = 30)

	UTEP	ACE	DeLeT	Total
Career				
Stayer	6*	0	8	14
Mover	4	8	1	13
Leaver	0	2	1	3
Current school (sector and type)				
Urban public	7	–	–	7
Urban charter	2	–	–	2
Other	1	–	–	1
Catholic (low income)	–	5	–	5
Catholic (upper income)	–	3	–	5
Jewish day school	–	–	10	10

* Teacher stated intention to leave teaching by the end of the academic year.

were well established with strong leadership and ties to philanthropists and the community; others were impoverished and were on the brink of closure.

All ten ACE teachers started to teach in Catholic schools serving primarily low-income Latino families. After four years of teaching in urban Catholic schools, only 5 teachers remained in similar schools; 2 decided to leave teaching, and the other 3 decided to pursue teaching positions in Catholic schools serving middle- and upper-class families.

The 10 DeLeT teachers taught in Jewish day schools serving mostly middle- and upper-class families of religiously liberal Jews. The schools varied in size, quality of leadership, and financial stability. Most taught in community schools; 2 got jobs in schools affiliated with the Conservative movement, and 1 worked in an Orthodox school. Only 1 of these teachers left the profession.

Staying, Moving, or Leaving Teaching

This chapter advances the hypothesis that teachers' personal commitments, preparation, and school conditions shape their learning and practice and, ultimately, affect whether they choose to stay, move to other schools, or leave teaching altogether.[19]

Stayers

Only teachers from DeLeT and UTEP programs stayed at their original schools. The fact that both programs not only offered an elaborated vision of practice but also provided specific pedagogical preparation and mentoring for teaching in specific kinds of schools catering to particular families and students may help account for this. ACE, however, with its vision of service and fast-track preparation, provided less pedagogical training, including fewer site-specific strategies and approaches to inform teachers' practices. All programs actively pursued larger social/religious causes that largely defined their missions. It can be argued that UTEP's and DeLeT's combination of a clear vision of teaching along with specific pedagogical training facilitated stronger attachments and commitments and the ability to teach in their respective school sectors.

Another set of factors that helps explain teacher retention has to do with the school environment itself, including the support available to teachers. Those who stayed in their schools reported receiving substantial support from school administrators and colleagues in formal and informal mentoring and induction. Stayers also praised their schools for respecting the needs of beginning teachers and for creating structures that enabled strong collaboration and peer learning.

For example, when we asked David, a DeLeT graduate, about his decision to stay in the school that hired him after graduation, he mentioned specific school conditions:

> One important consideration is, Do I see myself growing as a teacher in this environment? Do I have mentors here, formal and informal mentors? Are there role models here for me and people who I feel I'm still learning a lot from. And the answer is yes, absolutely. And, of course, there's a little wallet check . . . my timing seems to have been good because we've increased teacher salaries the last two years in a row . . . And then . . . there's just the gut check of like, Am I happy? Am I doing something from day to day that feels good and feels satisfying? Yes . . . the first year had its challenges and the second year was much easier, but there were still

things that I was hoping would change . . . Each of those times the administration has been very responsive to thinking about considering those changes and listening to those challenges and taking that into consideration for the future, so I've been happy.

David stayed in teaching because working in his school felt satisfying to him and because his professional concerns and needs were taken seriously and were properly addressed by his colleagues and the school administration.

Linda, another DeLeT teacher, offered a similar account of her experience in a different school. Besides having mentors and principals to help her grow professionally, she commended her school's culture for encouraging teachers to use their creativity and explore ways to strengthen their practice.

> I feel like the school has been a place where I've been able to do everything that I wanted to try . . . I've also felt like there have been different people in different years that have been huge supports, like work with a particular special educator one year, work with a particular principal for a few years. That was extremely supportive. This year the school is supporting me in a curriculum development about values in collaboration with the DeLeT program, so I feel like it's just a very supportive place, although it's very far away [from where I live], but that's a downfall. But that's why I stayed as opposed to looking at another Boston-area school.

Besides praising her school and peers, Linda credited DeLeT for supporting her continuing professional development. These two responses from DeLeT teachers reflected a pervasive agreement among DeLeT teachers who stayed in teaching that their Jewish day schools were playing a positive role in helping them grow professionally.

UTEP teachers who decided to stay taught in different schools and had mixed experiences in terms of school support. Some mentioned supportive relationships with colleagues and/or administrators along with opportunities for professional development. On balance, however, their experiences were not as positive as those of the DeLeT teachers. Some UTEP teachers chose to stay in what they described as "completely dysfunctional schools," while others stayed on in new, exciting schools, which they helped to establish but where experience, mentoring, and professional development of veteran teachers was scarce.

Sylvia, a teacher in a charter school, found it easy to stay in her school. The school's mission was closely aligned with her own early commitments to social justice as reinforced by UTEP: "My school actually aligns really well with the mission [of] UTEP . . . It's a social justice school. They want to close the achievement gap between minorities and white children. It has a lot of resources to do so." She conveyed a deep sense of ownership and pride in her school. She described herself as part of a select group that helped shape the school from the start and expressed strong feelings of attachment toward her principal and peers. "I feel good. I don't know how to encapsulate the emotion, but I just feel secure. I feel . . . [at] home or something. I couldn't imagine really teaching anywhere else, just because of the relationships I've built with the principal and the teachers and how smart everybody is, and I think it's a great decision for me." Thus, although she recognized the downsides of teaching at her school, in particular the long hours and reduced paycheck, as compared to CPS teachers, she had no second thoughts.

Not all UTEP teachers who stayed at their original schools felt as supported as Sylvia did. Yet, their choice to stay was often fueled by the same desire that brought them to teaching in the first place: to see their students grow and succeed. In the absence of appropriate institutional infrastructure and a willingness to support new teachers, some UTEP teachers took it on themselves to find alternative learning opportunities to facilitate their professional growth. Take the example of Lara, who debated the pros and cons of staying at her school:

> I felt like they [the administrators] were incompetent . . . They really didn't understand what classroom community, what school community, should look like. So I was really sort of [wondering] if I'm going to stay. I know students need teachers like me . . . but I think I might need a more supportive environment where the administration knows what they're doing . . . However, toward the end of the year, I felt [a sense of continuity]. I had student taught at this school . . . [and] now I'm actually receiving about seven or eight students from that classroom [where I did my internship]. . . . So I was excited about seeing where they went after I

left them . . . and where I can take them again in the year that's coming. Another thing that influenced my decision was that I feel like I'm still establishing myself as a teacher. And even though I feel like I have grown over the past couple of years, I feel like I need one more year, at least, if not another one more year, to sort of work out different content areas and . . . improve myself and know that . . . if I went to another school, regardless of the administration or what type of demographic it was, that I would be able to teach there and teach well.

Despite an unsupportive administration, Lara found comfort and professional support in collaborating with another UTEP teacher at her school. Together they found ways to advance their students' learning, using the skills and knowledge acquired in their teacher education program.

Other major thing that influenced my decision to stay . . . was the other teacher from UTEP . . . Even just yesterday we got together to start planning a reading workshop. And we both kind of looked at each other when we were finished, and we said like, "Wow, that feels so much better." It's so much easier, in a way, because we both have the same vision. We both know where we want to take our kids . . . Whereas last year . . . I didn't have someone to sort of bounce those ideas off of.

Lara's account is powerful, but she is an outlier, an exception that proves the rule. She persevered despite teaching in an unsupportive school and decided to stay in a place that most teachers would probably leave. Her case underscores the power of serious collaboration among like-minded teachers, suggesting a promising policy avenue: teacher networks created by teacher preparation programs for their graduates or induction initiatives that support collaboration among beginning, midcareer, and veteran teachers.

Overall, administrative support and professional culture were important factors in shaping UTEP teachers' future careers. When beginning teachers felt supported by their administration and colleagues, they stayed. Yet, a few UTEP teachers chose to stay in their schools despite working under extreme conditions and with a complete lack of support. These teachers were highly motivated to make a difference in the lives of students and, as did Lara, managed to stay afloat by forming their own support system with like-minded colleagues who shared their commitments, passion for teaching, and orientation to practice. These UTEP teachers were in their third year of teaching at the time of the Choosing to Teach Study; it remains to be seen how long these highly motivated teachers will remain in unsupportive school environments.

Movers

Moving from school to school was a common practice, particularly among ACE teachers after they finished their first two years of teaching. This pattern of moving from urban schools with low-income, minority students to suburban schools that paid higher salaries and offered better working conditions is consistent with research on urban public school teachers.[20] Movers and leavers are often dissatisfied with their school culture and with the lack of support from their administration. These factors also influenced ACE and UTEP teachers who moved or considered moving from their schools. For ACE teachers, moving also likely meant that, having completed their two years of service, they could decide where they wanted to teach.

One fact, however, is beyond debate: two years after we first interviewed ACE teachers in their initial school placements, most had decided to move and teach in a different Catholic school. Some wanted to work in a Catholic community more culturally familiar to them. This parallels the move of many white, middle-class teachers from urban to suburban schools where they encounter greater cultural congruence between their own and the students' backgrounds. An alternative explanation is that ACE preparation did not adequately prepare culturally responsive teachers.[21]

John was one ACE teacher who returned to the familiar, in his case teaching in his hometown in the urban Catholic school his parents attended. He was enthusiastic about moving back to a familiar environment:

> It has been wonderful. It's so easy [to teach here] . . . I was greeted kind of like a homecoming. When people found out that I was coming . . . they were really excited . . . It has made it a great joy to be able to put together lessons for these kids 'cause I feel like . . . they are kind of my people . . . they are my kids. So I'm pretty happy about that.

Yet, reading between the lines, John's decision to return to his hometown may also relate to the cultural/racial challenges he experienced in his first school, where the low-income, Latino students were different from the peers he grew up with.

Tami told a somewhat different story. Her first urban Catholic school presented many challenges, and she, too, experienced a lack of administrative support. She chose to move to a new school but stayed in a similar neighborhood in the same city. In her second school she still felt overwhelmed by the intense demands of teaching in a poverty-stricken neighborhood, particularly dealing with a population of African American students and their families. However, when asked how her current school differs from her first school, Tami noted, "Well, St. George is 100 percent Afro-American . . . And I guess parental involvement is a lot less than St. Luke's Parish, but we have a wonderful administrator here. That really makes the difference."

Her experience underscores the important role that a strong, supportive principal can play in helping new teachers' to overcome their initial cultural misconceptions and learn to deal more effectively with the challenges of teaching in a cultural environment different from the one familiar to the teacher. Interestingly, in both Tami's and John's cases, ACE teachers felt a lack of parental involvement in the school. This led John to move, while Tami chose to stay because her principal backed her up and offered tools to help address some of the challenges she faced.

The story of Mark, a third ACE teacher, further emphasizes the importance of the school administration in creating a supportive professional culture. Mark described a complete lack of administrative support and isolation in the urban Catholic school where he began teaching. This prompted his move to a school in the same city where he could collaborate with peers and form a culture of learning:

> It was just a sad story of inner-city school leadership. This happened at the end of my third year . . . I had a lot of constraints. [I was] stuck in the same place . . . [where I could] just literally lock [my] door because of the chaos outside of that one classroom . . . The thing is, in my opinion, the culture of learning extends beyond just one classroom and can be enhanced if the whole school is involved in it.

Beth, an ACE teacher who moved from an urban school serving low-income Latino students to an urban school serving white upper-class students, described her career decision:

> I moved to Raytown after I finished the ACE program, and I was not sure what I wanted to do . . . I did not know if I wanted to be in the classroom. I liked my time in Calexno, but it was very difficult . . . There is definitely a stronger focus here on professional development, on professionalism. I feel held accountable for student learning a lot more here . . . I felt there that I was more of a caretaker . . . so [the move] has been a huge difference in the leadership.

Moving to the new school allowed her to feel satisfied with her work—"here I feel like a professional"—since her school provided rigorous professional development and held high expectations both for staff and students. Beth's story parallels those of other ACE teachers who left schools serving minority low-income students to teach in schools with students from well-to-do families. This pattern illustrates the interaction of condensed preparation, poor school leadership, low teacher satisfaction, and the lure of improved professional opportunities.

In contrast, UTEP and DeLeT teachers had a considerably lower rate of movement. The few teachers who did leave their initial schools reported poor student conduct and/or a lack of support by their administrators. While these teachers continued to experience challenges in their second school, particularly tensions with veteran peers, they joined schools with administrators who were willing to back them, which made a big difference in teachers' motivation to continue teaching and to advance small-scale changes in their schools.

The case of Melissa, a DeLeT graduate who was let go by her first school because of budgetary constraints, illustrates this pattern. Melissa believed in integrating general studies and Jewish studies and opposed the rigid curricular separation in her school. Yet, she felt she could neither express nor act on this view. Her beacon of hope was the new head of school, who was trying to bring change by recruiting "progressive" women teachers. This soft wind of change encouraged Melissa to take a stand and lead small-scale changes, despite challenges from veteran colleagues.

I should mention that the staff has changed significantly. The first year that I was hired, there were only [a few] women . . . and then this past year women [more than doubled their number], and so every year they've been hiring more women, more progressive teachers . . . [who help change the way the school] think[s] students should be educated . . . So that's made a big difference in who my colleagues are and who I can ask to pull together. So the seventh grade teachers tend to be really open-minded, very progressive teachers, and so to come together and actually communicate and work together has been something that I've seen a lot of interest in . . . They just need leadership . . . So I kind of feel like I need to pick my battles, and the first place I want to start is uniting the secular studies teachers and hoping that we'll be able to have more of those connections.

This is also a story about a head of school who embraced distributive leadership and a teacher who used this opportunity to develop her leadership skills and to ground them further in her long-term commitment to day school teaching.

The story of Tran, a graduate of the UTEP program, shows how inflated expectations and a lack of a professional culture and administrative support can shape a teacher's career choices. As a first-year teacher, Tran taught in an all-black urban public school serving middle- and upper-class families as well as working-class families. Tran felt that the school's staff expected him to be a master teacher from day one, based on his UTEP preparation. The teachers constantly asked for his professional advice, and administrators expected him to succeed without offering any kind of support. These inflated expectations also meant that his teaching was closely scrutinized for errors or mistakes. At the end of the year Tran resigned and moved to a new school on Chicago's South Side. In comparing his previous school with his current school, he made the following observation:

[In my first school] every little thing I did . . . people would judge it and critique it. Here [in the new school], I get more space to just develop, and then I get more space to fail and it's acceptable. They don't expect me to be the best teacher here . . . At the other school, they expected me to be this super teacher in my first year because I was coming out of the University of Chicago and all that . . . I did not like it because it was my first year, so it's kind of setting you up for failure if they think you are an expert and then you are not performing like an expert . . . Here I am more supported.

Unfortunately, Tran's methods and approaches were not received well by veteran colleagues at his new school: "Other teachers are not doing [guided reading], so there is a sense of resentment when a new teacher comes in and does something different and not the same old traditional teaching that they are used to. So they kind of don't like that, because progressive education, it's a lot more work than traditional ways of teaching." Nevertheless, when asked if he can be the teacher he wants to be in his current school, and what makes that possible, Tran replied, "The principal supports what I do and allows me to do what I want to do and she is not pushing any specific curriculum or anything like that."

That almost all the participating ACE teachers moved from their initial school placements to a new school is particularly noteworthy in that it exposes critical tensions among the teachers' own strengths, weaknesses, motivations, and commitments and the preparation they received and, most prominently, the level of support they encountered in their schools.

Challenging school conditions also shaped the career decisions of UTEP and DeLeT teachers. Yet, DeLeT teachers experienced minimal culture shock when they entered Jewish day schools since they were teaching in schools that were similar to those they attended and working with children from families similar to their own. The few DeLeT teachers who did not attend day schools themselves had the opportunity to gradually learn about the school's organizational and cultural environment during their yearlong internship. And while UTEP teachers experienced similar challenge to those of ACE teachers in terms of fitting in with their schools, like DeLeT teachers, they enjoyed the advantage of a yearlong internship in several Chicago public schools before taking a job in the district. Teaching in the same district where they trained also allowed these graduates to stay connected to program alumni and faculty and to participate in professional development opportunities offered by UTEP.

Leavers

Despite the higher tendency of beginning teachers from selective colleges to leave teaching positions in hard-to-staff schools early on, very few teachers in our study left teaching altogether. Even more surprising is the fact that only two ACE teachers left teaching, even though the program recruits individuals for just two years of service.

Nancy, one of the two ACE teachers who left, went to law school, a career she wanted to pursue before enrolling in ACE. As she explained, "While I loved the experience and I loved doing it, teaching was really not what I was meant to be doing. So I decided to go to law school because I'm still really interested in education policy and want to use my love for education in a way that I can also use the law." While her decision to leave teaching may stem from a desire to become a lawyer, it may also partly relate to her teaching experiences. She felt that "the administration was very hands-off, for better or worse . . . [which] is difficult your first year, because you don't really feel like you know anything and you would like a little bit of guidance." She also described feeling lonely being away from her family, as did many of her program peers, and because of this she knew she "wouldn't stay there." Being a young, unsupported professional far away from family and friends may discourage many beginning teachers, even those who are well prepared to teach in their school and highly motivated to stay. An additional contributive factor for leaving in the case of ACE teachers is that many join the program in order to do two years of "service" before moving on to their "real" careers.

The two UTEP teachers who planned to leave teaching the following academic year were somewhat more apologetic about their decision. They felt badly about leaving their colleagues and students and failing to realize their program's expectations. They described a complex set of experiences that led to their decision. Joyce reported feeling supported by school leaders and by most of her colleagues, among them a UTEP alumna she helped to recruit; yet, she felt deceived after the administration went back on a promise not to increase the size of her class and added ten new students on top of the twenty students they already assigned her. When asked about the major factor that drove her out of teaching, she explained:

> Really, the main reason I'm leaving is because I kind of got tired of hearing kids tell each other they're gay all day and got tired of telling kids to sit down and be quiet and get back to work . . . Actually, the nine- and ten-year-olds have gotten in the way more of me teaching than the adminis-

tration has. The administration has said, "Go for it" and has given me as many resources as they can.

Joyce echoed the feelings of other beginning teachers who reported leaving teaching because of challenging student behaviors.[22] Yet, although Joyce is careful not to blame the administration, her story raises concerns about the passive role that the administration took, its lack of initiative in offering classroom management support, and its blunt decision to increase the class size of a struggling beginning teacher.

Ella, another UTEP teacher, decided to leave teaching for similar reasons. She, too, experienced difficulties with student behavior, but, unlike Joyce, she felt she was not being adequately supported by her administration. Ella mentioned the overemphasis on testing but credited the principal for letting her teach outside the prescribed curriculum. Looking back on her decision to enter teaching, she did not recall having a real passion to teach; rather, she convinced herself that teaching was the right path for her.

> To some extent I had a great deal of autonomy to plan units or lessons and that sort of thing. There's a significant emphasis on testing, but there's also a lot of creativity, and I guess I got on [the principal's] good side in the beginning, and so she's been pretty hands-off with me. Other people have had different experiences, but I've been able to do units on things like hunger and homelessness and the environment and a much more drawn-out African American history unit than other people I've spoken to have had the opportunity to do. But there are also significant challenges there, such as student behavior and lack of support from the administration regarding that.

These two cases reflect the complexity involved with making (and interpreting) a decision to leave teaching. Both Joyce and Ella described dissatisfaction with teaching and working in largely unwelcoming school environments. Based on their accounts, it's clear that they did not receive appropriate support consistent with their needs and could not find opportunities to grow professionally.

The story of Karen, a DeLeT teacher, shares some common themes with the other stories of teachers who decided to leave teaching. Throughout her preparation and internship, she felt ambivalent about teaching: "It wasn't like, 'Oh, my God, this has been my dream to be a teacher my whole life. And it's finally coming true.' It's sort of, I'm going to try this and I'm going to see." The first year of teaching was very difficult for Karen, who said she did not have enough preparation time at her school. As a result, she reported that teaching "consumed" her life, "to a degree that I didn't think was healthy." The fact that she and her co-teacher did not get along professionally exacerbated the situation. They had very different approaches to teaching, and the administration did not try to intervene or find ways to facilitate a more productive relationship. As a result, Karen felt increasingly dissatisfied with her job and the support she received and became disillusioned about pursuing a teaching career.

On the surface, the teachers who left teaching might seem less committed to teaching in hard-to-staff schools than those who stayed or moved. However, a close look at their experiences reveals a less clear-cut pattern. One way to interpret these stories is to read them as missed opportunities by administrators, mentors, and peers to form supportive professional cultures that acknowledge beginning teachers as learners by offering them formal and informal opportunities to interact with colleagues who are passionate about teaching and want to help them grow into effective teachers.

The Importance of Support and Community

Previous studies have pointed to school organizational variables, like administration support and professional culture, as paramount in understanding teacher retention and attrition. Findings from the Choosing to Teach Study partially corroborate this research. By and large, those teachers in our study who did not receive adequate support from administrators and peers, regardless of their school affiliation, were more likely to move or leave teaching early on.

Furthermore, even when other factors entered in, administrative support and professional community shaped teachers' career plans in profound ways. While the service mission of the ACE program may partly explain why many ACE teachers moved from their initial placements, a close look at what teachers said reveals that a school's working conditions and culture—

particularly the lack of collaboration with peers and the absence of a unified vision for the school, as well as weak administrative involvement and guidance (which could have helped some teachers overcome their cultural deficit perceptions)—were all essential components in determining teacher transition and attrition.

Finally, although the study's findings demonstrate the primary role of school conditions in the decision to stay, move, or leave and that teacher preparation takes a back seat in terms of its impact on teacher career choices, teacher preparation can affect teachers' preparedness to teach in culturally diverse environments and/or their ability to adapt to challenging demands in hard-to-staff schools. This suggests a more nuanced reality, one in which teacher motivations, preparation, and school conditions are tightly interwoven. For example, we demonstrated that the teachers came to their programs with strong social and religious commitments, and being prepared to teach in a specific school sector helped strengthen these initial commitments to their schools, students, the community, and to teaching, which, in turn, may have resulted in longer teaching service.[23] Yet, these new teachers craved the guiding hand of mentors and the support of administrators. When they found this, they thrived; when they did not, they tried building on their preparation or reaching out to peers from their programs. And when that did not work, they often decided to try teaching in a different school with more hospitable working conditions or, on rare occasions, to leave teaching.[24]

Inspiring Teaching

SHARON FEIMAN-NEMSER

This final chapter draws lessons from the longitudinal study of beginning teachers, the programs where they prepared to teach, and the schools where they worked and asks: What can we learn from three mission-driven, context-specific teacher education programs and from a sample of teachers who graduated from them? And how can the Choosing to Teach Study's concepts, theories, and empirical findings inform teacher education practice, policy and research?

Organized around the interactive theory that informed the study—namely, that teachers' learning, practice, and career trajectories result from the interaction of person, program, and school setting—the chapter first reviews important findings regarding the teachers, the programs, and the schools and then considers how these three elements interact to influence teachers' practices, retention, and career aspirations.

Contemporary policy debates about how to get teachers for our nation's schools tend to emphasize either recruitment and selection or professional preparation. This either-or approach, however, ignores a more complex and dynamic reality. Who goes into teaching matters, but so do the character and quality of their preparation and the working conditions in the schools.

Teachers

The thirty teachers who participated in the Choosing to Teach Study resemble the kinds of candidates many educators and policy makers are eager to recruit into the field. Demographically, they were mostly young, middle-class, white, and female (see chapter 4). And as college graduates, they met the entrance requirements for master's programs in teacher education at elite institutions of higher education—the University of Chicago, the University of Notre Dame, and Brandeis University. Thus, one important issue in their preparation concerns the similarities and differences in background between these new teachers and their students.

Both the UTEP and ACE teachers taught poor minority students, and the differences in race, ethnicity, and social class between themselves and their students posed critical challenges in teaching and learning to teach. While DeLeT teachers taught students whose religious, ethnic, and social class backgrounds resembled their own, they often encountered differences between their personal religious orientation and that of their students. ACE teachers also experienced such differences in religious beliefs and practices. Furthermore, teachers in all the programs worked with students with special learning needs.

Not surprisingly, most of the teachers identified with their program's mission. ACE and DeLeT teacher candidates expressed a strong desire to serve the Catholic or Jewish communities; UTEP candidates were committed to social justice. These commitments mirrored the candidates' upbringing as well as the selection criteria of the programs. Connecting teaching to a broader social cause helped fuel the teachers' decisions to teach in a particular school sector but was not sufficient to keep them there without adequate preparation.

Although it might be assumed that all thirty teachers were committed to becoming teachers before they embarked on their teacher education, that was not the case. Teachers' accounts of how they ended up in their respective programs revealed that some had always wanted to teach, others came with a more provisional, exploratory attitude, and a few got there by accident (see chapter 4). These different reasons for entering the teaching profession underscore the importance of learning about the teacher education programs and their impact.

Programs That Make a Difference

Program features that researchers have linked to effective teaching—or that are strong candidates for further study—include opportunities to learn the practice of teaching, the power of mission and vision, and identity formation as a central element of professional education. These aspects of teacher education programs are also linked to various program outcomes.

Teaching Context

The Choosing to Teach Study did not begin with the concept of context-specific teacher education. Rather, it started with a general understanding that the programs being studied prepared teachers for different school sectors. As the research team investigated what that meant and how it was enacted in each program, we began to see that the labels "urban," "Catholic," and "Jewish" lacked nuance. "Urban" was often used as a code for poor, deficient schools. And "Catholic" and "Jewish" presumed a commonality related to faith (as in "faith-based schools"), which does not work for liberal Jewish day schools, and a uniformity that does not reflect the diversity among Catholic and Jewish schools.

Placing three context-specific teacher education programs in dialogue with one another sharpened the team's understanding of what "teaching context" means in practice. Based on a model of context as a set of dynamic, nested layers, we saw both similarities and differences in the aspects of context that each of the three teacher education programs explicitly addressed and in the ways that each program taught its context (see figure C.1). By and large, the similarities related to the work of teaching and learning to teach, while the differences derived mainly from program mission and structure.

The University of Chicago's Urban Teacher Education Program gave explicit attention to five layers of context: federal/state policy, urban public

FIGURE C.1 Layers of contexts addressed by programs

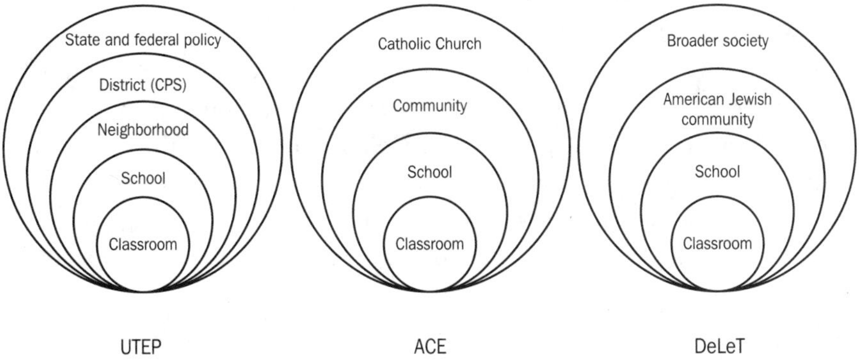

UTEP — State and federal policy / District (CPS) / Neighborhood / School / Classroom

ACE — Catholic Church / Community / School / Classroom

DeLeT — Broader society / American Jewish community / School / Classroom schools, neighborhoods/communities, the Chicago Public Schools, school and classroom. In year one, the program focused on the broad contexts of educational policy and politics, the characteristics and constraints of large urban schools, and the racial, economic, and cultural history and diversity of Chicago and its neighborhoods. Teacher candidates learned about these layers of context and what they implied for their professional identity as social justice teachers by reading works on urban schools, developing school portraits, participating in community walks, and reflecting on the forms of privilege and oppression that have shaped their personal experiences.

In the second year, the program honed in on local knowledge, such as district curricula and procedures. Placements at University of Chicago/ CPS charter partner schools enabled teacher candidates to see and practice the kind of teaching introduced in their courses. Since children are key to understanding the classroom and school context, UTEP students learned to see individual pupils in terms of their strengths and capacities and to appreciate the social and cultural forces that influence their development.

In chapter 1, Kavita Kapadia Matso and Karen Hammerness show how the program's approach to teaching the context of CPS dismantles stereotypic thinking and prepares teacher candidates to establish respectful relation-ships with students, families and communities. Moreover, grappling with different aspects of the Chicago context helped teacher candidates learn a particular stance toward social justice, come to know themselves, and learn to enact pedagogies with the specifics of students and their surroundings in mind. They conclude that the specific instructional practices UTEP taught (e.g., balanced literacy) were neither "urban" nor Chicago-specific. Rather, their enactment was context specific because it was informed by "local" knowledge.

The Alliance for Catholic Education attended to three layers of context: the classroom, the Catholic school context, and the community. Accord-ing to Christian Dallavis and Anthony Holter in chapter 2, the condensed nature of the program made it difficult to address multiple layers. As a result, the three layers that were addressed "compete[d] for programmatic attention," and some salient dimensions of context were "overlooked or underconsidered."

ACE had one seven-week summer session to prepare students to teach in Catholic schools in distant, unfamiliar locales. Most of the coursework focused on the pressing demands of classroom teaching. Students took courses in subject-specific pedagogy, classroom management, assessment, and child/adolescent development and learning. They also participated in a summer school practicum where they observed and practiced teaching with a mentor.

To learn the Catholic school context, ACE students participated in an Integrative Seminar, in which they discussed the philosophical founda-tions of Catholic education, the social justice teachings of the Church, and research on the effectiveness of Catholic schools. They also talked with peers about what it means to be a teacher in a Catholic school. A second course, Teaching in a Catholic School, explored "social and political issues, moral dilemmas, and church teachings that could inform situations they may face in the classroom."

Like UTEP teachers, ACE teachers taught in urban communities serving low-income minority students, and their pupils' backgrounds differed from their own. Unlike UTEP candidates, however, ACE teachers had more limited opportunities to learn the cultural, ethnic, and geographic contexts of their new community *before* they moved there or to work through any misconceptions about the communities, families, and students they were to serve *before* they encountered them.

Some pedagogy courses introduced the concepts of culturally responsive pedagogy and cultural competence. ACE teachers also met with future prin-cipals and housemates to learn about the cultures of the communities and schools where they were to live and teach. During the first retreat, they considered their own cultural identities in relation to the cultural contexts they would soon encounter. Mostly, however, ACE teachers learned about the ethnic, racial, geographic, and Catholic cultures of their new school and community through firsthand experience: teaching full time, living in the community, and doing community service. As a result, ACE students often "struggled to adapt to particular cultural and geographic contexts of their schools while also adapting to the Catholic school context."

The Day School Leadership Through Teaching Program had thirteen months to teach the contexts of Jewish day schools. The program concentrated on the classroom and school contexts with some limited attention paid to the broader civic and cultural milieus of the United States, Israel, and the Jewish people. It shared responsibility for teaching these contexts with its partner day schools.

Four of the five strands in the DeLeT curriculum—teaching fundamentals, subject-specific pedagogy, clinical studies, learners and learning—had direct bearing on the teacher's classroom responsibilities. The fifth strand, Jewish literacy and identity, related to the teacher's role as Jewish educator, which is enacted across all three layers of context. DeLeT students learned these contexts through formal study, guided practice, focused inquiry, and personal reflection.

The dual curriculum of the day school paralleled the dual curriculum of DeLeT with its courses on the learning and teaching of general studies (e.g., math, language arts, science) and Jewish studies (e.g., Bible, holidays, Israel). It encouraged teachers to integrate Jewish content into general studies and promoted the creation of classroom learning communities infused with Jewish values and experiences. The program drew parallels between the professional learning community in DeLeT, fostered through a week of intensive text study in pairs, and classroom learning communities and between an inquiry-oriented stance toward text study and an inquiry-oriented stance toward the study of learners and teaching.[1]

DeLeT relied on the yearlong internship to induct students into the distinctive culture of Jewish day schools, where parental expectations loom large and the diversity of learning needs and religious beliefs and practices surprise and challenge. Knowing the day school context meant understanding the interplay and sometimes tension among religious, communal, and academic expectations for both teachers and students. Mentor teachers and field instructors helped DeLeT interns interpret and navigate these realities. Encounters with religious and cultural diversity in the schools and in the program raised questions about Jewish practices and beliefs and the place of day schools in the Jewish community and in American society.

A comparison of how the three programs defined and taught the content of their respective contexts reveals some similarities and differences. The fact that all three programs attended to classroom context is not surprising, since that is the primary locus of teachers' work. But the programs differed in how deeply and specifically they contextualized classroom teaching.

UTEP deeply contextualized the main elements of classroom teaching—teacher, students, pedagogy, curriculum—in self-awareness, local culture and demographics, district curriculum and politics, state and federal policies, and the history of urban public schools. Within a two-year time frame, UTEP worked from the macro to the micro layers of context to foster an understanding of urban public schooling and to infuse such teaching with local knowledge.

DeLeT contextualized the elements of classroom teaching through a Jewish independent school lens. Pupils, ambitious pedagogy, the dual curriculum, day school culture, and community all became increasingly familiar to students through formal study, observation, participation, and guided practice. The Jewish journeys of DeLeT students were a context for understanding themselves and others. The fact that each day school was independent encouraged a focus on learning the local context.

ACE contextualized classroom teaching in terms of grade level and subject matter more than local geography, ethnicity, and culture, which were mainly learned in situ through teaching, living, and working in the community. Because ACE teachers were expected to be ethical role models, the program taught the religious context of Catholic education so that ACE teaches could addresses contemporary issues and problems through a Catholic lens. The program offered limited formal learning opportunities to develop cultural competence.

Learning the nested contexts of teaching helps teachers navigate local realities, form respectful relationships with families and colleagues, know students as individuals, and make curriculum relevant. One purpose of teaching context is to help new teachers make a smooth transition into schools as they are. An equally important purpose, one shared by the three teacher education programs in this study, is to prepare teachers who can contribute to school change. To realize that purpose, teachers need a vision of what could be along with an understanding of what is as well as the capacity and commitment to enact that vision in practice, what we call *teacher agency*.

Learning Practice in Practice

Well-planned, carefully guided field experiences are widely viewed as a sine qua non in good teacher education. They enable teacher candidates to observe and practice the kind of teaching envisioned by the program. In addition, learning to teach in a community of practice where teachers work together to improve their teaching and their students' learning sends an important message about professional responsibility and colleagueship. When clinical experiences are aligned with coursework and teacher candidates have opportunities to study and rehearse core practices before taking them to the classroom, they are more likely to make those practices part of their repertoire and enact them in their teaching.

In the three programs we studied, the nature and timing of clinical experiences varied. Teacher candidates in UTEP and DeLeT participated in a year of guided practice in carefully selected schools before they moved into full-time, independent teaching jobs. These extended internships or residencies were integrated with courses where teacher learning was situated in records of practice: classroom videotapes, curricula, student work, lesson plans. Teacher candidates gradually assumed classroom responsibilities in keeping with their growing confidence and competence. Both programs worked closely with mentor teachers, many of whom were program graduates, so that the teaching they modeled and nurtured reflected the vision of teaching endorsed by the program.

The condensed structure of ACE did not allow for such learning opportunities. Students became full-time teachers after an initial summer of preparation. While they did some student teaching in the first summer, the context was different and distant from the ones they taught in. Program faculty supported ACE teachers through periodic site visits and online courses, and the schools where ACE candidates taught were supposed to provide mentoring. But ACE teachers learned to teach by jumping directly into teaching, adapting generic skills of classroom management and instruction encountered in their methods courses to their unfamiliar teaching contexts.

DeLeT and UTEP preserved the distinction between preservice preparation and new teacher induction while also helping novices make a smooth transition into full-time teaching. Both programs supported graduates during their early years of teaching, although this did not always compensate for schools that neglected their responsibility for new teacher induction. The ACE program merged the two stages. ACE teachers received an abbreviated preparation and then did most of their learning on the job, where they were inducted into their schools by default or design, depending on administrative leadership.

The consequences of these differences play out in teachers' patterns of retention and in the nature of their practice. After completing their two years of service, many of the ACE teachers in our study sought teaching positions in schools more like the ones they attended, while UTEP and DeLeT teachers continued to teach in the schools for which they were prepared. These patterns suggest that teachers are more likely to stay, even in challenging settings, if they have opportunities to learn to teach in those contexts before they are responsible for teaching on their own. As Karen Hammerness writes in chapter 5, variation in "opportunities to learn *in practice* . . . correlate with graduates' plans to stay in teaching."

Mission and Vision

The three programs are animated by clear missions that link teaching to a broader social purpose and emphasize graduates' impact on society. For the ACE teachers this meant serving the Catholic community through education; for the DeLeT teachers this meant serving the Jewish community through day school teaching; for the UTEP students this meant promoting social justice through teaching. Prominent in faculty discussions of aims and purposes, these missions were visible in the programs' courses, assignments, and learning opportunities (see chapter 5). Identification with their program's mission motivated the new teachers to pursue teacher preparation, but it did not always sustain them in the face of teaching challenges.

Two of the programs, UTEP and DeLeT, shared a clear vision of good teaching as a professional practice that can be taught and learned over time. The programs clearly specified this vision and gave teacher candidates opportunities to learn to enact it in practice. As a result, UTEP and DeLeT candidates were able to describe in some detail their teaching practices and the impact those practices could have on students. As they incorporated these visions of good teaching into their developing identity as classroom teachers, they pictured themselves teaching for a long time. Moreover, when Eran Tamir and Karen Hammerness observed the classroom teaching of graduates from the two programs, we found them enacting the kinds of practices they had learned in their preparation (see chapter 6). Some studies of effective teacher education programs identify a vision of good teaching as an important program feature, but teacher candidates also need opportunities to learn to enact that vision in practice.[2] UTEP and DeLeT helped their students learn to do that.

Soul Searching

Soul searching figured prominently in the three teacher education programs. Each program presumed that teachers must know themselves before they can know their students. For UTEP and, to a lesser extent, ACE, this meant confronting issues of race and class; for DeLeT and ACE it meant confronting issues of religious belief and practice. Each program helped teachers develop ways of knowing, being, and acting in the world as they forged a professional identity rooted in religious, cultural, and/or social commitments.

Identity work in UTEP happened primarily in the soul strand, although the integrated nature of the program, with its attention to self, children, teaching, and social justice, helped novice teachers develop a stance toward social justice teaching informed by the Chicago context. Identity work in ACE happened mainly through the informal curriculum of retreats, where students reflected on and deepened their spiritual growth, shared the journey of becoming a Catholic school teacher, and developed a sense of being called to serve the poor. Identity work in DeLeT happened mainly in the Jewish literacy and identity strand, where students explored their personal stances on basic theological and ideological issues and considered the implications for their identity and practice as day school teachers.

In a recent comparative study of preparation for the professions sponsored by the Carnegie Foundation for the Advancement of Teaching, researchers urge professional educators to pay more attention to the "normative apprenticeship where novices learn to be the kind of person entitled to serve others":

Normative knowledge must again become an important part of the knowledge base of all professionals. And since this kind of knowledge is so closely linked to practical skills, on the one hand, and deeply formed ways of perceiving and relating, on the other, developing more effective professionals for our time requires reshaping professional preparation to incorporate these skills and outlook—what in seminaries is called *formation*.[3]

The three programs in the Choosing to Teach Study are compelling examples of what it means to take professional identity formation seriously in teacher education. At the same time, the programs differ in the extent to which they integrate the acquisition of knowledge and skills with the development of habits and values to shape a coherent professional identity and practice. UTEP and DeLeT helped the study's participating teachers put those pieces together directly; ACE encouraged such integration but depended on the individual teachers to do it for themselves.

School Matters

In studying context-specific teacher education, we wanted to know how programs prepare teachers to teach in particular kinds of schools. We also wanted to know how prepared schools were to receive these new teachers (see chapters 7 and 8). The early years of teaching are a formative phase in learning to teach, often determining whether people stay in teaching and what kind of teachers they become. Schools have a responsibility to continue the process of teacher development begun by teacher preparation. We followed our thirty teachers into teaching in order to study how their backgrounds, preparation, and school environments aligned and how that, in turn, affected their career decisions, practices, and agency.

Two general points frame this discussion. First, schools as organizations are embedded in larger social contexts—districts, dioceses, states—that influence what goes on there. Urban public, urban Catholic, and Jewish day schools face unique pressures related to their sectors, as well as resource constraints and staffing challenges.[4] Second, we found significant variation not only between school sectors but also within them. In each sector there were schools with strong and weak principals, serious and negligible mentoring, inspiring and instrumental goals, collaborative and individualistic professional cultures, and these variations affected how beginning teachers felt about themselves and their work and whether they chose to stay, move, or leave.

In describing their school's mission, the principals who hired the teachers in our study named various goals—promoting academic excellence, serving the community, meeting the needs of students, teaching (religious) values, advancing social justice. Yet, the goals meant different things in different schools and sectors. For example, "promoting social justice" meant preparing students for high school or changing the world. "Serving the community" meant building a cohesive religious community or providing extended services to the neighborhood. "Promoting academic excellence" meant raising test scores, seeing that students complete college, or helping students become knowledgeable critical thinkers.

Teachers valued the opportunity to teach in schools where they had a stake in the broader mission. One UTEP teacher put it this way: "My school actually aligns really well with the mission of UTEP. It's a social justice school . . . In some CPS schools, you may feel like you're the only teacher trying to, you know, teach for social justice." We heard similar statements from DeLeT and ACE teachers. Such alignment contributed to teachers' sense that their work was valued. But mission alignment was not the only factor determining whether a given school was a good fit. Equally important was the extent to which schools took the learning needs of beginning teachers seriously and provided the conditions and guidance to help them succeed.

We know a lot about the elements of strong induction that correlate with new teacher retention, effectiveness, and satisfaction.[5] New teachers want appropriate classroom assignments, regular opportunities to work with like-minded colleagues, a timely orientation to the school, and support from administrators. Under these conditions, new teachers are more likely to thrive.

Unfortunately, the schools in our study did not uniformly provide these supports. For example, all the principals we interviewed said they assigned mentors to new teachers. In some schools, mentoring was a serious professional role with regularly scheduled times for novices and mentors to meet. In other schools, mentoring took the form of an informal buddy system.

There were also wide differences in the way principals oriented new teachers to their school and in the professional cultures they fostered.

How did these differing school conditions influence new teachers' decisions to remain in their original school, move to a new school, or leave teaching? Drilling down on that question led to important insights about the interaction of person, program, and setting. In chapter 8, Eran Tamir discusses the waning influence of teacher preparation and the growing school effects on teachers' career plans. We saw this general pattern play out over time as the teachers in our study, like all teachers, sought school environments where they could be successful. Teachers who did not find such support from administrators and peers, regardless of their sector affiliation, were more likely to move or leave teaching early on.

Yet, some teachers stayed in their schools despite the unsupportive conditions. These exceptions suggest the power of vision-guided, context-specific, practice-centered teacher preparation in strengthening teachers' resolve and equipping them with a culturally responsive practice.

At the end of their first year of teaching, nine UTEP teachers, nine DeLeT teachers, and four ACE teachers said that they intended to teach for more than five years.[6] Two years later, the UTEP and DeLeT teachers were still committed to teaching at the same schools, and six ACE teachers also expressed a commitment to teach for more than five years but not necessarily in the kinds of schools for which they were prepared.[7] This finding is particularly striking, since two-thirds of the participants were teaching in urban schools serving poor minority students.

The fact that so many UTEP teachers stayed on, even in schools with challenging conditions, suggests that the program helped them develop the vision, knowledge, practical tools, and agency to sustain themselves as social justice teachers in a Chicago public school. In the case of DeLeT, the day schools and program were more closely synchronized. The program provided context-specific preparation, the schools offered acceptable conditions, and the teachers stayed. Both of these programs also had a strong presence in the local schools where some of their teachers were teaching. The kind of preparation UTEP and DeLeT offered and the programs' continuing involvement in new teacher development profoundly influenced their graduates' commitments, practices, and career decisions, in some cases even enabling new teachers to persist in challenging environments.

While ACE teachers remained committed to serving Catholic schools through teaching, some felt more comfortable doing so in more familiar settings. None of the ACE teachers stayed in their original schools. Five continued to teach in schools serving low-income minority students; three sought teaching positions in schools serving middle- and upper-class families; and two left teaching. Perhaps ACE teachers left their original placements because they finished their two years of required service as prescribed by the program. Perhaps they left because they could not be the kind of Catholic teachers they aspired to become in poorly led, underresourced, culturally different school settings. Perhaps they left because the condensed nature of their program did not allow time to develop the context-specific, culturally relevant understandings and skills they needed to be successful with their students.

These nuanced findings underscore the value of longitudinal, qualitative, comparative research to illuminate the dynamic interaction of teachers, teacher education programs, and school settings. Understanding this dynamic is key to figuring out how teacher education contributes to effective teaching and learning. Policy makers want to know which programs and pathways produce the most effective teachers as measured by standardized test scores. This desire rests on a narrow view of learning and teacher effectiveness. It also reflects the dubious assumption that the distance between teacher education and student learning is an uninterrupted straight line rather than a winding road that merges with working conditions in schools. We need research to light up this road by helping us understand what makes different programs attractive to different teacher candidates, how particular features of those programs influence specific learning outcomes for teachers and students, and how those outcomes are affected by various school contexts and school conditions.

Today, researchers question the usefulness of broad categories like "traditional" and "alternate" routes to differentiate teacher education programs. Similarly, from our study we learned that the labels "urban," "Catholic," and "Jewish" are not sufficiently nuanced to guide the design or study of context-specific teacher education, particularly when that context is culturally distant from teachers and presents significant challenges. Our research suggests that attending to the localness of school contexts in teacher education helps new teachers navigate the realities of school environments as they work to enact a vision of culturally responsive teaching.

Our research also highlights the motivating power of connecting teaching to a broad social mission and the essential requirement of ensuring that new teachers have the pedagogical repertoire they need to relate to diverse students and their families in respectful ways and to provide rigorous and relevant learning opportunities. Commitment and caring are important, but a sense of agency comes from knowing what to do.

Finally, our research reminds us that preparing teachers for schools that serve particular groups of students cannot happen without the thoughtful participation of school leaders and the purposeful design of clinical sites for learning to teach. Creating clinical settings where new teachers can see and practice context-sensitive teaching in the company of like-minded colleagues who care about the learning of all their students will go a long way toward improving both teaching and student learning. Without thoughtful participation on the part of schools in the orientation, support, and development of new teachers, we risk losing the gifts of bright, idealistic, socially committed teachers from teaching in areas of great need or from teaching completely.

Notes

Introduction

1. Marilyn Cochran-Smith and Kenneth Zeichner, eds., *Studying Teacher Education: The Report of the AERA Panel on Research and Teacher Education* (Mahwah, NJ: Lawrence Erlbaum, 2005); National Research Council, *How People Learn: Brain, Mind, Experience and School*, ed. J. Bransford, A. Brown, and R. Cocking (Washington, DC: National Academies Press, 2000); Suzanne Wilson, Robert Floden, and Joan Ferrini-Mundy, *Teacher Preparation Research: Current Knowledge, Gaps, and Recommendations* (Seattle: Center for the Study of Teaching Policy, 2001).

2. Donald I. Boyd et al., "Teacher Preparation and Student Achievement," *Educational Evaluation and Policy Analysis* 31, no. 4 (2009): 416–440.; Daniel C. Humphrey and Marjorie E. Wechsler, "Insights into Alternative Certification: Initial Findings from a National Study," *Teachers College Record* 109, no. 3 (2007): 483–530.

3. Pamela Grossman and Susanna Loeb, eds., *Alternative Routes to Teaching: Mapping the New Landscape of Teacher Education* (Cambridge, MA: Harvard Education Press, 2008), 204.

4. Wilson et al., *Teacher Preparation Research*; Robert Floden, "Teacher Value Added as a Measure of Program Quality: Interpret with Caution," *Journal of Teacher Education* 63, no. 5 (2012): 356–360; Edward Haertel, "Reliability and Validity of Inferences about Teachers Based on Student Test Scores" (14th William H. Angoff Memorial Lecture, National Press Club, Washington, DC, March 22, 2013), http://www.ets.org/Media/Research/pdf/PICANG14.pdf.

5. John Papay, "Different Tests, Different Answers: The Stability of Teacher Value-Added

6. Deborah L. Ball and Heather Hill, "Measuring Teacher Quality in Practice," in *Measurement Issues and Assessment for Teaching Quality*, ed. D. H. Gitomer (Thousand Oaks, CA: Sage, 2008), 80–98.

7. Sharon Feiman-Nemser and Margret Buchmann, "Describing Teacher Education: A Framework and Illustrative Findings from a Longitudinal Study of Six Students," *Elementary School Journal* 89, no. 3 (1989): 365–377; Grossman and Loeb, *Alternative Routes to Teaching,* 204; Daniel C. Humphrey and Marjorie E. Wechsler, "Insights into Alternative Certification: Initial Findings from a National Study," *Teachers College Record* 109, no. 3 (2007): 483–530.

8. Charles Foster, Lisa Dahill, Lawrence Goleman, and Barbara Tolentino, *Educating Clergy: Teaching Practices and Pastoral Imagination* (San Francisco: Jossey-Bass, 2006).

9. Kenneth R. Howey, Linda M. Post, and Nancy L. Zimpher, *Recruiting, Preparing, and*

Retaining Teachers for Urban Schools (Washington, DC: American Association of Colleges for Teacher Education, 2006); Linda Darling-Hammond, *Powerful Teacher Education Programs* (San Francisco: Jossey-Bass, 2006); Kenneth Zeichner and Hillary G. Conklin, "17 Teacher Education Programs as Sites for Teacher Preparation," in *Handbook of Research on Teacher Education*, 3rd ed., ed. Marilyn Cochran-Smith, Sharon Feiman-Nemser, and D. John McIntyre (New York: Routledge, 2008), 269–289; Daniel Humphrey, Marjorie Wechsler, and Heather Hough, "Characteristics of Effective Alternative Certification Programs," *Teachers College Record* 110, no. 1 (2008): 1–63.

10. Carol Rodgers, "'The Turning of One's Soul'—Learning to Teach for Social Justice: The Putney Graduate School of Teacher Education (1950–1964)," *Teachers College Record* 108, no. 7 (2008): 1266–1295; Jaime Grinberg, "'I Had Never Been Exposed to Teaching Like That': Progressive Teacher Education at Bank Street During the 1930's," *Teachers College Record* 104, no. 7 (2002): 1422–1460.

11. Laurence Boggess, "Tailoring New Urban Teachers for Character and Activism," *American Educational Research Journal* 47, no. 1 (2010): 65–95.

12. Robert Corwin, *Reform and Organizational Survival: The Teacher Corps as an Instrument of Educational Change* (New York: Wiley, 1973).

13. Karen Noordhoff and Judith Kleinfeld, "Preparing Teachers for Multicultural Classrooms," *Teaching and Teacher Education* 9, no. 1 (1993): 27–40; Kathryn Au, "Communities of Practice: Engagement, Imagination, and Alignment in Research on Teacher Education," *Journal of Teacher Education* 53, no. 3 (2002): 222–227; Brad Olsen and Lauren Anderson, "Courses of Action: A Qualitative Investigation in Urban Teacher Retention and Career Development," *Urban Education* 42 (2007): 5–29; Karen Hunter Quartz and TEP Research Group, "Too Angry to Leave: Supporting New Teachers' Commitment to Transform Urban Schools," *Journal of Teacher Education* 54, no. 2 (2003): 99–111; Karen Hunter Quartz et al., "Careers in Motion: A Longitudinal Retention Study of Role Changing among Early Career Urban Educators," *Teachers College Record* 110, no. 1 (2008): 218–250; Marilyn Cochran-Smith et al., "Good and Just Teaching: The Case for Social Justice in Teacher Education," *American Journal of Education* 115, no. 3 (2009): 347–377; Morva McDonald, "The Joint Enterprise of Social Justice in Teacher Education," *Teachers College Record* 109, no. 8 (2007): 2047–2081; Kimberley Alkins et al., "Project Quest: A Journey of Discovery with Beginning Teachers in Urban Schools," *Equity and Excellence in Education* 39, no. 1 (2006): 65–80.

14. The label "faith-based school" does not really work for non-Orthodox Jewish day schools where faith or belief is not a requirement for either students or teachers.

15. The term "context-specific teacher education" came to us as we analyzed the program data and began to think about what was distinctively urban about UTEP, distinctively

Catholic about the ACE program, and distinctively Jewish about DeLeT. Miriam Ben Peretz, a visiting scholar at the Mandel Center for Studies in Jewish Education at the time, proposed the label after learning about the study.

16. We transcribed and coded the interviews using Atlas.ti. Throughout the book we use pseudonyms for all teachers, principals, pupils, and schools.

17. Marvin Haberman, "Selecting and Preparing Culturally Competent Teachers for Urban Schools," in *Handbook of Research on Teacher Education,* 2nd ed., ed. J. Sikula, T. J. Buttery, and E. Guyton (New York: Macmillan, 1996), 747–760.

18. Urie Bronfenbrenner, "Nature-Nurture Reconceptionalized in Developmental Perspective: A Bioecological Model," *Psychological Review* 101, no. 4 (1994): 568–586; National Research Council, *How People Learn: Brain, Mind, Experience and School,* ed. J. Bransford, A. Brown, and R. Cocking (Washington, DC: National Academies Press, 2000); Jean Lave and Etienne Wenger, *Situated Learning: Legitimate Peripheral Participation* (Cambridge: Cambridge University Press, 1991); Joseph J. Schwab, "The Practical: Arts of the Eclectic," in *Science, Curriculum and Liberal Education,* ed. Ian Westbury and Neil J. Wilkof (Chicago: University of Chicago Press, 1978).

19. Au, "Communities of Practice," 80–114; Viv Ellis, Anne Edwards, and Peter Smagorinsky, eds., *Cultural-Historical Perspectives on Teacher Education and Development* (London: Routledge, 2010).

20. Linda Darling-Hammond et al., eds., *Preparing Teachers for a Changing World: What Teachers Should Learn and Be Able to Do* (San Francisco: Jossey-Bass, 2005); Karen Hammerness, *Seeing Through Teachers' Eyes: Professional Ideals and Classroom Practices* (New York: Teachers College Press, 2006); Darling-Hammond, *Powerful Teacher Education Programs;* Kavita Kapadia Matsko and Karen Hammerness, "Unpacking the 'Urban' in Urban Teacher Education: Making a Case for Context-Specific Preparation," *Journal of Teacher Education* 65, no. 2 (2013): 128–144, doi:10.1177/0022487113511645. http://jte.sagepub.com/cgi/content/long/65/2/128; Mary M. Kennedy, "Knowledge and Vision in Teaching," *Journal of Teacher Education* 57, no. 3 (2006): 205–211.

21. Parker Palmer, *The Courage to Teach: Exploring the Inner Landscape of a Teacher's Life* (San Francisco: Jossey Bass, 1998), 13.

22. Charles Foster, Lisa Dahill, Lawrence Golemon, and Barbara Wang, *Educating Clergy: Teaching Practices and the Pastoral Imagination* (San Francisco: Jossey Bass, 2006).

23. Lee Shulman, "Signature Pedagogies in the Professions," *Daedalus* 134, no. 3 (2005): 52–59.

24. Pam Grossman et al., "Redefining Teacher: Re-imagining Teacher Education," *Teachers and Teaching: Theory and Practice* 15, no. 2 (2009): 273–290; Herminia Ibarra, "Provisional Selves: Experimenting with Image and Identity in Professional Adaptation," *Administrative Science Quarterly* 44 (1999):764–791; Elliot G. Mishler, *Storylines: Craftartists' Narratives of Identity* (Cambridge, MA: Harvard University

Press, 1999); Dan C. Lortie, *School Teacher* (Chicago: University of Chicago Press, 1975); Pierre Bourdieu, *Outline of a Theory of Practice* (Cambridge: Cambridge University Press, 1977); Richard D. Ashmore, Kay Deaux, and Tracy McLaughlin-Volpe, "An Organizing Framework for Collective Identity: Articulation and Significance of Multidimensionality," *Psychological Bulletin* 130, no. 1 (2004): 80–114; Dorothy C. Holland, *Identity and Agency in Cultural Worlds* (Cambridge, MA: Harvard University Press, 2001).

25. Lortie, *School Teacher;* Michael A. Huberman, Marie-Madeleine Grounauer, and Jürg Marti, *The Lives of Teachers* (New York: Teachers College Press, 1993); Donald I. Boyd et al., "The Influence of School Administrators on Teacher Retention Decisions"; Richard M. Ingersoll, "Teacher Turnover andTeacher Shortages: An Organizational Analysis," *American Educational Research Journal* 38, no. 3 (2001): 499–534; Hunter Quartz and TEP Research Group, "Too Angry to Leave: Supporting New Teachers' Commitment to Transform Urban Schools," *Journal of Teacher Education* 54, no. 2 (2003): 99–111; Susan Moore Johnson and The Project on the Next Generation of Teachers, *Finders and Keepers: Helping New Teachers Survive and Thrive in Our Schools* (San Francisco: Jossey-Bass, 2006).

26. Richard M. Ingersoll, *Is There Really a Teacher Shortage?* (Seattle: Center for the Study of Teaching and Policy, University of Washington, 2003); Eran Tamir, "What Keeps Teachers in and What Drives Them out: Findings from a Longitudinal Comparative Case-Based Study of Beginning Teachers in Urban-Public, Urban-Catholic, and Jewish Day Schools," *Teachers College Record* 115, no. 6 (2013), http://www.tcrecord.org; Eran Tamir, "Choosing Teaching as a Career in Urban Public, Catholic and Jewish Schools by Graduates of Elite Colleges," *Journal of Educational Change.* Advance online publication (2013). doi: 10.1007/s10833-013-92229, http://link.springer.com/article/10.1007/s10833-013-9222-9.

27. Johnson et al., *Finders and Keepers.*

28. Darling-Hammond et al., *Preparing Teachers for a Changing World.*

29. Gerald G. Duffy, "Visioning and the Development of Outstanding Teachers," *Reading Research and Instruction* 41, no. 4 (2002): 331–344; Sharon Feiman-Nemser, "From Preparation to Practice: Designing a Continuum to Strengthen and Sustain Teaching," *Teachers College Record* 103, no. 6 (2001): 1013–1055; Hammerness, *Seeing Through Teachers' Eyes;* Kennedy, "Knowledge and Vision in Teaching," 205–211; Dot McElhone et al., "The Role of Vision in Trajectories of Literacy Practice Among New Teachers" (paper, American Educational Research Association, New York, April 2008).

30. Deborah Ball and David Cohen, "Developing Practice, Developing Practitioners: Toward a Practice-Based Theory of Professional Development," *Teaching as a Learning Profession* (San Francisco: Jossey Bass, 1999), 3–33; Pam Grossman, "A Framework

for Teaching Practice: A Brief History of an Idea." *Teachers College Record* 113, no. 12 (2012): 2836–2843; Ken Zeichner, "The Turn Once Again Toward Practice-Based Teacher Education," *Journal of Teacher Education* 63, no. 5 (2012): 376–382.

31. Boyd et al., "The Influence of School Administrators on Teacher Retention Decisions"; Tamir, "What Keeps Teachers in and What Drives Them out"; Richard Ingersoll and Jeffrey Kralik, "The Impact of Mentoring on Teacher Retention: What the Research Says," *ECS Research Review* (February 2004): 1–24; Susan M. Kardos and Susan Moore Johnson, "On Their Own and Presumed Expert: New Teachers' Experience with their Colleagues," *Teachers College Record* 109, no. 9 (2007): 2083–2106.

Chapter 1

1. Victoria Chou and Steven E. Tozer, "What's Urban Got to Do with It? Meanings of 'Urban' in Urban Teacher Preparation and Development," in *Partnering to Prepare Urban Teachers: A Call to Activism,* ed. Francine P. Petermann (New York: Peter Lang, 2008); Etta R. Hollins, *Learning to Teach in Urban Schools: The Transition from Preparation to Practice* (New York: Teachers College Press, 2012); Lois Weiner, "Evidence and Inquiry in Teacher Education: What's Needed for Urban Schools," *Journal of Teacher Education* 53, no. 3 (2002): 254–261.

2. Comparing the student populations of New York and Chicago illustrates how significantly urban districts can vary demographically. New York City's student enrollment consists of 14.35 percent white, 32.44 percent black, 13.56 percent Latino, and 39.19 percent Asian, while the enrollment of Chicago Public Schools has fewer white (8.84 percent) and Asian students (3.25 percent) and more black (49.82 percent) and Latino (38.52%) students. Erica Frankenberg, "The demographic context of urban schools," *Equity and Excellence in Education* 42, no. 3 (2009): 262; Chicago Public Schools: Stats and Facts, http://www.cps.edu/About_CPS/At-a-glance/Pages/Stats_and_facts.aspx.

3. Karen Hammerness and Kavita Kapadia Matsko, "When Context Has Content: A Case Study of New Teacher Induction in the University of Chicago's Urban Teacher Education Program," *Urban Education* 48 (July 2013): 557–584.

4. Richard M. Ingersoll, "Teacher Turnover and Teacher Shortages: An Organizational Analysis," *American Educational Research Journal* 38, no. 3 (2001): 499–534.

5. Jonathan Kozol, *The Shame of the Nation* (New York: Crown, 2005); Charles M. Payne, *So Much Reform, So Little Change: The Persistence of Failure in Urban Schools* (Cambridge, MA: Harvard Education Press, 2008).

6. Bill Rankin, "Chicago Boundaries: A Taxonomy of Transitions," http://www.radical cartography.net/index.html?chicagodots.

7. St. Clair Drake and Horace R. Cayton, *Black Metropolis: A Study of Negro Life in a Northern City* (Chicago: University of Chicago Press, 1993).

8. William Julius Wilson, *When Work Disappears: The World of the New Urban Poor* (New York: Random House, 1996).

9. Chou and Tozer, "What's Urban Got to Do with It?" 1.

10. Demographics of the four University of Chicago Charter School campuses reflect those of nearby CPS schools in terms of racial makeup (99 percent African American) and SES (85 percent receiving free or reduced-price lunch). Students are admitted to the charter school through an open lottery process.

11. Lois C. Moll, Cathy Amanti, Deborah Neff, and Norma Gonzalez, "Funds of Knowledge for Teaching: Using a Qualitative Approach to Combine Homes and Classrooms," *Theory into Practice* 31, no. 1 (1992): 132–141.

12. The phrase "context has content" emerged from a study of preparation for the clergy that is one of the studies of professions conducted by the Carnegie Foundation for the Advancement of Teaching. Charles Foster, Lisa Dahill, Larry Goleman, and Barbara Wang Talantino, *Educating Clergy: Teaching Practices and Pastoral Imagination* (San Francisco: Jossey-Bass, 2006).

Chapter 2

1. Dale McDonald and Margaret M. Schultz, *United States Catholic Elementary and Secondary Schools: The Annual Statistical Report on Schools, Enrollment, and Staffing* (Washington, DC: National Catholic Education Association, 2013).

2. White House Domestic Policy Council, *Preserving a Critical National Asset: America's Disadvantaged Students and the Crisis in Faith-Based Urban Schools* (Washington, DC: U.S. Department of Education, 2008).

3. Lauren Budzichowski et al., *The Spirit of ACE: Celebrating 15 Years* (Notre Dame, IN: Alliance for Catholic Education Press, 2008); Christian M. Dallavis, "Career Paths of Alternative Teacher Education Graduates," in *Beyond Alternative Teacher Education: Integrating Teaching, Community, Spirituality, and Leadership*, ed. John L. Watzke (Notre Dame, IN: Alliance for Catholic Education Press, 2007), 33–52.

4. Sonia Nieto and Patricia Bode, *Affirming Diversity: The Sociopolitical Context of Multicultural Education* (Boston: Pearson Allyn & Bacon, 2007), 171.

5. Victoria S. Haviland, "Things Get Glossed Over: Rearticulating the Silencing Power of Whiteness in Education," *Journal of Teacher Education* 59, no. 1 (2008): 40–54.

6. Geneva Gay, *Culturally Responsive Teaching: Theory, Research, and Practice* (New York: Teachers College Press, 2000); Jacqueline J. Irvine, *Educating Teachers for Diversity: Seeing with a Cultural Eye* (New York: Teachers College Press, 2003); Gloria Ladson-Billings, *The Dreamkeepers: Successful Teachers of African American Children* (San Francisco: Jossey-Bass, 1994); Gloria Ladson-Billings, *Crossing Over to Canaan: The Journey of New Teachers in Diverse Classrooms* (San Francisco: Jossey-Bass, 2001); Nieto and Bode, *Affirming Diversity*; Ana M. Villegas and Tamara Lucas, *Educating*

Culturally Responsive Teachers: A Coherent Approach (Albany: State University of New York Press, 2002).

7. Gay, *Culturally Responsive Teaching,* 29.

8. Christian M. Dallavis, "Extending Theories of Culturally Responsive Pedagogy: An Ethnographic Examination of Catholic Schooling in an Immigrant Community in Chicago" (PhD diss., University of Michigan, 2008), 36.

9. Gay, *Culturally Responsive Teaching,* 44.

10. Jill Constantine et al., *An Evaluation of Teachers Trained Through Different Routes to Certification* (Washington, DC: U.S. Department of Education, 2009), 27.

11. Anthony S. Bryk, Valerie E. Lee, and Peter B. Holland, *Catholic Schools and the Common Good* (Cambridge, MA: Harvard University Press, 1993); William H. Jeynes, "Religion, Intact Families, and the Achievement Gap," *Interdisciplinary Journal of Research on Religion* 3 (2007): 1–24; Vivian Louie and Jennifer Holdaway, "Catholic Schools and Immigrant Students: A New Generation," *Teachers College Record* 111, no. 3 (2009): 783–816; Derek Neal, "The Effects of Catholic Secondary Schooling on Educational Achievement," *Journal of Labor Economics* 15, no. 1 (1997): 98–123.

12. Geneva Gay, "Educational Quality for Students of Color," in *Multicultural Education: Issues and Perspectives,* 3rd ed., ed. James A. Banks and Cherry A. McGee Banks (Toronto: Allyn & Bacon, 1999), 223.

13. The indicators and rubric used for evaluating performance are available online at http://ace.nd.edu/downloads/academic-supervision.

14. Louis A. DelFra and Timothy R. Scully, "Come and You Will See: Spirituality in ACE," in *Teaching Service and Alternative Teacher Education: Notre Dame's Alliance for Catholic Education,* ed. G. Michael Pressley (Notre Dame, IN: University of Notre Dame Press, 2002), 184–214.

15. *To Teach as Jesus Did: A Pastoral Message on Catholic Education* (Washington, DC: U.S. Conference of Catholic Bishops, 1972), 4; *Renewing Our Commitment to Catholic Elementary and Secondary Schools in the Third Millennium* (Washington, DC: U.S. Conference of Catholic Bishops, 2005).

16. Bryk et al., *Catholic Schools and the Common Good.*

17. Delfra and Scully, "Come and You Will See," 191.

18. Anne R. Gere, Jennifer L. Buehler, Christian M. Dallavis, and Victoria S. Haviland, "A Visibility Project: Learning to See How Preservice Teachers Take up Culturally Responsive Pedagogy," *American Educational Research Journal* 46, no. 3 (2009): 816–852.

19. Christian Dallavis, "'Because That's Who I Am': Extending Theories of Culturally Responsive Pedagogy to Consider Religious Identity, Belief, and Practice," *Multicultural Perspectives* 13, no. 3 (2011): 140.

20. Gay, *Culturally Responsive Teaching.*

21. M. Reardon, *Catholic Schools Then and Now* (Oregon, WI: Badger Books, 2005).

22. Alliance for Catholic Education, "About ACE," http://ace.nd.edu.

23. *Renewing Our Commitment*, 1.

Chapter 3

1. Marvin Schick, *A Survey of Day School Principals in the United States* (New York: AVI CHAI Foundation, 2007).

2. According to David Ellenson, "liberal" refers to Jewish day schools affiliated with (a) the Progressive Association of Reform Day Schools; (b) the Solomon Schechter Day School Association of the Conservative movement; and (c) the Network of Community Day Schools (RASAK). David Ellenson, "An Ideology for the Liberal Jewish School: A Philosophical-Sociological Investigation," *Journal of Jewish Education* 74, no. 3 (2008): 245–263.

3. Of the handful of Jewish teacher training programs created around the same time, the PARDES Educators Program in Jerusalem is still in operation. Others, like the Jewish Teacher Corps and Ha-Sha'ar, were short-lived.

4. While this study was under way, DeLeT became the day school concentration in the MAT program at Brandeis University. DeLeT now prepares general and Jewish studies teachers for both elementary and secondary grades, including teachers of Hebrew and the Bible.

5. Ezra Kapelowitz, Minna Wolf, and Stephen Markowitz, *Promoting Excellent Teaching in Jewish Day Schools: A Case Study of the DeLeT Program* (Jerusalem: Platforma, 2008).

6. DeLeT has had three faculty leaders over the twelve years of its existence and a core faculty that has nurtured the program's ongoing development.

7. Judah Pilch, *Study of Secondary and Higher Jewish Education in Cleveland* (Cleveland: Bureau of Jewish Education, 1964); Jonathan Krasner, "Jewish Education and American Jewish Education, Part 1," *Journal of Jewish Education* 71, no. 2 (2005): 121–177; Jonathan Sarna, "American Jewish Education in Historical Perspective," *Journal of Jewish Education* 64, nos.1–2 (1998): 8–21.

8. Gerald Graff, *And You Shall Teach Them Diligently: A Concise History of Jewish Education in the United States, 1776–2000* (New York: Jewish Theological Seminary Press, 2008); Sarna, "American Jewish Education in Historical Perspective."

9. Marvin Schick, *A Census of Jewish Day Schools in the United States* (New York: AVI CHAI Foundation, 2009).

10. Ibid. Schick classifies the rest as "Special Education" schools that are under Orthodox sponsorship.

11. Reform day school enrollments are stable, but Conservative day schools reported a 25 percent decline, which parallels a general weakening of the movement. Ibid., 11.

12. Alex Pomson and Howard Deitcher, eds., *Jewish Day Schools, Jewish Communities: A Reconsideration* (Oxford: Littman Library of Jewish Civilization, 2009), 12.

13. Since 2007 DeLeT has benefited from generous funding from the Jim Joseph Foundation.

14. The other academic site is the Hebrew Union College–Jewish Institute of Religion (HUC) in Los Angeles, which trains rabbis, canters, and Jewish educators for the Reform movement. Michael Zeldin, dean of the School of Education at HUC, partnered with Sharon Feiman-Nemser at Brandeis to plan and launch the DeLeT program.

15. At Brandeis, DeLeT became the Jewish day school concentration in the MAT program. At HUC, DeLeT became one of several certificate programs. For more information about DeLeT at HUC, see www.huc.edu/centers/delet. For more information about DeLeT at Brandeis, see www.brandeis.edu/programs/delet.

16. Eran Tamir et al., *The DeLeT Alumni Survey: A Comprehensive Report on the Journey of Beginning Jewish Day School Teachers* (Waltham, MA: Mandel Center for Studies in Jewish Education, 2010).

17. University rankings were based on SAT scores required for admission. For more details on the system, see ibid.

18. In 2012, DeLeT launched a track to prepare teachers of Hebrew.

19. According to an alumni survey administered in 2010, 40 percent of DeLeT alums teach general students, 40 percent teach Jewish studies, and 20 percent teach both. Eran Tamir, "The Retention Question in Context-Specific Teacher Education: Do Beginning Teachers and Their Program Leaders See Teachers' Future Career Eye to Eye?" *Teaching and Teacher Education* 26, no. 3 (2010): 665–678.

20. Mandel Center for Studies in Jewish Education, *MAT-JDS/DeLeT Handbook* (Waltham, MA: Brandeis University, 2002).

21. Sharon Feiman-Nemser and Michael Zeldin, "Final Report: The DeLeT Program at Brandeis University and Hebrew Union College–Jewish Institute of Religion, 2002–2007" (submitted to the National Advisory Committee, 2007).

22. Karen Hammerness, "To Seek, to Strive, to Find, and Not to Yield: A Look at Current Conceptions of Vision in Education," in *The Second International Handbook of Educational Change*, vol. 23, pt. 1, eds. Andy Hargreaves, Ann Leiberman, Michael Fullan, and David Hopkins (Amsterdam: Springer, 2010), 1033–1048.

23. In this twelfth year of the program, most of the mentors are graduates of the DeLeT program.

24. Jon A. Levisohn, "Community as a Means and an End in Jewish Education," in *Jewish Day Schools, Jewish Communities*, ed. Alex Pomson and Howard Deitcher (Portland, OR: Littman Library of Jewish Civilization, 2007), 90–105.

25. Sharon Feiman-Nemser, "From Preparation to Practice: Designing a Continuum to Strengthen and Sustain Teaching," *Teachers College Record* 103, no. 6 (2001): 1013–1055.

26. Mandel Center for Studies in Jewish Education, *DeLeT Program Teaching Standards and Continuum for Teacher Development* (Waltham, MA: Brandeis University, 2006).

27. Traditionally a *beit midrash* is a place where men study Talmudic texts, often in pairs (*havruta*). This traditional form of Jewish learning has been appropriate by many contemporary Jewish educational institutions and adapted to various purposes.

28. In the early years of the program, the Beit Midrash took place once or twice a week during both summers. Entering students were paired with graduating students. Currently the Beit Midrash occurs daily during a week of orientation before the formal start of the MAT program.

29. Brian Lord, "Teachers' Professional Development: Critical Colleagueship and the Role of Professional Community," in *The Future of Education: Perspectives on National Standards in America,* ed. Nina Cobb (New York: College Entrance Examination Board, 1994).

30. For a discussion of the Beit Midrash for Teachers as a form of professional development, see Sharon Feiman-Nemser, "Beit Midrash for Teachers: An Experiment in Professional Education," *Journal of Jewish Education,* 72, no.3 (2006): 161–181. For a discussion of the purposes and pedagogies used in the DeLeT Beit Midrash, see Elie Holzer with Orit Kent, *A Philosophy of Havruta: Understanding and Teaching the Art of Text Study in Pairs* (Boston: Academic Studies Press, 2013).

31. The Jewish Sabbath begins at sundown on Friday.

32. A Web case,"Third Graders Learn Jewish Values Through Havruta Study," created by Jocelyn Segal, DeLeT graduate, and Orit Kent, co-creator of the DeLeT Beit Midrash, can be found at the Mandel Center for Studies in Jewish Education, www.brandeis.edu/mandel/projects/beitmidrash/Jewishvaluesandhavruta.html.

33. Rosh HaShanah, the Jewish new year, and Yom Kippur, the Day of Atonement, come early in the fall and are a major focus of attention in the opening weeks of school.

34. Grant P.Wiggins and Jay McTighe, *Understanding by Design* (Alexandria, VA: Association for Supervision and Curriculum Development, 2005).

35. Draft Rubric for Integrated Units, DeLeT Program, 2002–2003.

36. Michael Zeldin, "Integration and Interaction in the Jewish Day School," *The Jewish Educational Leader's Handbook,* ed. Robert Tornberg (Denver: A.R.E., 1998), 579–590; Alex Pomson, *Making the Best of the Worst of Times: Thinking of Schools as Vehicles of Meaning for Teachers* (New York: Coalition for the Advancement of Jewish Education, 2001); Jonathan Sarna, "American Jewish Education in Historical Perspective," *Journal of Jewish Education* 64 (Winter/Spring 1998): 8.

37. Jon A. Levisohn. "From the Integration of Curricula to the Pedagogy of Integrity," *Journal of Jewish Education* 73, no. 3 (2009): 288

38. The requirement to develop an integrated unit was changed because many of the partner day schools had trouble finding time for such units. While students still design and teach a major unit, they are encouraged, but not required, to integrate secular and Jewish content.

39. DeLeT faculty, focus group discussion with the author, April 27, 2009.

40. Judy Elkin, interview with the author, November 19, 2007.

41. Abraham Joshua Heschel, "Jewish Education," *The Insecurity of Freedom.* (Philadelphia: Jewish Publication Society, 1966), 223–241, emphasis added.

42. A *succah* is a temporary structure that some Jews build during the eight day fall holiday of Succot. Traditional Jews follow the injunction to eat in the succah during the holiday in remembrance of the transitional structures that the Israelites built for shelter as they wandered in the desert for forty days.

43. Judy Elkin, "Vision Behind the Jewish Journeys Project" (working paper, Mandel Center for Studies in Jewish Education, Waltham, MA: Brandeis University, 2007).

44. Judy Elkin, focus group discussion with the author, April 27, 2009.

45. Judy Elkin, focus group discussion with the author, April 27, 2009.

46. These findings come from a longitudinal survey of DeLeT graduates from Brandeis and Hebrew Union College–Jewish Institute of Religion, in Tamir et al., *The DeLeT Alumni Survey.*

47. Jon Levisohn, syllabus, Philosophy of Jewish Education: Educational Visions in Theory and Practice, July 2007.

48. Daniel Pekarsky, *Vision at Work: Theory and Practice at Beit Raban* (New York: Jewish Theological Seminary, 2006); Deborah Meier, *The Power of Their Ideas: Lessons for America from a Small School in Harlem* (Boston: Beacon Press, 2002).

49. Sharon Feiman-Nemser, "From Preparation to Practice: Designing a Continuum to Strengthen and Sustain Teaching," *Teachers College Record* 103, no. 6 (2001): 1013–1055.

50. All MAT students present their research at an annual teacher research conference that precedes graduation in the second summer of the program.

Chapter 4

1. James Gee, "Identity as an Analytic Lens for Research in Education," in *Review of Research in Education,* ed. W. G. Secada (Washington, DC: American Educational Research Association, 2001), 99–125; Anna Sfard and Anna Prusak, "Telling Identities: In Search of an Analytic Tool for Investigating Learning as a Culturally Shaped Activity," *Educational Researcher* 34, no. 4 (2004): 14–22.

2. Deborah P. Britzman, *Practice Makes Practice* (Albany: State University of New York Press, 1991); Seymour Sarason, *Teaching as a Performing Art* (New York: Teachers College Press, 1999); Jane Danielewicz, *Teaching Selves: Identity, Pedagogy and Teacher Education* (Albany: State University of New York Press, 2001); Douwe Beijaard, Paulien Meijer, and Nico Verloop, "Reconsidering Research on Teachers' Professional Identity," *Teaching and Teacher Education* 20, no. 2 (2003): 107–128; Matt Ronfeld and Pamela Grossman, "Becoming a Professional: Experimenting with Possible Selves in Professional Preparation," *Teacher Education Quarterly* 35, no. 3 (2008): 41–60.

3. Janet Alsup, *Teacher Identity Discourses: Negotiating Personal and Professional Spaces* (Mahwah, NJ: Lawrence Erlbaum and the National Council of Teachers of English, 2006); Colleen M. Fairbanks et al., "Beyond Knowledge: Exploring Why Some Teachers Are More Thoughtfully Adaptive Than Others," *Journal of Teacher Education* 61, nos. 1–2 (2010): 161–171.

4. Presumably, more typical teacher education programs bring together trainees from diverse backgrounds and prepare them for schools that are also quite diverse, so that the possibility of examining how becoming a teacher fits with other aspects of the person's life has been more elusive.

5. Jeffrey Arnett, *Emerging Adulthood: The Winding Road from the Late Teens Through the Twenties* (New York: Oxford University Press, 2004); Frances Goldscheider and Calvin Goldscheider, *The Changing Transition to Adulthood: Leaving and Returning Home* (Thousand Oaks, CA: Sage, 1999); Richard A. Setterstein, Frank F. Furstenberg, and Rubén G. Rumbaut, eds., *On the Frontier of Adulthood: Theory, Research, and Public Policy* (Chicago: University of Chicago Press, 2005); Seth Schwartz, James Cote, and Jeffrey Arnett, "Identity and Agency in Emerging Adulthood: Two Developmental Routes in the Individualization Process," *Youth and Society* 37, no. 2 (2005): 201–229; Steve Hitlin and G. Elder, "Agency: An Empirical Model of an Abstract Concept." in *Constructing Adulthood: Agency and Subjectivity in Adolescence and Adulthood; Advances in Life Course Research*, vol. 11, ed. Ross Macmillan (Amsterdam: JAI Press, 2007), 33–67.

6. Bethamie Horowitz, *Connections and Journeys: Assessing Critical Opportunities for Enhancing Jewish Identity* (New York: UJA–Federation of Jewish Philanthropies of New York, 2000); Paul Wink and Michele Dillon, "Spiritual Development across the Adult Life Course: Findings from a Longitudinal Study," *Journal of Adult Development* 9, no. 1 (2002): 79–94.

7. Pierre Bourdieu, *Outline of a Theory of Practice* (Cambridge: Cambridge University Press, 1977).

8. Dan Lortie, *Schoolteacher* (Chicago: University of Chicago Press, 1975).

9. Theorists have defined "agency" in several different ways. First is a more macro- sociological tradition of viewing agency as "the ability to operate independently of deter-

mining constraints of social structure" (Craig Calhoun, ed., *Dictionary of the Social Sciences* [New York: Oxford University Press, 2002]), but this stance does not specify what it is about the person that makes such autonomy possible. Second are the more sociopsychological approaches that emphasize the ability of the individual to act on and even to transform the context, rather than only reacting to it (Ronald Berger, "Agency, Structure, and the Transition to Disability," *Sociological Quarterly* 49, no. 2 [2008]: 309–333). Mustafa Emirbayer and Ann Mische ("What Is Agency?" *American Journal of Sociology* 103, no. 4 [1998]: 962–1023) have described three features that together comprise agency: past-oriented habit, present-oriented consideration of the way things stand, and future-oriented purpose.

10. When we designed the interviews, agency was not something we were planning to investigate. It only emerged as a topic in the course of tracing people's evolving identities.

11. The one exception was an individual who had completed college about a decade earlier.

12. This compares to 62 percent of entering undergraduates at the University of Chicago who come from public high schools. See https://collegeadmissions.uchicago.edu/viewchicago/facts.shtml.

13. I coded participants' entrance accounts in terms of their explicit interest in going into teaching as a career at the time they began the program. I created a measure of personal agency based on three different features from their accounts about how they decided to enter the programs: (1) the quality of clarity or serendipity (some "always knew" they wanted to become teachers; some "fell into" the possibility of going into teaching; some "winnowed down" their career exploration to focus on teaching); (2) the use of clear, decisive language (some said they "wanted" to be teachers; some used more tentative language, like "should," "could," or "kind of" around the decision); (3) their motivation and personal goals/planfulness (the number of substantive reasons or rationales offered about why going into teaching appealed to them, such as interest in education, the focal context, neither, or both).

14. In the few cases where they subsequently came up against school conditions that were problematic, they readjusted their plans, shifting their career goals in new, related directions (i.e., becoming a principal or moving into education in another setting).

15. The study's protocol with the program leaders included a question about which graduates among the ten participants from each program were viewed as exemplary.

16. Only at the end of the 2008 interview did Mark mention in passing that he comes from a Hispanic background.

17. In passing, she juxtaposed doing service to "going abroad in college"—something she didn't do—as if to say these were somehow related.

18. The study focused on only two of her many "partial" selves—her teacher/educator self and her Jewish self—while leaving out her parent self, etc.

Chapter 5

1. National Research Council, Committee on the Study of Teacher Preparation Programs in the United States, *Preparing Teachers: Building Evidence for Sound Policy* (Washington, DC: National Academies Press, 2010).

2. Grant Wiggins and Jay McTighe, *Understanding by Design,* 2nd ed. (New York: Pearson, 2005).

3. Linda Darling-Hammond et al., eds., *Preparing Teachers for a Changing World: What Teachers Should Learn and Be Able to Do* (San Francisco: Jossey-Bass, 2005).

4. Recently, some teacher educators have begun to argue that these kinds of practices and strategies should be at the center of teacher preparation curriculum and should be the basis of all coursework and clinical work. See, for example, Deborah Ball and Francesca Forzani, "The Work of Teaching and the Challenge for Teacher Education," *Journal of Teacher Education* 60, no. 5 (2009): 497–511; Pam Grossman, Karen Hammerness, and Morva McDonald, "Redefining Teaching, Reimagining Teacher Education," *Teachers and Teaching: Theory and Practice* 15, no. 2 (2009): 273–289; Morva McDonald, Elham Kazemi, and Sarah Schneider Kavanagh, "Core Practices and Pedagogies of Teacher Education: A Call for a Common Language and Collective Activity," *Journal of Teacher Education* 64, no. 5 (2013): 378–386.

5. The DeLeT program also includes a child study as one of its main assignments.

6. For one elaboration of this vision for teacher education, see Grossman et al., "Redefining Teaching, Reimagining Teacher Education."

7. Sharon Feiman-Nemser and Janine Remillard, "Perspectives on Learning to Teach," in *The Teacher Educator's Handbook: Building a Knowledge Base for the Preparation of Teachers,* ed. Frank Murray (San Francisco: Jossey-Bass, 1995), 63–91.

8. Mary Kennedy, "Knowledge and Vision in Teaching," *Journal of Teacher Education* 57, no. 3 (2006): 205–211; Sharon Feiman-Nemser, "From Preparation to Practice: Designing a Continuum to Strengthen and Sustain Teaching," *Teachers College Record* 103, no. 6 (2001): 1013–1055.

9. Kennedy, "Knowledge and Vision in Teaching."

10. Grossman et al., "Redefining Teaching, Reimagining Teacher Education"; McDonald et al., "Core Practices and Pedagogies of Teacher Education."

Chapter 6

1. Pam Grossman, Karen Hammerness, and Morva McDonald, "Redefining Teacher: Reimagining Teacher Education," *Teacher and Teaching: Theory and Practice* 15, no. 2 (2009): 273–290; Ken Zeichner, "The Turn Once Again Toward Practice-Based Teacher Education," *Journal of Teacher Education* 63, no. 5 (2012): 376–382.

2. Mary M. Kennedy, "The Role of Preservice Teacher Education," in *Teaching as the Learning Profession: Handbook of Teaching and Policy,* ed. Linda Darling-Hammond

and Gary Sykes (San Francisco: Jossey-Bass, 1999), 54–86; Grossman et al., "Redefining Teacher."

3. Research on the preparation of novices for a variety of different professions including law, the clergy, and social work as well as teaching revealed that novices learning to teach had the fewest opportunities to learn in practice. Pam Grossman et al., "Teaching Practice: A Cross-Professional Perspective," *Teachers College Record* 111, no. 9 (2009): 2055–2100.

4. Blue Ribbon Panel on Clinical Preparation and Partnerships for Improved Student Learning, *Transforming Teacher Education Through Clinical Practice: A National Strategy to Prepare Effective Teachers* (Washington, DC: National Council for Accreditation of Teacher Education, 2010); Ken Zeichner, "Rethinking the Connections Between Campus Courses and Field Experiences in College- and University-Based Teacher Education," *Journal of Teacher Education* 61, nos. 1–2 (2010): 89–99.

5. Deborah Loewenberg Ball and Francesca Forzani, "The Work of Teaching and the Challenge of Teacher Education," *Journal of Teacher Education* 60, no. 5 (2009): 497–511; Grossman et al., "Redefining Teacher"; Morva McDonald, Elham Kazemi, and Sarah Schneider Kavanagh, "Core Practices and Teacher Education Pedagogies: A Call for Common Language and Collective Activity," *Journal of Teacher Education* 64, no. 5 (2013): 378–386.

6. Zeichner, "The Turn Once Again Toward Practice-Based Teacher Education."

7. We aimed for a sample of six teachers (two from each program). Identifying and observing two UTEP and two DeLeT teachers was relatively easy, because most of them remained in teaching and were concentrated in Chicago and Boston, respectively. However, all ten ACE teachers in our sample moved from Los Angeles; some left teaching for leadership positions or other occupations and were scattered around the country. As result, we were able to observe only one teacher.

8. In order to validate our observations of teachers' practices, we shared drafts of their cases and asked whether they felt the text accurately described their practice. We received detailed responses from all five teachers. Overall, they felt that the written cases accurately reflected their practice. In some cases they offered minor correction to details that were misrepresented. Teachers also helped us with demographic details about their schools or with a missing title of a poster. While we tried to incorporate teachers' feedback, the results reflect our own views.

9. The aims are cited from the school's mission statement, drafted July 31, 2012.

10. The antagonist in the Book of Esther.

11. Erin Turner, Sylvia Celedon-Pattichis, and Mary Marshall, "Opportunities to Learn Problem Solving and Mathematics Discourse among Latino/a Kindergarten Students," in *Promoting High Participation and Success in Mathematics by Hispanic Students: Examining Opportunities and Probing Promising Practices*, ed. Richard S.

Kitchen and Edward A. Silver (Washington, DC: National Education Association Press, 2008).

12. *Investigations in Number, Data and Space: Implementing Investigations in Kindergarten,* 2nd ed. (New York: Pearson, 2008).

13. Grossman et al., "Teaching Practice."

14. Elizabeth G. Cohen and Rachel A. Lotan, eds., *Working for Equity in Heterogeneous Classrooms: Sociological Theory in Practice* (New York: Teachers College Press, 1997).

15. Ibid.

16. Grossman et al, "Teaching Practice"; David Pearson and Linda Fielding, "Comprehension Instruction," in *Handbook of Reading Research 2,* ed. R. Barr, M. L. Kamil, P. Mosenthal, & P. David Pearson (White Plains, NY: Longman, 1991), 815–860.

17. Pam Grossman, Peter Smagorinsky, and Sheila Valencia, "Appropriating Tools for Teaching English: A Theoretical Framework for Research on Learning to Teach," *American Journal of Education* 108, no. 1 (1999): 1–29; Martin Nystrand, *Opening Dialogue: Understanding the Dynamics of Language and Learning in the English Classroom* (New York: Teachers College Press, 1997); Mary Catherine O'Connor and Sarah Michaels, "Aligning Academic Task and Participation Status Through Revoicing: Analysis of a Classroom Discourse Strategy," *Anthropology and Education Quarterly* 24, no. 4 (1993): 318–335; Catherine Snow, Peg Griffin, Susan Burns, and the NAE Subcommittee on Teaching Reading, *Knowledge to Support the Teaching of Reading: Preparing Teachers for a Changing World* (San Francisco: Jossey-Bass, 2005).

18. Household income data is for 2010 and was retrieved from http://www.city-data.com/neighborhood/XXXXX-Chicago-IL.html.

19. Students were able to purchase and use laptops paid for over the course of their three years. Teachers are explicit about when students can and cannot use laptops.

20. Richard M. Ryan and Edward L. Deci, "Intrinsic and Extrinsic Motivations: Classic Definitions and New Directions," *Contemporary Educational Psychology* 25, no. 1 (2000): 54–67; Gloria Ladson-Billings, *The Dreamkeepers: Successful Teachers for African-American Children* (San Francisco: Jossey-Bass, 1994).

21. Just as a side note, this class took place before the start of the Arab Spring in Tunisia in 2011.

22. This type of interaction, where a teacher invites a single-word response from students, may suggest a relatively limited conversation that doesn't support the development of students' ideas. A different interpretation is that Thomas chose this activity as a hook to stimulate students' participation and interest, as the subject of the West was already discussed in prior classes.

23. For more details on the career paths of ACE teachers, see chapter 8.

24. National Research Council, *Preparing Teachers* (Washington, DC: National Academies Press, 2011).

25. Susan Moore Johnson, *Finders and Keepers: Helping New Teachers Survive and Thrive in Our Schools* (San Francisco: Jossey-Bass, 2004); Eran Tamir, "What Keeps Teachers In and What Drives Them Out: Findings from a Longitudinal Comparative Case-Based Study of Beginning Teachers in Urban-Public, Urban-Catholic, and Jewish Day Schools," *Teachers College Record* 115, no. 6 (2013), http://www.tcrecord.org.

Chapter 7

1. Since the Choosing to Teach participating teachers taught in twenty-four schools, the initial plan was to interview all twenty-four school principals. While most principals were eager to participate in this study, one Jewish day school principal refused to participate. In addition, we were unable to locate four of the ten Catholic school principals, who left their positions and whose schools reported having no contact information for them. We did contact the urban public school principals, all of whom agreed to participate. In fact, for one of the urban schools, we interviewed both the principal and assistant principal.

2. Three of the five principals who stayed longer than five years in their jobs were from Jewish day schools, and two were from urban public schools. None of the Catholic school principals stayed in their schools for that length of time.

3. Thomas M. Smith and Richard Ingersoll, "The Wrong Solution to the Teacher Shortage," *Educational Leadership: Keeping Good Teachers* 60, no. 8 (2003): 30–33.

4. Richard Ingersoll and Jeffrey Kralik, "The Impact of Mentoring on Teacher Retention: What the Research Says," *Education Commission of the States Research Review*, 2004, http://www.gse.upenn.edu/pdf/rmi/ECS-RMI-2004.pdf.

5. Susan M. Kardos and Susan Moore Johnson, "On Their Own and Presumed Expert: New Teachers' Experience with Their Colleagues," *Teachers College Record* 109, no. 9 (2007): 2083–2106.

6. In contrast to these personnel-centered interventions, studies suggest that teacher retention is also explained by some school conditions, which are constant and, for the most part, beyond the principal's reach. For example, teacher attrition is closely linked to the demographic profile of the students. As a result, teachers who work in urban schools serving low-income and minority students are far more likely to leave their schools early on in their tenure. This can be seen in Donald Boyd et al., "The Influence of School Administrators on Teacher Retention Decisions," *American Educational Research Journal* 48, no. 2 (2011): 303–333; Thomas Smith and Richard Ingersoll, "What Are the Effects of Induction and Mentoring on Beginning Teacher Turnover?" *American Educational Research Journal* 41, no. 3 (2004): 681–714.

7. Anthony Bryk, Eric Camburn, and Karen Seashore Louis, "Professional Community in Chicago Elementary Schools: Facilitating Factors and Organizational Conse-

quences," *Educational Administration Quarterly* 35, no. 5 (1999): 751–781; Kardos and Johnson, "On Their Own and Presumed Expert."

8. Keith Leithwood, Karen Seashore Louis, Stephen Anderson, and Kyla Wahlstrom, *Review of Research: How Leadership Influences Student Learning,* The Wallace Foundation, 2004, http://www.wallace foundation.org/knowledge-center/school-leadership/key-research/Documents/How-Leadership-Influences-Student-Learning.pdf.

9. The additional four principals did not mention the term "social justice," or related phrases concerning social inequality, as a goal for their school.

10. See chapter 1 for a discussion of how UTEP prepares its teachers for the urban context; also see chapter 8, which describes how UTEP teachers implemented a social justice–oriented curriculum in their classes.

11. Three of the eight principals in our sample did not mention "serving the community" as a significant aim for their school.

12. The other four principals did not mention "developing childrens' character" as a goal for their school.

13. For research on late hiring in public schools and its negative impact on the quality of instruction and cohesion of urban public schools, see *What Matters Most: Teaching for America's Future* (New York: National Commission on Teaching and America's Future, 1996); Susan Watson, *Recruiting and Retaining Teachers: Keys to Improving the Philadelphia Public Schools* (Philadelphia: Consortium for Policy Research in Education, 2001), http://www.cpre.org/sites/default/files/researchreport/797_children01.pdf.

14. In addition to their school-based mentorship, UTEP teachers were assigned in their first year a UTEP coach and a district mentor.

15. See, for example, Smith and Ingersoll, "The Wrong Solution to the Teacher Shortage"; Jonah Rockoff, "Does Mentoring Reduce Turnover and Improve Skills of New Employees? Evidence from Teachers in New York City" (NBER Working Paper No. 13868, 2008), http://www.nber.org/papers/w13868.pdf?new_window=1; Sharon Feiman-Nemser, "From Preparation to Practice: Designing a Continuum to Strengthen and Sustain Teaching," *Teachers College Record* 103, no. 6 (2001): 1013–1055.

16. Sarah Birkeland and Sharon Feiman-Nemser, "Helping School Leaders Help New Teachers: A Tool for Transforming School-Based Induction," *The New Educator* 8, (2012): 109–138; Susan Moore Johnson and The Project on the Next Generation of Teachers, *Finders and Keepers: Helping New Teachers Survive and Thrive in Our Schools* (San Francisco: Jossey-Bass, 2004).

17. While the term "social justice" was never used by Catholic principals to denote a school aim or goal, other phrases, like "serving underserved populations" or "serving the poor," which demonstrate a similar commitment, did come up in the interviews.

18. This orientation plan was weak compared to the standards of other Jewish day schools, but it seemed stronger compared to some Catholic and urban public schools

that were unable to bring their teachers together during the summer and/or hired them late in the summer.

Chapter 8

1. Sharon Feiman-Nemser, "From Preparation to Practice: Designing a Continuum toStrengthen and Sustain Teaching," *Teachers College Record* 103, no. 6 (2001): 1013–1055.

2. Texas State Board for Educator Certification, *The Cost of Teacher Turnover* (Austin: Texas Center for Educational Research, 2000).

3. Susan Kardos and Susan Moore Johnson, "On Their Own and Presumed Expert: New Teachers' Experience with Their Colleagues," *Teachers College Record* 109, no. 9 (2008): 2083–2106.

4. Matthew Ronfeldt, Susanna Loeb, and James Wyckoff, "How Teacher Turnover Harms Student Achievement," *American Educational Research Journal* 50, no. 1 (2013): 4–36.

5. Ed Boe, Lynne H. Cook, and Robert J. Sunderland, "Teacher Turnover: Examining Exit Attrition, Teaching Area Transfer, and School Migration," *Exceptional Children* 75, no. 1 (2008): 7–31; Richard Ingersoll, "The Teacher Shortage: A Case of Wrong Diagnosis and Wrong Prescription," *NASSP Bulletin* 86, no. 631 (2002): 16–31.

6. Ashley Keigher, "Teacher Attrition and Mobility: Results from the 2008–09 Teacher Follow-Up Survey" (NCES Report No. 2010-353, National Center for Education Statistics, Washington, DC, 2010), http://nces.ed.gov/pubs2010/2010353.pdf.

7. Ingersoll, "The Teacher Shortage"; National Commission on Teaching for America's Future, "No Dream Denied: A Pledge to America's Children," 2003, http://www.nctaf.org/article/index.

8. Susan Aud et al., "The Condition of Education 2013" (NCES Report No. 2013-037, National Center for Education Statistics, Washington, DC, 2013), http://nces.ed.gov/pubs2013/2013037.pdf. Included in the 45 percent are teachers who left the profession, teachers who moved within their school district, and teachers who moved to schools outside their district. While we acknowledge the differences between these categories, the assumption behind adding the categories is that the damage to schools and students happens when teachers leave or move, no matter where these teachers end up working.

9. Aud et al., "The Condition of Education 2013."

10. National Commission on Teaching for America's Future, "The High Cost of Teacher Turnover," 2007, http://nctaf.org/wp-content/uploads/2012/01/NCTAF-Cost-of-Teacher-Turnover-2007-policy-brief.pdf.

11. In some cities, like New York, Washington, DC, and Chicago, there are often funding inequities between neighborhood schools, which serve primarily low-income and minorities students, and magnet selective schools, which cater to middle- and

upper-class families. Major works illuminating such inequities include Jonathan Kozol, *Savage Inequalities* (New York: Harper Perennial, 1991); Pauline Lipman, *The New Political Economy of Urban Education: Neoliberalism, Race, and the Right to the City* (New York: Routledge, 2011). Bruce D. Baker and Sean P. Corcoran, "The Stealth Inequalities of School Funding: How Local Tax Systems and State Aid Formulas Undermine Equality," September 2012, http://www.americanprogress.org/wpcontent/uploads/2012/09/StealthInequities.pdf. A succinct literature review of teacher attrition in public schools can be found in Geoffrey D. Borman and N. Maritza Dowling, "Teacher Attrition and Retention: A Meta-Analytic and Narrative Review of the Research," *Review of Educational Research* 78, no. 3 (2008): 367–409.

12. Charles T. Clotfelter et al., "Do School Accountability Systems Make It More Difficult for Low-Performing Schools to Attract and Retain High-Quality Teachers?" *Journal of Policy Analysis and Management* 23, no. 2 (2004): 251–271; Richard Murnane and John Papay, "Teachers' Views on No Child Left Behind: Support for the Principles, Concerns about the Practices," *Journal of Economic Perspectives* 24, no. 3 (2010): 151–166.

13. Emily Useem, Robert Offenberg, and Elizabeth Farley, *Closing the Teacher Quality Gap in Philadelphia: New Hope and Old Hurdles,* Research for Action, 2007, http://files.eric.ed.gov/fulltext/ED496638.pdf.

14. Denise McDonald, *United States Catholic Elementary and Secondary Schools 2007–2008: The Annual Statistical Report on Schools, Enrollment, and Staffing,* http://www.ncea.org/news/AnnualDataReport.asp. According to some estimates, to date only 4 percent of the teaching staff left in Catholic schools is from the clergy. For details see *Preserving a Critical National Asset: America's Disadvantaged Students and the Crisis in Faith-Based Urban Schools* (Washington, DC: U.S. Department of Education, 2008).

15. Stephen Provasnik and Scott Dorfman, "Mobility in the Teacher Workforce: Findings from the Condition of Education" (NCES Report No. 2005-114, National Center for Education Statistics, Washington, DC, 2005), http://nces.ed.gov/pubs2005/2005114.pdf.

16. Michael Ben-Avie and Jeff Kress, A North American Study of Educators in Jewish Day and Congregational Schools (New York: Jewish Education Service of North America, 2008); Adam Gamoran et al., The Teachers Report: A Portrait of Teachers in Jewish Schools (New York: Council for Initiatives in Jewish Education, 1998); Eran Tamir and Raquel Magidin de-Kramer, "Teacher Retention and Career Commitments among DeLeT Graduates: The Intersection of Teachers' Background, Preparation to Teaching, and School Context," Journal of Jewish Education 77, no. 2 (2011): 76–97; Eran Tamir and Sally Lesik, "Jewish Day School Teachers: Career Commitments in the 21st Century," Journal of Jewish Education 79, no. 2 (2013): 131–156.

17. Eran Tamir, "The Retention Question in Context-Specific Teacher Education: Do

Beginning Teachers and Their Program Directors See Teachers' Future Career Eye to Eye?" *Teaching and Teacher Education* 26, no. 3 (2010): 665–678; Richard Ingersoll, "Teacher Turnover and Teacher Shortages: An Organizational Analysis," American Educational Research Journal 38, no. 3 (2001): 499–534.

18. In order to retain the anonymity of this teacher, we are unable to offer additional details.

19. Sharon Feiman-Nemser and Margaret Buchmann, "Describing Teacher Education: A Framework and Illustrative Findings from a Longitudinal Study of Six Students," *Elementary School Journal* 89, no. 3 (1989): 365–377; Pam Grossman and Susanna Loeb, *Alternative Routes to Teaching: Mapping the New Landscape of Teacher Education* (Cambridge, MA: Harvard Education Press, 2008); Daniel Humphrey and Marjorie Wechsler, "Insights into Alternative Certification: Initial Findings from a National Study," *Teachers College Record* 109, no.3 (2007): 483–530.

20. Geoffrey D. Borman and N. Maritza Dowling, "Teacher Attrition and Retention: A Meta-Analytic and Narrative Review of the Research," *Review of Educational Research* 78, no. 3 (2008): 367–409.

21. For more on this, see chapters 2 and 5. A year after these interviews with ACE teachers, the study team visited the ACE program, interviewed faculty and leaders, and collected program documents and course syllabi. We found some evidence that ACE was aware of the need to prepare culturally responsive teachers and had been trying to address this through the program's curriculum. See also a study that advocates the need for Catholic teachers to adopt cultural responsive pedagogy; Christian Dallavis, "Qualifying Sociopolitical Consciousness: Complicating Culturally Responsive Pedagogy for Faith-Based Schools," *Education and Urban Society* 45, no. 2 (2011): doi: 10.1177/0013124511408597.

22. Richard Ingersoll, *Is there Really a Teacher Shortage? A Report Co-Sponsored by the Center for the Study of Teaching and Policy and the Center for Policy Research in Education* (Seattle: University of Washington, Center for the Study of Teaching and Policy, 2003).

23. Eran Tamir, "What Keeps Teachers In and What Drives Them Out: Findings from a Longitudinal Comparative Case-Based Study of Beginning Teachers in Urban-Public, Urban-Catholic, and Jewish Day Schools," *Teachers College Record* 115, no. 6 (2013), http://www.tcrecord.org; Kavita Kapadia Matsko and Karen Hammerness, "Unpacking the 'Urban' in Urban Teacher Education: Making a Case for Context-Specific Preparation," *Journal of Teacher Education* 20, no. 10 (2013): 1–17; Eran Tamir, "Choosing to Teach in Urban Schools Among Graduates of Elite Colleges," *Urban Education* 44, no. 5 (2009): 522–544; Tamir, "The Retention Question in Context-Specific Teacher Education"; Tamir, "What Keeps Teachers In and What Drives Them Out"; Eran Tamir, "Choosing Teaching as a Career in Urban Public Catholic and Jewish Schools

by Graduates of Elite Colleges," *Journal of Educational Change,* (2013), http://link. springer.com/article/10.1007/s10833-013-9222-9.

24. I do not imply here that schools in all three sectors offered similar working conditions to teachers in the Choosing to Teach Study. As shown earlier, teachers from UTEP and, in particular, from ACE were far more exposed to harsh school environments, which, in part, resulted in the transition of all ACE teachers from their initial placements.

Conclusion

1. See Sharon Feiman-Nemser, "Beit Midrash for Teachers: An Experiment in Professional Education," *Journal of Jewish Education* 72, no. 3 (2006): 161–181.

2. Linda Darling-Hammond and Karen Hammerness, "The Design of Teacher Education Programs," in Preparing Teachers for a Changing World, ed. L. Darling-Hammond and J. Bransford (San Francisco: Jossey-Bass, 2005), 390–441.

3. Charles Foster, Lisa Dahill, Lawrence Golemon, and Barbara Tolentino, *Educating Clergy: Teaching Practices and the Pastoral Imagination* (San Francisco: Jossey-Bass, 2006), p. 11.

4. Public schools experience the pressure to raise test scores and meet annual yearly progress; Catholic schools, especially in poor, urban areas, have limited resources and severe staffing challenges; Jewish day schools are dealing with economic sustainability.

5. Susan Moore Johnson and The Project of the Next Generation of Teachers, *Finder and Keepers: Helping New Teachers Survive and Thrive in Our Schools* (San Francisco: Jossey-Bass, 2004).

6. Eran Tamir, "Choosing to Teach in Urban Schools Among Graduates of Elite Colleges," *Urban Education* 44, no. 5 (2009): 522–544; Eran Tamir, "The Retention Question in Context-Specific Teacher Education: Do Beginning Teachers and Their Program Directors See Teachers' Future Careers Eye to Eye," *Teaching and Teacher Education* 26, no. 3 (2010): 665–678.

7. Eran Tamir, "What Keeps Teachers In and What Drives Them Out: Findings from a Longitudinal Comparative Case-Based Study of Beginning Teachers in Urban-Public, Urban-Catholic, and Jewish Day Schools," *Teachers College Record* 115, no. 6 (2013), http://www.tcrecord.org.

Acknowledgments

This book is the product of the Choosing to Teach Project, a research initiative at Brandeis University's Jack, Joseph and Morton Mandel Center for Studies in Jewish Education. The study brought together researchers from five universities to study three unique teacher education programs and a sample of their graduates. We want to thank the many people who contributed to the Choosing to Teach project and to this book.

Father Tim Scully, CSC, director of the Institute for Educational Initiatives at the University of Notre Dame and founder of the Alliance for Catholic Education (ACE) at the University of Notre Dame helped conceive the project. We especially appreciate his leadership and vision in bringing together faculty and graduates from the ACE program with faculty and graduates from the Day School Leadership Through Teaching (DeLeT) program at Brandeis University in two retreats. The open discussions at those retreat seeded the idea of a joint study.

Susan Kardos from the Mandel Center and John Watzke from the Institute for Educational Initiatives planned and conducted an initial study of graduates from ACE, UTEP, and DeLeT. When Kardos and Watske took new positions, Eran Tamir stepped in as project leader. Tamir, who oversaw all aspects of the project, including design, data collection, and analysis, was joined by Karen Hammerness, Bethamie Horowitz, and Sharon Feiman Nemser. We also welcomed Karita Kapadia Matsko, Christian Dallavis, and Anthony Holter. Doing research with such thoughtful and energetic colleagues has been a true delight for all of us.

Our work benefited greatly from the administrative and research assistance of Marcie Quaroni, Ai Morrita, Galit Higgins, Elizabeth Dinolfo, Michael Emmerson, and Lauren Davis, who spent many hours arranging meetings and conference calls, coding and analyzing data, and assisting in the preparation of conference presentations and articles. Their contribution to the project has been invaluable. We are also grateful to Renee Rubin Ross, who worked with Eran Tamir on developing and conducting interviews with school principals during her postdoctoral fellowship at the Mandel Center.

In addition to administrative and research assistance, we received endless support from our colleagues at the Mandel Center for Studies in Jewish Education at Brandeis University, UTEP at the University of Chicago, and the Alliance for Catholic Education at the University of Notre Dame. Here is a partial list of colleagues who contributed to our thinking: At Brandeis: Sarah Birkeland, Sue

Fendrick, Orit Kent, Marya Levenson, Jon Levison, Nili Pearlmutter, Joe Reimer, Vivian Troen, Judy Elkin, Cindy Shulak-Rome, Serene Victor, Noreen Leibson. At the University of Chicago: Marvin Hoffman and Susan Stodolsky. At the University of Notre Dame: Fr. Tim Scully, Tom Doyle, John Staud, and Sr. Gail Mayotte.

Along the way we received invaluable external feedback from Miriam Ben Peretz, Mary Diez, Pam Grossman, Lee Shulman, Diana Turk, and Ken Zeichner, who graciously read and offered critical commentary on our work as discussants and reviewers. We also benefited from the thoughtful advice of many anonymous reviewers who read earlier products of the Choosing to Teach Project. This book builds on some of that work. While we cannot acknowledge these reviewers by name, we are indebted to their constructive critiques.

We could not have pursued this research without the enthusiastic participation of the thirty teachers from DeLeT, ACE, and UTEP who opened their hearts and shared their dreams, personal histories, and professional experiences. We are also indebted to the directors and faculty at ACE, DeLeT, and UTEP who took the time to be interviewed and willingly participated in focus group discussions. Finally, we are grateful to the numerous school principals and assistant principals who graciously agreed to meet with us to discuss their perceptions, beliefs, and actions regarding issues related to beginning teachers.

Caroline Chauncey, editor-in-chief at Harvard Education Press, deserves special thanks for her faith in the project and her continuing support and guidance throughout the entire process.

The Choosing to Teach Project received generous funding from the Jack, Joseph and Morton Mandel Center for Studies in Jewish Education, a partnership between the Jack, Joseph and Morton Mandel Foundation of Cleveland and Brandeis University. We are also grateful to the Spencer Foundation for a research grant that enabled us to carry out the last phase of data collection in schools.

Finally, we thank our families for their patient support and good humor.

About the Editors

Sharon Feiman-Nemser is the Jack, Joseph and Morton Mandel Professor of Jewish Education at Brandeis University with a joint appointment in the Education Studies Program and the Department of Near Eastern and Judaic Studies. She began her career as a high school English teacher. At Brandeis she has founded the Jack, Joseph and Morton Mandel Center for Studies in Jewish Education and started the master of arts in teaching (MAT) program, which prepares teachers for public schools and Jewish day schools. Feiman-Nemser has written extensively on teacher education, learning to teach, mentoring, and new teacher induction. Her most recent book, *Teachers as Learners*, was published by Harvard Education Press in 2012.

Eran Tamir is a senior research associate at the Jack, Joseph and Morton Mandel Center for Studies in Jewish Education and a lecturer in education at Brandeis University. A sociologist and an educational policy scholar, he focuses his research on the social context of educational policy, teacher education policy, and the politics of education at the federal, state, and school levels. Tamir studied New Jersey's first alternate route to teaching in the United States, has led the Choosing to Teach project since 2006, and founded the Longitudinal Survey of Day School Teachers. He is currently working on multiple research projects focusing on school leadership and culture, teacher careers, politics of education, and teacher preparation for financial literacy.

Karen Hammerness is an associate professor and the director of program research in the Master of Arts in Teaching Program at Bard College. Her research focuses on the design and pedagogy of teacher education in the United States and internationally with particular interest in the role of vision in teaching and teacher education and features of strong teacher education programs. Hammerness is doing comparative research on teacher education in five countries and studying context-specific teacher preparation for New York City. Her book, *Seeing Through Teachers' Eyes: Professional Ideals and Classroom Practices*, was published in 2006 by Teachers College Press.

About the Contributors

Christian Dallavis is senior director of Leadership Programs for the Alliance for Catholic Education (ACE) at the University of Notre Dame. He is the founder and director of the Notre Dame ACE Academies, a comprehensive university-school partnership that puts disadvantaged children on the path to college and heaven by mobilizing the resources of the University of Notre Dame, local dioceses, and parental choice scholarship programs. He directs Notre Dame's K–12 school leader formation program, the Mary Ann Remick Leadership Program, and leads the university's effort to establish the Center for Transformational Educational Leadership.

Anthony Holter is the executive director of the Fulcrum Foundation in Seattle, which was founded to leverage support for Catholic schools in the Archdiocese of Seattle. Prior to his appointment at Fulcrum, he was a faculty member of the Mary Ann Remick Leadership Program in the Alliance for Catholic Education at the University of Notre Dame, where he was also director of program evaluation and research, and focused his own research on how Catholic school principals use inquiry and data to make important decisions in their school communities.

Bethamie Horowitz is a sociopsychologist on the research faculty of New York University's Steinhardt School, where she teaches in the doctoral program in Education and Jewish Studies. She came to NYU in 2011 after two decades working in a variety of applied contexts in the United States and Israel. As research director at United Jewish Appeal (UJA) Federation of New York, she developed a multi-method investigation to study the changing patterns of Jewish engagement in the lives of baby boomer and younger American Jews, entitled "Connections and Journeys." As research director of the Mandel Foundation Israel, Horowitz conducted a longitudinal study of the careers of graduates of its professional programs. Her current research focuses on emerging adults and how they construct their lives in light of their background, their aspirations, and the changing contexts they encounter.

Kavita Kapadia Matsko is an assistant clinical professor and the founding director of the University of Chicago Urban Teacher Education Program (UTEP), which is part of the Urban Education Institute. In addition to her interest in context-specific preparation, her research focuses on new teacher preparation and development in urban schools. Kavita's portfolio includes working with the University of Chicago Consortium on Chicago School Research on projects related to new teacher induction, teacher evaluation, and teacher effectiveness.

Index